# North Carolina Getaways

## A Guide to
## Bed & Breakfasts and Inns

by Don Vandeventer

Published by
**Down Home Publications**
P.O. Box 1899-B
Candler, NC 28715

Distributed to the book trade by
**John F. Blair, Publishing**
1406 Plaza Drive
Winston-Salem, NC 27103
(800) 222-9796

DISCLAIMER

Although the author has researched exhaustively to ensure the accuracy and completeness of the information contained in this book, we assume no responsibility for errors, inaccuracies, omissions, or any other inconsistency herein.

Published by:

Down Home Publications
P.O. Box 1899-B
Candler, NC 28715

Distributed to the book trade by:

John F. Blair, Publisher
1406 Plaza Drive
Winston-Salem, NC 27103
(800) 222-9796

Copyright © 1996 by Don Vandeventer.
Printed in the United States of America
10  9  8  7  6  5  4  3  2  1

Maps copyright © 1993/1994 North Carolina Travel and Tourism Division, used and modified with permission


Publisher's Cataloging-in-Publication Data
Vandeventer, Don.
North Carolina Getaways: a guide to bed & breakfasts and inns / by Don Vandeventer
    Includes index.
    1. Bed and breakfast accomodations—North Carolina—Directories.
2. North Carolina—Guidebooks.    I. Title.    II. Series.
ISBN 1-886443-01-7

# Contents

## RATES

$ ........................ 50 and under
$$ ....................... 51-100
$$$ ..................... 101-150
$$$$ ................... 151-250
$$$$$ ................. 251 and over

## AFFILIATIONS

AAA .................. American Automobile Association
AB&BA ............ American Bed & Breakfast Association
AHA ................. American Hotel Association
AHMA .............. American Hotel & Motel Association
CCHMA ........... Crystal Coast Hotel & Motel Association
IIA ...................... Independent Innkeepers Association
NB&BA ............ National Bed & Breakfast Association
NCBBI .............. North Carolina Bed & Breakfasts & Inns
NCHMA ........... North Carolina Hotel & Motel Association
OBHMA ........... Outer Banks Hotel & Motel Association
PAII ................... Professional Association of Innkeepers International
SIA ..................... Southern Innkeepers Association
USB&B ............. United States Bed & Breakfast Association

## KEY TO SYMBOLS
### PAYMENT

$$$=Cash

CHECKS=Checks

MC=Master Card®

VISA=Visa®

AMEX=American Express®

DISCOVER=Discover®

CARTE BLANCHE=Carte Blanche®

Diner's Club=Diner's Club®

### AMENITIES

A/C=Air Conditioned

=Full Breakfast

=Continental Breakfast

=Lunch and/or Dinner Available

=Fireplace Available

=Hot Tubs

=Jacuzzi in room

=Phone in room

=TV in rooms

VCR=VCR Available

=Wheelchair access

# What is a Bed and Breakfast or Inn?

First, let me tell you how to best understand the basic differences between inns by giving you some definitions....

**Reservation Service Organizations (RSO's):** These are individual businesses that represent several inns, bed & breakfasts, etc. They allow the consumer to call one telephone number, usually a toll-free line, and make reservations at a number of inns in a variety of locations. The inns they represent pay them directly for their services and you should not have to pay anything. RSO's are usually the choice for someone who does not want to bother with the details of a trip and wants someone else to make the selection for them.

**Homestays or Bed & Breakfast Houses:** These are smaller, homelike facilities that are usually operated by a single innkeeper or a couple. You will be made to feel like part of the family and may even eat in the family dining room or watch TV with the innkeepers. In this European atmosphere you can expect the innkeepers to have outside jobs and interests during the day with clean, comfortable accommodations being afforded you each evening. These homes take guests in because they enjoy meeting new people and sharing the uniqueness of their life-style with others.

**Bed & Breakfast Inns:** Usually larger than Homestays, these inns are operated on a commercial basis with innkeepers who generally spend all of their time working as full-time innkeepers. They offer a wide range of types and styles of facilities ranging from rustic to elegant. They serve breakfast exclusively to the guests that spend the night there with the occasional opportunity to get a picnic lunch for your daily excursion. Afternoon teas, evening social hours, and other amenities are often included as part of your stay with the emphasis on professional hospitality. You can expect assistance and interaction from the innkeepers of these inns but you probably can find some places in each facility where you can have some privacy from others if that is what you want.

**Country Inns:** These inns have all the benefits of Bed & Breakfast Inns but serve additional meals such as lunch and dinner, too. Open to the public, Country Inns can be run by innkeepers and their staff or by a manager hired by the owners to act as host/hostess as well as direct the staff. You can expect an even wider range of amenities at this type of inn than is usually available at other types of properties but you will not suffer from lack of attention. Innkeepers and staffs at these facilities are well trained and oftentimes quite sophisticated with their levels of service.

# How to Pick the Right Place

Well, now you know how to understand the terminology when reviewing possible places to venture to. Let me also give you a suggested list of questions for you to ask when you call the inn:

1.   **Rates:** What are the rates and what is included in that rate? Rate shopping is very popular these days but believe me, just because two inns quote different rates, does not mean that one is better or worse. Everything is relative and that includes a rate. Be sure to LISTEN to what the innkeeper tells you about what is included. If you have a question about what you heard, do not hesitate to ask for clarification. It is the little things that add up to a great inn experience. Most innkeepers will be more than happy to tell you what makes their inn special.

2.   **Baths:** Do the guest rooms have private baths? While this is not a priority for everyone, it is still important to know whether or not to take a robe.

3.   **Bedrooms:** What are the sizes of the beds? Most inns have a variety of bed sizes ranging from twins to kings. If you do not specify the size bed you prefer, you may not have a choice by the time you arrive. Remember that people were smaller in the 18th and 19th century than they are today. King- and queen-sized beds are really a creation of the modern era. Do not expect the innkeeper to provide you with both a king-sized bed for your 6'4" husband and an antique bed for your aesthetic pleasure.

4.   **The Area:** What is there to do in the area? How far from the inn is it? Innkeepers know exactly what attractions are most liked by the typical customer and are prepared to tell you all about them. They also have a deep pool of knowledge about some of the more unique things available in their area. Keep in mind that YOU need to give the innkeeper an idea what you are looking for so they can then marry the information they give you to your needs. You will get more information that is of use to you if you will share what you want out of your experience right up front.

5.   **Amenities:** Miscellaneous items that are important to you. If a fireplace is what you really want, then make that the first question you ask. Same thing goes if you just cannot live without a jacuzzi. If you are leaving a sick child with grandmother so you can get away, then having a telephone available is important to you. Whatever it is that means the most to you, save yourself a lot of time and energy by making yourself a short list of questions to ask BEFORE you begin calling around.

# How to Get the Most out of Your Stay

1.  **Reservations:** Try to call the inn for information/reservations during off-peak hours. Keep in mind that most innkeepers are busy preparing breakfast and serving guests between the hours of 7 a.m. and 10 p.m.

2.  **Check-in:** Ask about check-in and checkout policies for each inn. Every operation is unique and each inn has its own policy. Some inns can be flexible and adjust to your needs and some cannot.

3.  **Cancellations:** What is the cancellation policy of the inn? How does the inn handle credit card guarantees? If you have to cancel, what is the inn's refund policy? Again, each inn has its own policy.

4.  **Payments:** What types of payment are acceptable at the inn? Most inns these days accept some type of credit card as well as personal checks. It takes only a moment to mention what kind of payment you would like to make and ask whether that is acceptable to that particular inn.

5.  **Rules:** The rules are the rules! Each inn has its own set of rules regarding things like children, smoking, alcoholic beverages, etc. Find an inn whose rules are to your liking.

6.  **Phone Numbers:** When leaving a number where you can be reached, DO NOT leave the inn's toll-free number. These 800 numbers are for reservations and information only. Each inn has a regular direct dial number that is usually on the brochure and other materials.

7.  **Comment Cards:** Take time to write comments about the inn and leave it for (or mail it to) the innkeeper(s). Please take the time to tell us what we did right, as well as what we could be doing to make your next experience better.

So there you have it! I really did not set out to write so much but being a true innkeeper. I only wanted to make sure you knew everything you needed to know to make your stay in a bed and breakfast the best it could possibly be. Please carry this guidebook with you and use it often. Some of the best experiences of your life are sitting right here in your hands!

Diane Sheiry
North Carolina Bed Breakfast and Inns Association,
President, 1996

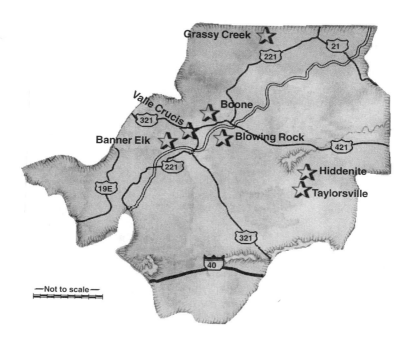

# Northern Mountains

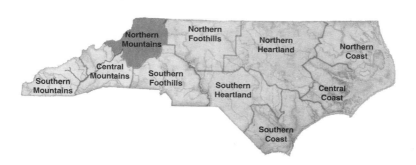

## Hummingbird Lodge Bed & Breakfast
## Banner Elk

Located in the high country of the northern mountains, the Hummingbird Lodge is a spacious 3,000 square foot mountain lodge. Built of red cedar, this open-air lodge sits on over five acres of woodlands at 4,100 feet, just 2.4 miles from Banner Elk.

Banner Elk is the center of some of the best outdoor recreation in the western part of the state. The mountain peaks towering above Banner Elk reach elevations of 5,000 to 6,000 feet.

The area is well known for its skiing. Less than six miles to the north of the Lodge is Beech Mountain, the highest incorporated city east of the Mississippi River. The fourteen slopes of Ski Beech (at 5,500-foot elevation) provide 830 feet of vertical drop at the largest ski resort in North Carolina. To the south of the Lodge, Sugar Mountain has eighteen slopes with a vertical drop of 1,200 feet. Also to the south is Ski Hawksnest with eleven slopes. They offer "Nighthawk" skiing Saturday night only from 11 p.m.-4 a.m.

Skiing is not the only activity in Banner Elk. It is also a center for horseback riding, river rafting, gemstone mining, trout fishing, hiking, and, of course, golf. Eight miles southeast is Grandfather Mountain Park, a private park that encompasses the 5,964-foot Grandfather Mountain. Here visitors will find an excellent Nature Museum, natural wildlife habitats, hiking trails, and the Mile-High Swinging bridge. It is also the home of the annual Highland Games each July.

The Hummingbird Lodge opened in late 1991. Susan and Randy Hutchins took over the operation early in 1993. They had been

traveling the United States for more than two years. Since they enjoyed traveling and meeting new people, they were afraid that living in one place would be a big letdown. The ever-changing mountains have provided constant new adventures, and the Lodge has provided them a way to continue to meet and entertain new friends. Like us, you will quickly find there is no such thing as a guest at the Lodge, only new friends enjoying the beauty of the mountains.

Each morning at the Hummingbird Lodge brings a full breakfast in the large, open dining room overlooking the valley. Weather permitting, you may dine on the breakfast terrace outside. Sunday breakfast includes blueberry pancakes, bacon, sausage, bread, fruit, juice, coffee and milk. Other mornings you may find French toast (it has a caramel base which requires no syrup) or hash brown casseroles, bacon, eggs, eggs Benedict or souffles on the table. Susan plans each breakfast to provide plenty of energy for you to enjoy a day in the mountains. Randy and Susan will gladly plan breakfast around special dietary needs as well.

Be sure to ask to see the toy shop at the base of the drive. Randy likes puzzles and is putting the finishing touches on one right now. Susan is the artist. Together they plan to use the toy shop that was built by the original owners.

---

**Hummingbird Lodge Bed & Breakfast**
**Rt. 4, Box 403; NC Hwy. 194; Banner Elk, NC 28604**
**(704) 963-7210**
**Innkeepers: Randy & Susan Hutchins**
Rooms: 4; Private Baths: 2; Shared Baths: 2; Rates: $$
Affiliations: Banner Elk Chamber, Boone Area Chamber
Payment: $$$ CHECKS  Amenities:  VCR

## Gideon Ridge Inn
## Blowing Rock

Dramatic mountain scenery is one of the inn's best features. The inn sits atop a 4,000-foot ridge overlooking the Blackberry and John's River gorges. Paraphrasing a popular song, on a clear day it seems as though you can see forever. My favorite place was sitting on one of the six stone terraces and watching the ever-changing vista before me.

The building was started in 1939 and completed in 1942 as a private summer home for the nephew of Moses Cone. Built of stone from Grandfather Mountain, the inn is located on a secluded five-acre tract just south of the town of Blowing Rock. Less than a mile away is North Carolina's oldest tourist attraction, Blowing Rock. It has attracted visitors since the early 1840s.

Cobb and Jane Milner, the innkeepers, came to Blowing Rock from New Jersey to find a home in Jane's home state. After discovering the house, they realized it was too large for just the two of them. Yet they knew they couldn't give it up. They became innkeepers overnight.

Together, with help from their daughter Susan, and daughter-in-law, Cindy, they have created a first-class inn. Each room within the two-story building is so tastefully decorated with family heirlooms and antiques, it creates an ambiance I have seldom known. The central point within the inn is the library. There are chairs grouped around the large stone fireplace, Oriental rugs, rough-hewn beams, and a baby grand piano. Here guests get together to visit with each other, play games, or to relax with a good book. Just off

the library is the dining room where Jane and Cobb serve a full breakfast at individual tables. This allows guests to dine and enjoy the beauty of the mountains.

The community of Blowing Rock was already developing into a summer resort community as early as 1880. Over the last century the town has maintained its summer resort status, yet has not been commercially abused. There are few fast-food restaurants and no mall. The town consists of quaint shops and cafes.

Within a short drive of downtown, you find the Blue Ridge Parkway, the Moses H. Cone Manor House and Estate and the Julian Price Park. The oldest theme park in the state, Tweetsie Railroad, is located just north of town, and one of the state's largest outlet centers is at the town's edge. Mystery Hill and the Appalachian Heritage Museum and Military Museum are also located a short drive from the Gideon Ridge Inn.

Appalachian State University is an easy ten-minute drive away in Boone. Here you also will find the Daniel Boone Native Gardens, Hickory Ridge Homestead (an eighteenth century home site) and *Horn in the West*, the nation's third oldest outdoor drama.

**Gideon Ridge Inn**
**P.O. Box 1929; 6148 Gideon Ridge Rd.; Blowing Rock, NC 28605**
**(704) 295-3644; Fax: (704) 295-4586**
**Innkeepers: Jane & Cobb Milner/Cindy & Cobb Milner, III**
Rooms: 10; Private Baths: 10; Rates: $$-$$$; children over 12
Affiliations: IIA
Payment:      Amenities:

# The Lindridge House Bed & Breakfast
# Blowing Rock

High on a ridge just five miles from Blowing Rock, the Lindridge House is convenient to everything there is to see and do in the area. This two-story home, sitting on 7½ acres, has some of the most spectacular views that you will find of the mountains. This is where innkeepers Suzann French and Lou Gutheil created a perfect mountain retreat. The two guest rooms and suite they have created have commanding views of the mountains. The rooms are decorated with an electric blend of country and antique furnishings each has its own style and personality, yet with all of the modern conveniences of private bath and even cable television.

Walking trails on the property will lead you past many native plants and wildflowers to a creek and pool created by an underground spring. From the picnic area to the large stone fireplace in the great room, the Lindridge House offers peace and quiet.

Breakfast is a specialty at the Lindridge, and it shows in the variety of treats that Suzann and Lou offer each morning. While you may never have the same breakfast two days in a row, there is always fresh fruit such as baked apples with vanilla cream, blueberries, blackberries or strawberries that are grown on the property. Entrees to help you start your day might include a vegetable egg strata, stuffed puffy French toast or walnut sausage rolls. Other mornings might bring the house favorite: apple-walnut pancakes.

When you're ready to explore the area you will quickly find out why Blowing Rock is one of our favorite communities along the Blue Ridge Parkway. As early as the 1880s the community was already developing into a summer resort community; however it has not been commercially abused. Its quaint shops and cafes are a delight in our fast-paced society. The community was named for the 3,000-foot cliff that overlooks the Johns River Gorge. The updraft from the Gorge appears to make snow fall upside down and light-weight objects tossed over the edge, to come back.

For those who love the outdoors, the Blue Ridge Parkway is almost at your doorstep. A short drive will take you to Julian Price Park or to the Moses H. Cone Manor House and Estate that covers 3,500 acres and includes two trout fishing lakes and 25 miles of horseback riding trails. The Blowing Rock Stables offer guided trail rides around the Manor House and past Bass Lake, known for its fishing.

For history lovers, a stop at The Appalachian Heritage Museum will give you an overview of the mountain culture from the early settlement through the Depression Era. It's only a short drive from Blowing Rock to Boone where the outdoor drama, *Horn in the West* depicts early settlers in their struggle for independence from Britain. The two-hour production combines history, entertainment and excitement all into one.

For the most incredible views in all of western North Carolina, Grandfather Mountain is only nine miles from the Lindridge. Here in addition to spectacular scenery, you'll find the mile-high swinging bridge, a nature museum and a wild animal habitat. Also only a short drive from the Lindridge House is Linville Falls. This is perhaps the best known waterfall in the entire Appalachian Mountains, and certainly one of the most scenic. The falls are at the beginning of one of the deepest canyons east of the Mississippi, with walls nearly 2,000 feet in some areas.

Our only regret at the Lindridge House—so much to do in the area, we didn't have time to try out their antique pool table.

---

**The Lindridge House Bed & Breakfast**
**5447 US Hwy 221 S.; Blowing Rock, NC 28605**
**(704) 295-7343**
**Innkeepers: Suzann French & Lou Gutheil**
Rooms: 2; Private baths: 2; Suites: 1; Rates: $$-$$$; children over 12
Affiliations: NCBBI, Blowing Rock Chamber, High Country Host
Payment:    Amenities:

# Maple Lodge
# Blowing Rock

While the Maple Lodge is not the oldest operating bed & breakfast in North Carolina, it is definitely high on the list. Originally built prior to 1930 as a one-story home, Jo Greene added a second floor in 1946 so she could take in boarders. Her children named the lodge for the two maple trees that were in the front yard. One of the trees still remains.

When the second floor was finally finished in 1946, there were seven bedrooms with six bathrooms. Pine panelling was used in the parlors and each of the rooms had hardwood floors. The Wildflower Room has cherry flooring while the rest of the lodge has red oak.

While the Lodge has been in continuous operation as a bed & breakfast since 1946, David and Marilyn Bateman (and Leroy, the cat) are newcomers. They purchased Maple Lodge in 1993, but Marilyn is not new to bed & breakfasts. Her maternal great-grandmother ran a rooming house in Illinois, and her grandmother ran a boarding house in Virginia. Another ancestor was the innkeeper at "The Sign of the Mermaid" in Kingston, NJ, an inn operating before the Revolutionary War. Marilyn also owned a bed & breakfast for several years in Annapolis, Maryland before moving to Blowing Rock.

Today, the Lodge has a total of eight guest rooms and one suite. Each has private bath and full, queen, or king sized beds, some with canopies. The rooms are furnished with family heirlooms, Oriental carpets and country antiques. In keeping with the theme of an old country inn, the Lodge has two parlors, one with a stone fireplace and the other an old-time pump organ.

A single glance around Blowing Rock and the visitor will quickly understand why David and Marilyn moved to this charming village located off the Blue Ridge Parkway. The town is rich with craft shops, art galleries, and antiques. Restaurants provide home-style cooking as well as elegant continental cuisine. Woodlands Bar-B-Que is one of our favorite places to eat.

In Blowing Rock you can enjoy professional summer theater, concerts in the park or just relax in the city's gazebo at Memorial Park. Within a short drive you can wander miles of trails along the Blue Ridge Parkway. Blowing Rock Stables offers horseback riding at Moses Cone Park. You may want to take a ride on the Tweetsie Railroad at the oldest theme park in the mountains. Another favorite place is the Blowing Rock itself, a privately owned park located at the edge of town.

Breakfast each morning at the Maple Lodge is served in the Garden Room. The glass wall lets you enjoy the wildflower garden during breakfast. In the fall when the air is a bit nippy, there is always a fire in the wood-burning stove. Served buffet style, the full breakfast includes home-baked breads and muffins, fresh fruit, hot oatmeal-apple baked cereal, and other treats such as sausage or bacon fritatas, orange-pecan French toast, waffles, and egg casseroles.

---

**Maple Lodge**
**P.O. Box 1236; Sunset Dr.; Blowing Rock, NC 28605**
**(704) 295-3331**
**Innkeepers: Marilyn & David Bateman**
Rooms: 10; Private Baths: 10; Suites: 1; Rates: $$-$$$;
Affiliations: PAII, Blowing Rock Chamber, Boone Area Chamber, High Country Host
Payment:      Amenities:

## Stone Pillar Bed & Breakfast
## Blowing Rock

Located a half block from Main Street, Stone Pillar is an easy walk to downtown Blowing Rock. The location and homelike atmosphere drew Angel and me to the bed and breakfast.

Being an innkeeper was the fulfillment of a lifelong dream for George Van Nuys. The care and attention shown to guests is a reflection of that dream.

His vision really started coming into focus after a trip to the area in 1986. By 1988, George and his partner, Ron Tharp, were in a position to move to the area. After several months of renovating, they opened the Stone Pillar as a bed and breakfast in July of 1989. George takes care of the day-to-day operations at the inn. Ron is a goldsmith and operates the Fovea Gallery on Sunset Drive in downtown Blowing Rock.

Built in the early 1920s as a summer home, George and Ron have decorated the inn to reflect the feel of a village home. Each of the six guest rooms in the 5,500-square-foot home are decorated with heirlooms and antiques. Fireplaces and a cast-iron open hearth stove add to the ambiance. The custom designed green willow furniture, such as the headboard in the Country Room and the porch furniture, compliment the picture. While keeping with the overall theme of the bed and breakfast, Laura's Room (located on the main floor) is completely handicap-accessible.

The village of Blowing Rock sits at an elevation of 3,700 feet and is on the Eastern Continental Divide. Many (including the author) con-

sider the Blue Ridge Parkway one of the most scenic drives in the United States. Beginning at the Shenandoah Park in Virginia, it stretches 469 miles to the Great Smoky Mountains in North Carolina.

Along the Parkway and just outside of Blowing Rock is the Moses H. Cone Memorial Park. Here the visitor can enjoy the Craft Center (operated by the Southern Highlands Handicraft Guild) hiking or horseback riding. Or you may want to fish in the 22-acre Bass Lake or 16-acre Trout Lake. Another park along the Parkway is the Julian Price Memorial Park, covering more than 3,900 acres.

To the north of Blowing Rock is Tweetsie Railroad, the first theme park in Western North Carolina. A bit further north is the community of Boone with its summer outdoor drama *Horn In The West*.

Blowing Rock supplies the visitor with comfortable days to shop or sight-see. The shops and galleries offer crafts, antiques and art. Restaurants in the area provide foods ranging from mountain fare to fine dining. A good selection of restaurants are within walking distance of Stone Pillar.

Of course, no stay at the Stone Pillar would be complete without George's full breakfast, served family-style in the dining room. Omelets, pancakes or stuffed French toasts are only part of the treat. With notice, he will try to meet special dietary needs.

**Stone Pillar Bed & Breakfast**
**P.O. Box 1881; 144 Pine St.; Blowing Rock, NC 28605**
**(704) 295-4141**
**Innkeepers: George Van Nuys & Ron Tharp**
Rooms: 6; Private Baths: 6; Rates: $-$$
Payment: $$$ CHECKS MC VISA  Amenities: 🐾 📷 ♿

# The Gragg House
# Boone

Judy and Robert Gragg refer to the style of their home as a fancy farmhouse with casual elegant furnishings. Located just outside of Boone, on property that has been in the family for years, The Gragg House offers city convenience with country peace. They are blessed with mountain views, surrounded by woods and a landscape of native wildflowers, rhododendron and mountain laurel. While sitting on the deck, the only sound we could hear was birdsong.

The large home is spacious and immaculate with the decorating scheme flowing from room to room. Other than the private living quarters downstairs, guests have the majority of the home to themselves. Comfort and privacy are more assured as The Gragg House is a true bed and breakfast home.

The rooms, named for their grown daughters, Annette and Elizabeth, are large and comfortably furnished. We stayed in Annette's room (pictured). It featured an iron bed from Charleston Forge dressed in Laura Ashley linens and an eclectic mix of country antiques. Elizabeth's room, offers guest flexibility with twin beds that can be made into a king.

Upon arrival, Judy and Robert offer The Gragg House with southern hospitality in its truest sense. Their home does not lack for any attention to detail in regard to decor, cuisine and comfort.

Boone will always be one of my favorite places to visit. It is a year-round destination for visitors from all over the world. Sitting on a plateau with high peaks on all sides, the days are warm and evenings cool enough to be comfortable.

The out-of-doors offers an endless variety of activities to be enjoyed by all ages. The mountain scenery and cool summer temperatures are per-

fect to enjoy the areas fishing, canoeing, hiking, horseback riding and whitewater rafting. Gem mining is a year round activity and golf enjoys a long season from early winter until late in the fall. Skiing is the favorite winter sport, with four of the best ski resorts in the southeast and numerous cross-country ski trails just moments away.

As fireflies flicker on cool summer nights, the past comes alive at the *Horn in the West* Amphitheater as Daniel Boone takes the stage. This, the third-oldest outdoor drama, recounts the story of Daniel Boone and the mountain men in their conflict with the British Militia and the Cherokee Indians.

The Appalachian Cultural Museum, helps bring an understanding of the people and history of the area. Displays include Native American artifacts, tools and furnishings of the early settlers. Another display is dedicated to the Wizard of Oz theme park that was once located in the area.

Before you begin your travels around Boone and the area, Judy makes sure you're served a splendid breakfast that is both healthful and delicious. Breakfast may be served in the formal dining room, in the sunroom or outside on the deck. Croissant French toast served with cinnamon whipping cream syrup and a side dish of orange glazed mixed fresh fruit always prompts recipe requests. Whatever the morning fare, it is always unusual, creative, and appetizing.

---

**The Gragg House**
**210 Ridge Point Drive; Rt. 6, Box 1205; Boone, NC 28607**
**(704) 264-7289; Fax: (704) 264-7289**
**Innkeepers: Robert & Judy Gragg**
Rooms: 3; Private bath: 1; Shared Baths: 2; Rates: $$
Payment: $$$ CHECKS Amenities:

## Lovill House Inn
## Boone

It was Daniel Boone, Indian fighter and explorer who blazed the first trail over the mountains. While Daniel never actually lived in the area, he did have a hunting cabin here. Over the years following his exploration, settlers moved into the area and formed a settlement located on a plateau with high peaks on all sides.

When decorated Confederate officer, Capt. Edward Francis Lovill arrived to settle in 1875, just ten years after the Civil War, Boone was a sleepy little community in an area known as the "Lost Providence." Their settlement, named for Daniel Boone, was destined to become not only the county seat but the very heart of the High Country.

There is little doubt that Edward Lovill contributed to the growth of Boone, first as a North Carolina state senator and later, when he drew up the papers with B.B. Daugherty that established the forerunner of today's Appalachian State University.

For the next 100 years, the Lovill family lived in the home the Captain built, while the town of Boone grew up around them. By 1993, when Tim and Lori Shahen arrived, one of the most historic homes in Boone had fallen into disrepair. However, Tim and Lori had a vision for the two-story farmhouse. With its wide wraparound porches, pine and maple flooring and arched doorways, they saw the bed and breakfast of their dreams.

Extensive renovation and restoration have brought the Lovill House back to life. Modern baths were added and double insulation between walls and floors was installed to insure privacy for guests. Three of the original five brick fireplaces were salvaged and most of the wormy chestnut woodwork was preserved. Tim and Lori have added fine antiques, original works of art and quality reproductions that work together to highlight the warmth and charm of this traditional farmhouse.

In the evenings, the Shahens invite their guests to join them for a hosted social hour. When the weather is warm, they often move onto the wide veranda with high-backed rockers or stroll out to the garden to gather near the stream. In the winter, guests are welcome to enjoy social hour in front of the open-hearth fireplace in the big country kitchen.

Mornings bring hot coffee or tea outside your door as you prepare for a full gourmet breakfast. Offerings vary day to day and throughout the season. Fruits, home-baked breads, and entrées of Belgian waffles, omelets or eggs Benedict accompanied by country ham, sausage or bacon are all a part of Lori's bountiful menu.

For the traveler, Boone is rich in its cultural heritage, and arts and craft shops abound in the area. In 1883, eight years before Sears and Roebuck became partners, a small general store was opened in the community of Valle Crucis. Recently the Mast General Store has opened a second store in Boone on Main Street just a short drive from the Lovill House.

For the history buff, the Appalachian Cultural Museum offers a glimpse of Mountain Culture from the early settlements to the present time. The nation's third oldest outdoor drama, *Horn in the West*, follows Daniel Boone and the Mountain Men in their conflict with the British Militia and the Cherokee Indians. For the outdoor enthusiasts, the area is rich with parks, whitewater rafting, mountain biking and hiking trails. A favorite of all who visit the area is the Daniel Boone Native Garden that covers eight acres and features mountain plants, shrubs, trees and rocks indigenous to North Carolina.

---

**Lovill House Inn**
**404 Old Bristol Rd.; Boone, NC 28607**
**(800) 849-9466; (704) 264-4204**
**Innkeepers: Tim & Lori Shahen**
Rooms: 5; Private baths: 5; Rates: $$-$$$; children over 12
Affiliations: PAII, NCBBI, AAA◆◆◆, Mobil, Boone Chamber, High Country Host
Payment:  CHECKS M/C VISA Amenities:

# River House
# Grassy Creek

There are so many words that describe River House. "Peaceful" and "relaxing" are the first that come to mind. Good food, comfortable rooms and quiet walks are just a few of the others I use when describing the River House.

Nestled in the natural bowl of the Blue Ridge Mountains of Ashe County at an elevation of 3,000 feet, River House sits on 125 acres that include wooded lands, a pasture, an orchard and several springs. The New River, flowing along the front of the property, is said to be older than the Nile.

The main house faces the river. It includes two guest rooms that look out over the river and the mountain, a library, two dining rooms and kitchen. The 1870 house was restored in the late 1930s by local a doctor, James Ballou, as the show house for Ashe County. Like others before me, I fell in love with its porch that offers a splendid view of the river. It was here that we made new friends; a doctor and his wife from Atlanta, a minister on sabbatical, and an Australian author. I don't think I'll ever know which I enjoyed most; resting on the porch after an excellent dinner in the award-winning four-star dining room, the conversation with new my friends, fireflies dancing in the cool evening air under a 400-year-old sycamore, or the calming sounds of the river. I just know this porch is one of my favorite memories of the summer.

Behind the main house is a seven-room cottage. It provides an additional four guest rooms, one of them having its own sitting room and two with private porches. The seventh guest room (where we stayed) is in the building that used to be Doctor Ballou's office. Beyond the cottage, a stroll up the hill will take you past the old scale house (once used for weighing livestock), a large barn complex, and several other

buildings, including a 40 by 100 foot tobacco barn. At the top of the hill you will find several trails that offer panoramic views of the river and mountains.

Innkeeper Gayle Winston was born in Ashe County. Before becoming a world-class chef, she was a Broadway producer. Her first restaurant venture was the Troutdale Dining Room, in Troutdale, Virginia. It was here, and later at other historic restaurants, such as the Glendale Springs Inn in Ashe County, and the Old Salem Tavern in Winston-Salem, that Gayle won her much-deserved reputation.

A short drive from the Blue Ridge Parkway and the Virginia border, River House is located in an area that is rich in history. Daniel Boone slept here, and the Moravians passed through on their way to Winston-Salem. Many of the peaks in the area are over 4,000 feet, the highest being Three Top Mountain, at 5,195 feet. Several parks, such as E. B. Jefferess, Mt. Jefferson, New River and Grayson Highlands, offer outdoor activities and miles of trails. The only cheese factory in North Carolina is located in West Jefferson, just south of River House, as are the world-famous Ashe County Frescoes.

Since 1980, River House has held the high country's most memorable weddings, including the site for the ceremony, the decorations, the flowers, the cake, the food and the drink. They can even furnish the photographer, musicians and minister if needed!

---

**River House**
**1896 Old Field Creek Road; Grassy Creek, NC 28631**
**(910) 982-2109; Fax: (910) 982-2109**
**River House, Inc.; Innkeeper: Gayle Winston**
Rooms: 9; Private baths: 9; Rates: $$-$$$
Affiliations: Chamber members in three counties
Payment:  Amenities:

# Hidden Crystal Inn
# Hiddenite

Eileen Lackey Sharpe, the octogenarian owner of The Hidden Crystal Inn and founder of the adjacent Lucas Mansion Museum and Hiddenite Center for Folklife and Cultural Arts, established the inn in 1989. Housed in a nearly fifty-year-old southern plantation style house, the two-building complex provides the first public lodgings in Hiddenite since fire destroyed the famous Sulphur Springs Hotel and Spa in the 1920s.

Rock hounds know about Hiddenite with its gemstone-rich earth. The serene scenery of wooded foothills and farms often are overlooked because visitors to the area walk with their heads bent downward searching for gemstones. An ancient fault line makes the area one of the most mineral-rich in the nation. The town of Hiddenite is named after the stone that ranges from pale greenish-yellow to almost emerald green.

While the Hidden Crystal Inn is named for the stones found in the area, you quickly realize that the Hidden Crystal Inn is a gem itself. Each room is exquisitely appointed, the attention to detail as precise as the gem cutter's tools. Personal attention, to the point of pampering, is a trademark of the inn. Each of the twelve rooms and the one suite is filled with art, antiques and area gemstones. Guests enjoy the library that features an exhibit of local minerals. The pool and patio are favorite places to lounge on sunny days. Evenings are often spent around the antique player Grand Piano. There is croquet, badminton, and an English Country garden complete with gazebo to help you shed the stress of day-to-day living.

Presenters of small meetings and retreats have discovered that the inn's small conference facility, The Crystal Cottage, is an ideal place for

meetings. The Conference Center provides audiovisual equipment, fax, copier, modem and all guest rooms have in-room phones. The inn offers big hotel amenities while retaining old world charm.

The inn's restaurant, which serves three meals a day (a full gourmet breakfast is included in the room rate) is noted in the Unifour (Gateway to the Blue Ridge) region as an outstanding fine dining establishment. Executive Chef Ken Martin, formerly Chef at Winston-Salem's Zevely House and La Chaudiere, offers very creative New American and Continental cuisine

*Inn Business Review* rated Hidden Crystal as one of the ten outstanding new inns of 1991. By 1994, The American Bed & Breakfast Association listed the Hidden Crystal Inn as one of the top sixteen bed and breakfasts or inns in North America.

Stop at the Hiddenite Center for Folklife and Cultural Arts. Events at the Center include dinner theater, music and dance performances. Part of the Center is the Lucas Mansion Museum and Galleries. Once home of "Diamond Jim" Lucas, this turn-of-the-century mansion houses a collection displaying Alexander County gems and minerals and the history and life-style of "Diamond Jim". Antiques, art and history are located on the second, and Eileen Sharpe's personal collection of international antique and modern dolls and toys are on the third floor.

---

**Hidden Crystal Inn**
**P.O. Box 58; Sulpher Springs Rd.; Hiddenite, NC 28636**
**(704) 632-0063; Fax: (704) 632-3562**
**Innkeeper: Lynn S. Hill**
Rooms: 12; Private Baths: 12; Shared Baths: 1; Suites: 1; Rates: $$-$$$
Affiliations: NCBBI, AB&BA
Payment:    Amenities:

## Barkley House Bed & Breakfast
## Taylorsville

Located a couple miles south of Taylorsville, the Barkley House is a great place for anniversaries, honeymoons or a fantasy weekend. Its innkeeper, Phyllis Barkley, loves to cater to her guests. With a bit of warning, Phyllis will get balloons or flowers. Special foods such as wine, cheese, strawberries, chocolate or whipped cream also can be made available in the room. She will light the candles if she knows when to expect you. To help relieve stress, a licensed massage therapist can even come to the Barkley House by appointment.

Raised in the area, Phyllis spent many years in Texas. She returned to the area with the idea of opening a bed and breakfast. In 1988, the dream came true with the opening of the Barkley House. The Barkley House, built in the late 1800s, is a Georgian style farmhouse filled with antiques and family heirlooms. Together they provide a quiet setting in which to enjoy the area.

Located in the center of Alexander county (known as the gem capital of North America) it is an area of pastoral beauty. It also provides many unique points of interest. You can dig or sluice for emeralds or other precious stones at the Emerald Hollow Gem Mine. You also could visit Hiddenite Center for Folklife and Cultural Arts. The Center presents dinner theater, music and dance performances. Each September an entire week of festivities takes place at the Center.

Also in the area is the Lucas Mansion Museum and Galleries. The museum, a part of the Hiddenite Center, is the former home of "Diamond Jim" Lucas. The Lucas Mansion Museum is the recipient of many awards for cultural excellence. The Mansion houses a permanent collection of Alexander County gems and minerals, including

the six-sided, 294-pound North Carolina Crystal. Antiques and collectibles provide an excellent view of life at the turn of the century. It also will give you an insight into "Diamond Jim", a world-traveler and internationally-known gem trader.

Elevations in the county range from 1,000 feet in the southeast corner to 2,500 feet in the northeast. The Brushy Mountains provide a barrier to cold winter winds and help to keep summer evenings cool and comfortable.

Rocky Face Mountain, located to the north of Hiddenite, is known for its rare flora and fauna. The land is owned by the Felburn Foundation, a nature conservancy organization. To the south of Taylorsville is Rink Dam that offers picnicking by the waterfall, boating and fishing.

Racing fans will remember Junior Johnson. He got his start driving moonshine in the 40s and 50s for the Burgess brothers. At one time Puff and Grafton Burgess owned the home. A blackjack table was found in pieces in the shed. If it could talk, it might tell you many secrets. Be sure to ask Phyllis about some local history while you're there.

Breakfast includes crepes, stuffed French toast, and waffles. *My* favorite was haystack eggs (scrambled eggs served on a bed of potato sticks and sour cream with a fence of bacon).

---

**Barkley House Bed & Breakfast**
**2522 NC Hwy 16 S.; Taylorsville, NC 28681**
**(800) 474-4652; (704) 632-9060**
**Innkeeper: Phyllis Barkley**
Rooms: 3; Private Baths: 3; Rates: $$
Payment: $$$ CHECKS MC VISA AMEX  Amenities: A/C ⬜ 🎿 👥 ✎

# Mast Farm Inn
# Valle Crucis

The history of the Mast Farm adds to the ambiance of the Inn. Joseph Mast left his home in Germany and migrated first to Switzerland and then to Lancaster County, PA. From there, he walked to the mountains of Western North Carolina. History tells us that he traded a dog, a rifle and a pair of leggings for a thousand acres of land. Yet there are no records of the first home built by Joseph on the property. The first known dwelling was a two-room cabin built by his son, David, about 1810. By the early 1880s, the main farm house had been built. Over the next 25 years, at least five additions were made to the main building. By the early 1900s, the first inn was operated on the property by Finley and Josephine Mast.

Finally the property became a boarding house and many of the out buildings needed work. In 1984, on their wedding anniversary, Francis and Sibyl discovered the Mast Farm. They had been searching for months to find a suitable place for a mountain inn. Today, the inn is on the National Register of Historic Places and one of the finest examples of a self-contained mountain homestead in North Carolina.

The 18-acre Mast Farm Inn includes a century-old farm house refurbished with nine guest rooms and the dining rooms. Outbuildings include a smoke house, the two-room log cabin, a spring house, an apple house, a blacksmith shop, woodworking shop, wash house, barn, and granary. Three of the outbuildings, the two-room cabin (loom house), woodworking shop and blacksmith shop, have been refurbished as minisuites.

They furnished all the rooms with turn-of-the-century antiques. I enjoyed going room to room looking for items that I had grown up with

on my grandparents farm. Quilts on pine-paneled walls, iron beds, and kerosene lanterns, to name a few. Even the porch swing and rockers helped to take me back to when life was less hurried and harried.

True to the country inn tradition, dinner is available at the Mast Farm Inn for both guests of the Inn as well as the public. Dinners are served Tuesday through Saturday at 6:00 and 7:45 p.m. and Sunday at 12:30 and 2:30 p.m. The four-course meals follow a rotating menu. Each dinner includes salad, a meat entree and a vegetarian entree. For example Tuesday's menu includes: an appetizer, fresh spinach salad, pot roast, or vegetable lasagna, mashed potato casserole, garden vegetables, rolls, dessert and beverages. *My* favorite is Sunday's menu with fried chicken and country ham.

Valle Crucis is home of the Mast General Store, just up the road from the Mast Farm Inn. Opened in 1883, eight years before Sears and Roebuck became partners, the Mast General Store has never closed.

It's a short drive from Valle Crucis to Boone, home of the third-oldest outdoor drama in the nation. *Horn in the West* tells of Daniel Boone and the Mountain men in their conflict with the British Militia and the Cherokee Indians.

---

**Mast Farm Inn**
**P.O. Box 704; Valle Crucis, NC 28691**
**(704) 963-5857; Fax: (704) 963-6404**
**Innkeepers: Sybil & Francis Pressly**
Rooms: 9; Private Baths: 7; Shared Baths: 1; Cabins: 3; Rates: $$-$$$$; children over 12
Affiliations: IIA, PAII
Payment:      Amenities: 🪑 📖 🍴

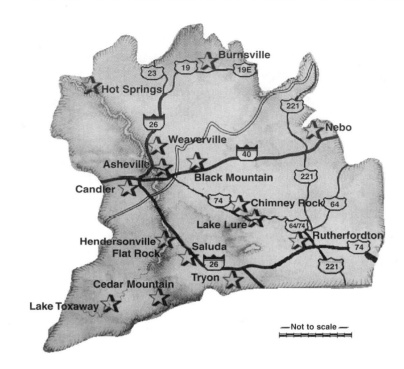

# Central Mountains

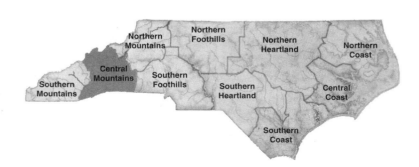

## Abbington Green Bed & Breakfast Inn
## Asheville

Abbington Green provides a touch of England in the heart of the Asheville historic Montford area. Valerie named her bed & breakfast for a place in England that was home to her father's family. She has lovingly furnished it with family heirlooms and named each room after parks and gardens around London.

The Wythe Peyton House, as it is called on the National Register of Historic Places, was built in 1908 for businessman David Latourette Jackson. For the last thirty years, the house had been rented and required major renovations to return it to its former glory. When Valerie purchased the home in February of 1993, she hired both an architect and an expert in historic restoration. By May of 1993 work began, and by October of the same year Abbington Green was open. Valerie won a Griffin Award from the Preservation Society for the renovation of the house.

Special care has been taken at Abbington Green to insure that each of the five rooms provide the best in amenities. Rooms include canopy-draped queen size beds, quality bedding, fine towels and soaps, and terry bathrobes. Three of the bedrooms even have fireplaces with gas-burning logs. The first of two suites, Eaton Square, has been completed in the carriage house. It is a duplex suite, has two bedrooms, one with a queen size bed and the other with twin beds. It also offers guests a sitting room, dining area and full kitchen. Valerie expects the second of the two suites, Hyde Park, to be finished soon.

Valerie serves breakfast each morning beginning at 8:30 in the formal dining room. Breakfast includes traditional English fare, stuffed crois-

sants or quiche Florentine. Her specialties are fruit soups and eggs Benedict.

Perfectly located in the Montford area, the Abbington Green provides easy access to the many attractions and points of interest in the Asheville area. It is less than five minutes from downtown Asheville and Pack Place with its Colburn Gem & Mineral Museum, the Asheville Art Museum, Health Adventure and the Diana Wortham Theater.

A few blocks from Pack Place is the Thomas Wolfe Memorial. This is the Dixieland boarding house of *Look Homeward Angel* and Thomas Wolfe's boyhood home. Also downtown is T.S. Morrison's, Asheville's oldest store, established in 1891.

Just south of downtown is Biltmore Estate. The Biltmore House is a 255-room French Renaissance chateau built in 1895 by George W. Vanderbilt. Today it is open to the public as a major attraction drawing more than 750,000 people a year.

Other area attractions that are close to Abbington Green include the Biltmore Homespun Shops, a ten-acre Botanical Garden, the Smith-McDowell House, the Antique Car Museum and the award-winning Nature Center. There are so many attractions that a stop at the Welcome Center is a must.

---

**Abbington Green Bed & Breakfast Inn**
**46 Cumberland Cir.; Asheville, NC 28801**
**(800) 251-2454; (704) 251-2454; Fax: (704) 251-2872**
**Innkeeper: Valerie Larrea**
Rooms: 5; Private Baths: 5; Suites: 1; Rates: $$-$$$; children over 10
Affiliations: NCBBI, PAII
Payment: $$$ CHECKS MC VISA AMEX Amenities: A/C 🖥 ⌨

## Albemarle Inn
## Asheville

Kathy and Dick Hemes fell in love with bed and breakfasts in 1983. With each inn or bed and breakfast they visited, they said, "If this were our inn, we'd do this, that or the other differently." Finally in March of 1992, they had the opportunity to change careers from the corporate world to what has proven to be the natural choice.

Kathy loves to spoil the guests. Dick enjoys the evening social hour when everyone gets acquainted. Together, they try to be as attentive to their guests as they can without being intrusive. Even breakfast is completely guest-oriented with Dick and Kathy personally serving a full breakfast of fresh fruits, juice, stuffed French toast, or brandied French toast with pecans. Other breakfast entrées include croissant a l'orange, omelettes, Eggs Moonstruck, and Eggs Albemarle.

The Greek Revival style mansion was built in 1909 for a doctor and his family. In 1920, they built another house (almost a perfect twin) in Biltmore Forest. When the family moved, the first house was converted to a private school. It first became an inn or, more correctly, a boarding house in 1941. Bela Bartok, the Hungarian composer, completed his Third Piano Concerto while staying at the Albemarle. In 1981, the boarding house changed hands and was converted to a bed and breakfast.

Loving care has been taken to restore the Albemarle to its early grandeur. The decorating reflects the years that Dick and Kathy lived in the Far East. There is a tasteful blend of antiques and accessories accented with oriental pieces throughout the inn. All eleven guest rooms are individually furnished in various styles. Each has a special feature such as the canopy bed pictured above. The marvelous carved-oak staircase with its curved-frame glass windows is another outstanding feature.

Kathy's love of decorating—especially details—can be seen everywhere. Dick's masterful needlepoint pillows accent the sitting areas.

Albemarle Inn is located in a beautiful and quiet residential area known as Grove Park. It is only five minutes from the downtown galleries, antique shops, the Thomas Wolfe Memorial, Pack Place Museum plus many excellent restaurants. The world-famous Biltmore Estate and the shops and galleries of Historic Biltmore Village are only ten minutes away.

Other notable attractions within an easy drive of Albemarle include the Southern Highlands Handicraft Guild and Folk Art Center on the Blue Ridge Parkway. The Smith-McDowell House, which contains two centuries of mountain history in Asheville's oldest brick structure, is a ten-minute drive.

Asheville is full of things to do, places to see and great restaurants in which to dine. Dick and Kathy know the area well and can help with everything from reservations for dinner or suggestions on day trips and tours.

**Albemarle Inn**
**86 Edgemont Rd.; Asheville, NC 28801**
**(800) 621-7435; (704) 255-0027**
**Innkeepers: Dick & Kathy Hemes**
Rooms: 10; Private Baths: 10; Suites: 1; Rates: $$-$$$; children over 14
Affiliations: NCBBI, PAII
Payment:      Amenities:

## Beaufort House Victorian Bed & Breakfast
## Asheville

Some people never realize their dreams. Before Robert and Jacqueline Glasgow were married, they knew that they would someday operate a bed and breakfast. After a two-year honeymoon around the world, the couple settled in Miami, Florida. When they made the decision to start a family, they felt that a bed and breakfast would be the best environment for their children. During a trip to Asheville they saw the Beaufort House. A few months later, the Glasgows began converting this magnificent home into a bed and breakfast.

To convert the home, Robert and Jacqueline installed nine new bathrooms and a new kitchen. A new roof plus new wiring and plumbing finished the major renovation. Wanting the work to meet their own exacting standards, they did most of the work themselves, calling in experts when the job demanded. With the renovations complete, they began on the cosmetic changes to make the house ready for guests. They wallpapered every room, selected oriental carpets, and purchased quality antiques and period reproductions.

Built in 1894, this 2½-story Queen Anne style mansion was designed by A.L. Melton for Theodore Fulton Davidson, a prominent attorney in Buncombe county. Davidson was very active in public service and served terms as Buncombe County judge, mayor of Asheville, attorney general and state senator. The house, named for his wife's home town of Beaufort, North Carolina, was often the site of private dinner parties, socials and political fund raisers. Today, Beaufort House is listed on the National Register of Historic Places, its charm and elegance recaptured by the efforts of Robert and Jacqueline.

As you drive through the gates onto carefully landscaped two acres of land, it's easy to forget that you are just a few blocks from downtown Asheville. From the shrubs, flower beds and magnificent oaks, to the wraparound porch,

bay windows and gingerbread trim, the house looks much as it did a hundred years ago.

It's easy to see that Robert and Jacqueline did a lot of research on colors, fabrics, and furnishings to help recreate the 1890's period within the home. They have also added the modern convenience of central air conditioning. Guest rooms have private baths, many with two-person Jacuzzis, cable TV/VCRs and phones. Several of the rooms in the main house also have wood-burning fireplaces. New to the Beaufort are three cottages. These feature private baths with Jacuzzis, wood-burning fireplaces, as well as cable TV/VCRs and phones.

The morning paper and Robert's freshly-squeezed orange juice greet you each morning. As you head for the dining room, the fragrance of fresh ground coffee wafts from the kitchen. While Robert greets you and introduces other guests, Jacqueline is putting the finishing touches on breakfast. Not only does she bake fresh bread each day, but Jacqueline also makes her own jams and jellies. The breakfast menu changes each day, but there is always a variety of fresh fruits and entrees to greet you. The five-course breakfast might include made-from-scratch Belgian waffles, French toast or "eggs Beaufort."

Asheville has many different "worlds" within the city. There is the Biltmore Estate and all its grandeur, Biltmore Village with its various quaint shops, and Pack Place with its many different museums under one roof. Throughout the city there are dozens of first-class restaurants from which to choose. Both Robert and Jacqueline can help with reservations and suggestions for almost anything you might want to do.

---

**Beaufort House Victorian Bed & Breakfast**
**61 N. Liberty St.; Asheville, NC 28801**
**(704) 254-8334; Fax: (704) 251-2082**
**Innkeepers: Robert & Jacqueline Glasgow**
Rooms: 8; Private baths: 12; Suites: 1, Cottages: 3; Rates: $$-$$$$; adults only
(25% off for AARP members Sun-Thu excluding July, Aug and Oct)
Payment:    Amenities:

## Dogwood Cottage Inn
## Asheville

The word cottage is so ambiguous, but rarely more so than it is with the Dogwood Cottage Inn. That's because the cottage contains more than 7,000 square feet of space. The cottage was built in the late 1890s in what is known as Appalachian rustic shingle style. An area visitor, Mr. Raoul, had five children and, upon coming to Asheville, found the local hotels would not let him book a room. His response was to build the Manor Hotel and this cottage to be his summer home. There are twenty other similar "cottages" in the area that were used as part of the hotel. Families would stay at the cottages with their children and servants. Then go down to the Manor for meals, socializing, and entertainment. Finally the cottage was sold to E.W. Grove of Grove Park Inn fame. Grove planned to use the cottage as his summer home, but died before he had the chance to move in. He left the cottage to his sons who in turn sold the property.

The Tracys, Joan and Don, had stayed in bed & breakfasts ever since the World's Fair in Knoxville. After thirty-nine years in data processing, the time came when they wanted out of the corporate structure. A visit to Asheville and the Biltmore Estate convinced Don and Joan that Asheville and a bed & breakfast was a natural for them as they loved the area and love to entertain. They purchased the cottage in 1989, but required three years to renovate. By August of 1993 they opened the doors and the Dogwood Cottage Inn was born.

Complete with swimming pool open to guests, a large fireplace in the parlor, polished wood floors and oak-beamed ceilings and a 42-foot veranda, the Dogwood is given over to large spaces. It is so peaceful, with only sounds of birdcalls and squirrels scampering around the trees that it is hard to imagine that you are less than 1½

miles from downtown Asheville. This is a perfect starting point for shopping or exploring.

Asheville is a place of many small worlds inside a larger one. Shopping areas, such as Biltmore Village, are plentiful. Architecture, from Art Deco to a 255-room French Renaissance chateau, can be found in the area. Museums like Pack Place, the Antique Car Museum, the Biltmore Village Museum, and the Smith-McDowell House are all within an easy drive of the Dogwood Cottage. For those who love the mountains, the Blue Ridge Parkway travels around $1/3$ of the city. Following the Parkway 14 miles to the northeast will take you to Mount Mitchell, the highest peak in the eastern U.S. at 6,684 feet. To the southwest, a 17-mile drive on the Parkway will take you to Mount Pisgah. From there you're only a stone's throw from the Cradle of Forestry, the birthplace of modern forestry in America.

Don and Joan will make sure that you're well fed before you begin your adventures. Breakfast brings fresh fruit (local, when in season), French toast, banana bread, sausage or ham biscuits, bacon, pancakes, or egg soufflés to the table. As both enjoy cooking, breakfast is a treat.

---

**Dogwood Cottage Inn**
**40 Canterbury Rd. N; Asheville, NC 28801**
**(704) 258-9725**
**Innkeepers: Joan & Don Tracy**
Rooms: 4; Private Baths: 4; Rates: $$
Affiliations: NCBBI
Payment:       Amenities: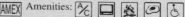

## The Inn on Montford
## Asheville

When the railroad came to Asheville in the 1880s, it brought great changes to the city. The population jumped from 2,500 to over 10,000 in less than 15 years. The wealthy found the mountains to be blissful relief from the heat of the lowlands. In 1895, the Biltmore Estate, a 100,000-acre estate with a 255-room mansion, was completed.

During the construction of the mansion at the Biltmore Estate, Richard Sharp Smith, an Englishman, was the supervising architect. When the project was completed, Smith went on to design a number of other buildings and homes in the area. In 1900, Sharpe designed an "Arts and Crafts" interpretation of a gabled English cottage for Dr. Charles Jordan at 296 Montford Avenue.

From the late 1800s and well into the twentieth century, the Montford district was Asheville's most prestigious area. It was home to the "movers and shakers" in Western North Carolina. Its broad avenue led from downtown Asheville, just five minutes away, to the home of Congressman and ambassador, Richmond Pearson. Thomas Wolfe immortalized the district in his books *Look Homeward, Angel* (1929) and *You Can't Go Home Again* (1940).

When America entered WWII, the Montford district began a forty year decline. During the last 15 years, the area has undergone extensive reclamation, and is now a National Historic District. Like most Historic Districts, restoration is an ongoing process. However, the extensive renovation of the Inn on Montford was completed several years ago.

Ripley Hotch (co-author of *How to Start and Run Your Own Bed and Breakfast Inn*) and Owen Sullivan opened the Inn on Montford as a bed and breakfast more than five years ago. In 1995, the mother/daughter team of Lynn and Alexa Royden purchased the B & B and added their own special touches. They created a bed and breakfast that is elegant yet comfortable by adding an

eclectic mix of antiques, period reproductions, overstuffed chairs and oriental rugs.

The four guest rooms, located on the second floor, are named for famous writers linked to the Asheville area: O. Henry, F. Scott Fitzgerald, Edith Wharton and, of course, Thomas Wolfe. The rooms are large and comfortable with private baths, three with whirlpool baths, and one with an old-fashioned clawfoot tub. The rooms all feature gas fireplaces, queen-size four poster beds, comfortable chairs and plenty of light for reading as well. As you walk up the stairs to the guest rooms, be sure to take time to look at the framed autographs on the walls. You will find letters and mementos signed by authors Tolstoy, Emerson, Longfellow, Mark Twain, Rudyard Kipling, Sir Arthur Conan Doyle, and George Bernard Shaw. Others you might recognize include Will Rogers, Buffalo Bill Cody and Charlie Chaplin. From the Civil War there are Ulysses S. Grant, William Sherman and Jefferson Davis. Lynn is an active collector of autographs, so the collection changes from time to time.

While a full breakfast is served family style in the formal dining room, Lynn and Alexa can handle the special needs of business travelers and well as vacationers who need an earlier continental breakfast. Those who have the opportunity to experience the treats of Bavarian puffed pancakes, raspberry filled croissants a l'orange or carefully prepared omelets, will find them exceptional.

Alexa has a world of knowledge about Asheville, and can help with recommendations on shopping, dining, or the best points of interest in the community. From having lived in Asheville for a number of years, I know that Alexa's suggestions are first-rate.

---

**The Inn On Montford**
**296 Montford Ave.; Asheville, NC 28801**
**(800) 254-9569; (704) 254-9569; Fax: (704) 254-9518**
**Innkeepers: Alexa & Lynn Royden**
Rooms: 4; Private baths: 4; Rates: $$$
Affiliations: PAII, NCBBI
Payment:       Amenities:

## Richmond Hill Inn
## Asheville

The Richmond Hill Inn is considered one of the best examples of a Queen Anne-style mansion in the country. Listed on the National Register of Historic Places, it provides an elegance of a bygone era.

James G. Hill, supervising architect of the United States Treasury Buildings, designed it as the private home of Congressman and ambassador Richmond Pearson and his wife, Gabrielle. It was one of the most elegant, and innovative, homes of its time. There was running water, its own communication system, and a pulley-operated elevator for transporting baggage from one floor to another. At the time of completion, it was a social and political activity center in the area.

Richmond Pearson lived at Richmond Hill until his death in 1923. Gabrielle survived him by one year. For the next twenty-seven years, the estate remained under a caretaker's charge. In 1951, the Pearsons' surviving children, Thomas and Marjorie, returned to the home and opened the mansion for public tours.

Neither Thomas nor Marjorie had children, and they left the house to their cousin, General Hayne Davis Boyden. In 1974, Boyden sold the estate. Over the next dozen years, many attempts were made to preserve the home. The first problem was moving the home 600 feet to the east. Weighing ½-million pounds, moving required more than a week. The Crouch-Mitch House Moving Company of Asheville received a national award for moving the largest structure in the U.S. in 1984.

In 1987, Dr. Albert J. Michel and his wife Margaret, then owners of the Education Center in Greensboro, purchased the property. In 1988, they also obtained 40 additional acres that were once a part of the original estate bringing the total to 47½.

The Michels preserved the building where possible, and restored or recreated where necessary. With 30,000 square feet, its generously-sized rooms, fine woodwork and the attention to detail have made it a perfect inn. Dr. and Mrs. Michel's choice of innkeeper has also helped to make the Richmond Hill Inn one of the top inns in America. They asked their daughter, Susan Michel, to run the inn for the first year. She fell in love with the inn and stayed.

The main house contains twelve bedrooms, the library, main hall, ball room and Gabrielle's, the inn's restaurant. The restaurant opened to the public in 1989. Each of the guest rooms is beautifully decorated with period antiques. They named the rooms after Pearson family members, important guests or Asheville-associated writers, such as F. Scott Fitzgerald.

In 1991 the Croquet Cottages were complete, adding an additional nine rooms to the inn. Then, in 1993, the Carriage House provided both a conference area and much-needed office space to the inn.

The American Bed & Breakfast Association selected the Richmond Hill Inn as one of the top sixteen inns in America. AAA gives it a four-diamond award, and this author considers it one of the top four he has ever visited.

---

**Richmond Hill Inn**
**87 Richmond Hill Dr.; Asheville, NC 28806**
**(704) 252-7313; Fax: (704) 252-8726**
**Innkeeper: Susan Michel**
Rooms: 33; Private Baths: 33; Suites: 3; Rates: $$$-$$$$$
Affiliations: PAII, IIA, AB&BA, AAA◆◆◆◆
Payment:     Amenities:

# The Scarlett Inn
# Asheville

This simplified Queen Anne-style home, located in the Historic Montford area of Asheville, was built in 1896 for Asheville businessman, Benjamin Jones. Associated with Carolina Power and Light, Jones involved himself with the early development and expansion of electric utilities in the area.

When Greg and Bridgett Bounds first saw the house in 1991, it needed major renovations. The work took almost two years with Greg doing all of the repairs himself. Finally, in October of 1993, the Scarlett Inn was ready to receive her first guest.

Named for their daughter, Victoria Scarlett, the inn offers three large rooms to the traveling public. One easily converts into a suite. Two of the rooms have queen-size beds, while the third has a standard full-size bed. Each room has been carefully decorated and furnished with period antiques and reproductions. Greg even serves breakfast on fine antique china accented with sterling silver in the formal dining room. During the summer, he serves wine & cheese on the large wraparound veranda. In the winter, you may have it in the front parlor.

Something that makes bed & breakfasts unique is that they become a reflection of the innkeeper. Some are formal, others are very casual. While the Bounds have recreated a home with a Victorian style, the feeling you have is one of visiting good friends. The inn is perfect for couples and families with children over twelve.

Since Bridgett still works full-time as a nurse, Greg takes care of most of the day-to-day operations of the Inn. However, Bridgett usually prepares the full breakfast each morning while Greg serves. Served family-style, breakfast might include French toast (made with real French bread), omelets, fresh fruit, homemade muffins, juices, herbal teas (from their herb garden) and, of course, coffee.

The Montford area of Asheville is north of the downtown business and shopping area. It is less than a five-minute drive to the area's visitor center. Greg and Bridgett can help with many suggestions of places to visit, shop or dine. There is so much in the area, however, that I would highly recommend a stop at the visitor's center, as well.

While downtown, you might want to visit Pack Place, the Thomas Wolfe Memorial, or take in one of the many activities at the Asheville Civic Center. One of Angel's and my favorite places is T.S. Morrison's, Asheville's oldest store. Morrison's has been in continuous operation since 1891 and is like a retail museum without an admission charge.

A short drive northeast of the Scarlett Inn and you will find the Biltmore Homespun Shops, Grovewood Gallery and the Antique Automobile Museum. Less than a mile southwest is Riverside Cemetery where you will find the graves of William Sidney Porter (O'Henry), Governors Zeb Vance and Locke Craig and Asheville's favorite son, Thomas Wolfe.

There's so much to do within the area, you should plan to spend several days at the Scarlett Inn. You also must remember to take in Biltmore Estate, the Smith-McDowell House, Botanical Gardens, Nature Center and the Biltmore Village Historic Museum.

---

**The Scarlett Inn**
**315 Pearson Dr.; Asheville, NC 28801**
**(704) 253-7888**
**Innkeepers: Greg & Bridgett Bounds**
Rooms: 3; Private Baths: 3; Cottages: 1; Rates: $$-$$$; children over 12
Affiliations: Asheville Chamber, Historical Preservation Society
Payment:   Amenities:

## The Wright Inn
## Asheville

In the late 1890s and well into the 1900s, the most fashionable area in Asheville was the Montford District. At that time, Pearson's Drive wandered from Montford Avenue along the crest of the hill. It then continued down and across the French Broad River to the Richmond Hill, home of Richmond Pearson. Many homes in the area were built by wealthy industrialists and real estate developers.

Several of the these Victorian-style homes were built in the Queen Anne style from 1880-1910. They had steeply-pitched roofs of irregular shape and used various methods to avoid smooth-walled appearances. Porches were usually one story high and extended along one or both side walls.

Many consider the Wright House one of the finest examples of the Queen Anne architecture. The home was built in the late 1890s for Osella B. and Leva Wright. Mr. Wright was the proprietor of the Carolina Carriage House in Asheville. His personal carriage house sheltered a fine carriage on the main floor, with quarters above for the groomsman and a stable below.

Unfortunately, the Wright fortunes declined. When there was no more money, Mr. Wright disappeared. From 1914 on, Mrs. Wright called herself a "widow." Mr. Wright secretly returned home when he was dying. Mrs. Wright buried him the day he died, and never revealed her secret. From 1914 until 1970, the fine home was a boarding house.

In 1987, Ed and Barbara Siler bought the house and spent more than a year restoring the home with careful attention to detail. In 1988 the Wright Inn opened its doors. Then, in 1994, Carol and Art Wenczel purchased the inn.

Art and Carol greet guests in the Coleman parlor which is beautifully decorated with period furniture, handmade oak trim, and a fireplace. Each of the eight rooms and one suite is decorated in turn-of-the-century style with fine antiques and family heirlooms. Each guest room has its own private bath, telephone and cable TV. Two of the rooms have fireplaces. The carriage house has a living room, dining room, kitchen, three bedrooms and two full baths.

Afternoon tea and cookies are served in front of a fire in the Willows drawing room or in the gazebo. Breakfast is also served in the gazebo, weather permitting. When the weather demands, breakfast is served in the formal dining room. Served individually, the full breakfast includes juices, coffee and teas, homemade breads, fresh fruits and main courses such as Bermuda pancakes with blueberry sauce, egg strata, or eggs Benedict.

The Wright Inn is a short drive to all of the Asheville area attractions. Carol and Art love to entertain and can help with information about the area as well as dinner suggestions and reservations.

The American Bed & Breakfast Association awarded the Wright Inn its distinguished triple crown. The Inn and Carriage House are both on the National Register of Historic Places.

---

**The Wright Inn**
**235 Pearson Drive; Asheville, NC 28801**
**(800) 552-5724; (704) 251-0789**
**Innkeepers: Carol & Art Wenczel**
Rooms: 8; Private Baths: 9; Carriage House: 1; Rates: $$-$$$$; children over 11
Affiliations: NCBBI, PAII, AB&BA
Payment:  Amenities:

## Black Mountain Inn
## Black Mountain

Every bed and breakfast is different. They are a reflection of the inn-keeper. Of their personality, taste, and interests. This is something that makes staying at a bed and breakfast wonderful. You can escape the "styrofoam world" of fast food and roadside motels.

There is something else that often makes a bed and breakfast unique; the history of the structure. The *when* and *why* it was built. Or *how* it was used. In some cases it's *who* stayed there. This is what first caught my attention about the Black Mountain Inn.

The B & B is a pleasant place to stay with its fireplace and comfortable rooms. June Bergeron has done a fantastic job of renovating this historic structure. She has decorated each of the seven rooms with an eclectic blend of styles. The moment you drive up the gravel lane, you move back to a time of quiet romance.

Built in the 1870s, it served as the stage coach stop for years. Later it was used as the Franklin Humanitarian Home, and even as part of a university. Then, in the early 1940s, Mrs. Mary Alshire purchased the house.

The previous owners had added the third-floor art studio and sunroom. Mrs. Alshire continued the remodeling. She had the landscaping done, and the house re-oriented toward the road. Purchased to be her summer home, it became a haven for artists and writers. Norman Rockwell, Joan Sutherland, Helen Keller, and Ann Sullivan all stayed at the home. In addition, two of my favorite authors, Ernest Hemingway and John Steinbeck, were frequent guests.

There is much to do in the Black Mountain area, and June provides a full breakfast to get you started. Her "homemade" granola is famous

with her guests. So are the pastries, breads, and muffins. Other breakfast favorites include soufflés, blintzes and crepes.

The village of Black Mountain is twelve miles east of Asheville in the Swannanoa Valley. For years, the Cherokees called it Grey Eagle. Early settlers labeled it the Dark Mountain. Today it is best known for its antique shops, galleries and especially for its music festivals.

The Historic District in downtown Black Mountain is commonly called "The Loop." This rectangular area includes not only shops, but also interesting places to eat such as My Father's Pizza. The Old Depot, for decades the focal point of Black Mountain, is now an arts and crafts gallery. One block west of the Loop is the Valley Museum, located in the old fire station.

Black Mountain has the distinction of being a small mountain community, yet close to everything. Within a thirty-minute drive you can ride mountain bikes, go llama trekking or whitewater rafting. You can visit a 255-room estate, or take the Blue Ridge Parkway to the highest peak east of the Mississippi, Mount Mitchell. The scenic drive down NC 9 will take you to Chimney Rock and through Hickory Nut Gorge. While the actual distance is less than 30 miles, it can take a couple of hours to drive it. This is partly because of the all the places there are to stop and look around. It is also because there is no such thing as a straight stretch of road during the drive.

---

**Black Mountain Inn**
**718 W. Old Hwy. 70; Black Mountain, NC 28711**
**(800) 735-6128; (704) 669-6528**
**Innkeepers: June Bergeron Colbert**
Rooms: 7; Private Baths: 7; Rates: $$
Affiliations: Black Mountain Chamber
Payment:  CHECKS Amenities:

## A Little Bit Of Heaven Bed & Breakfast
### Burnsville

It's been said, without much exaggeration, that you could throw darts at a map of the Burnsville area and hit a beautiful spot every time. With road names like Lickskillet, Hardscrabble, Possum Trot and others, there are bound to be some interesting places to explore. Your starting spot is Bearwallow Road.

John and Shelley Johnson with their co-innkeepers, Meghan (11) and Katie (9), have created a perfectly named bed and breakfast. Here, at an elevation of 3,000 feet, you will find "A Little Bit Of Heaven Bed and Breakfast." It sits on two acres adjacent to the South Toe River Valley and the Pisgah National Forest.

Opened as a bed and breakfast in 1992, the large stone home provides four comfortably-sized bedrooms each with private bath. The rooms, like the home itself, is decorated in country eclectic style. The living room features a huge fireplace built of local stone. Across the entire back of the house, a second-story deck provides magnificent views of Celo Knob, the second-highest peak (6,200 feet) east of the Mississippi. The highest, Mount Mitchell (6,684 feet) is just out of view.

Only three miles east of Burnsville and about the same distance west of the South Toe River Valley (Highway 80-S), A Little Bit of Heaven is located a stone's throw from 19 East. While in the area I would suggest taking the 15-mile drive south on NC-80 to the Blue Ridge Parkway. The road follows the river most of the way with the Black Mountains on one side and the Seven-Mile Ridge on the other. Along the way, the Lost Cove Picnic Area is a perfect place for a picnic. Shelley might even be able to help with the necessities. When you reach the Parkway at Buck Creek Gap, the drive to Mt. Mitchell is just 11 miles south.

Turning north will take you to Crabtree Meadows. There is a coffee-shop/campground on the 10-mile drive to Little Switzerland. Then go back under the Parkway and follow Crabtree Creek Road down the mountain back to 19 East. This drive is one of the most scenic in Western North Carolina.

The town of Burnsville reminds me more of a northeastern village than an Appalachian mountain community. Complete with town square, Burnsville is made up of small shops lining the main street. Here you will find antique dealers and specialty shops including an excellent quilt shop. The people of Burnsville are friendly and more than willing to stop and visit, provide directions and tell you about local history and gossip. A feature stop is the Parkway Playhouse Summer Theater, North Carolina's old professional summer theater.

Shelley knows that no trip to the area would be complete without a full breakfast. Your day will start with breakfast served family-style in the dining room with cheesy egg bake, waffles, omelets, or possibly stuffed French toast. There is always fresh home baked bread, coffee cake, or muffins, fresh fruits, coffee and teas.

---

**A Little Bit Of Heaven Bed & Breakfast**
**937 Bear Wallow Rd.; Burnsville, NC 28714**
**(704) 675-5379**
**Innkeepers: Shelley & John Johnson**
Rooms: 4; Private Baths: 4; Rates: $$
Payment:   Amenities: 🖥 ♨ ✆

## NuWray Inn
## Burnsville

The NuWray Inn has been the standard of southern hospitality since 1833. It is the oldest country inn in Western North Carolina. Owners Pam and Chris Strickland carry on its grand traditions.

Each of the Inn's twenty-six rooms and five suites is charming and comfortable. Its dining room is legendary and serves some of the best food in the south.

The original Inn was a two-story log structure operated by Bacchus Smith as a tavern and the local stage stop. You will find part of the original logs within the walls of today's imposing Colonial Revival style structure. The three-story clapboard inn takes up a large portion of one corner of Burnsville's Town Square. Its two-tiered porch is a favorite place for guests to retire. Rocking chairs allow them to meet one another while their generously-portioned meals settle.

With more than 150 years of history, every corner of the NuWray has a story to tell. Each guest room is unique with its own personality. Like the parlors and common rooms, they are decorated with period antiques and wrought iron. The decor blends perfectly with collections of glass and china that were carefully assembled by four generations of the Ray and Wray families. The fireplace in the main lobby, the Steinway Duo-Art player grand piano and the Reginaphone all help capture days most of us thought were lost forever.

NuWray has been a stopover for many writers and actors. Thomas Wolfe and O. Henry have tread the polished hardwood floors and this author will always treasure his time there.

The dining room is also an excellent reason to visit the NuWray. The family-style breakfasts and dinners have attracted visitors and local folk for years. (Dinner is not included in room rate) Specialties include pork roast, smothered steak, BBQ ribs, roast beef, turkey, ham and, of course, *real* southern fried chicken. With each main course there are 6-8 fresh vegetables, homemade biscuits, homemade dessert and a choice of coffee, tea or lemonade. Breakfast (open to the public) is also a treat with sausage, bacon, ham, grits, gravy, eggs, biscuits, honey and strawberry jam.

The town of Burnsville adds to the charm of NuWray. Located deep within the world's oldest mountains, antique dealers and specialty shops line the quiet streets. Just south of the Inn is one of Western North Carolina's most scenic drives. The road through the Toe River Valley meanders to the Blue Ridge Parkway. Along its route you will discover much of the beauty that has always been a part of the Appalachian Mountains. The people are friendly, the climate pleasant, and when you reach the top of Mount Mitchell, you'll see the most incredible views anywhere east of the Mississippi.

**Nu Wray Inn**
**P.O. Box 156; Town Square; Burnsville, NC 28714**
**(800) 368-9729; (704) 682-2329**
**Innkeepers: Chris & Pam Strickland**
Rooms: 26; Private Baths: 31; Suites: 5; Rates: $$-$$$
Affiliations: PAII, Mobil, AAA, AB&BA
Payment:     Amenities:

# Owl's Nest Inn at Engadine
# Candler

Part of the beauty of the Owl's Nest is that it is hidden from view. While located on Smokey Park Highway (U.S. 19/23) it sits high on a ridge surrounded by trees and shrubs. You know the road is down below—that you can be in Asheville to the east or Waynesville to the west in just 15 minutes—yet there is a peace and quiet at Owl's Nest that brings a variety of birds and the occasional deer into the meadow.

We had a feeling that we were onto something special the moment we turned into the tree-lined drive. After following the drive's twisting turns, we discovered a magnificent white Queen Anne mansion set off by turrets and balconies.

Captain Hoyt, the home's designer and first owner, was born in Washington, North Carolina. During the Civil War, he served as a cavalry officer in the famed Mobile Rifles. When the war was over, he went to New York City to seek his fortune. The fates were kind to him and he married a wealthy divorced woman with three daughters. When he returned to North Carolina with his family, they decided to settle in a small valley just west of Asheville. They began a new life and lived in a cabin while waiting for their new home, which they named Engadine for a valley in Switzerland, to be completed.

Wanting the same amenities that the rich families had in Asheville, yet desiring to be away from the city, proposed some interesting problems in construction for 1885. Running water for the water closets was provided by building a water storage tank in the attic. Servants would pump water into the storage tank, and fresh water was provided for in-home use. While the storage tank no longer exists (rooms have modern bathrooms), many of the water closets, complete with marble-topped counters, are still used by Inn guests at the Owl's Nest. Another novel, but practical, idea for its

day was the use of a dynamo powered by a stream to provide electricity to the home.

Within the home, the captain used floor-to-ceiling paneling taken from pine heartwood. Today, the floors, walls and woodwork remain much as they were more than 100 years ago. The glistening beauty of the wood is enriched by oriental rugs, antique furnishings and period reproductions.

For innkeeper Mary Melaugh, the dream of owning a bed and breakfast began more than seven years ago. Like many dreams, other things kept getting in the way. When her husband, Jim, was offered early retirement by the company for which he worked, they jumped at the chance. A course in innkeeping rekindled the dream, and a trip to North Carolina introduced them to the home they would open just a few months later as the Owl's Nest Inn at Engadine. Mary and Jim added the "Owl's Nest" for Mary's collection of nearly 100 owls that you will find throughout the house.

The largest of the four guest rooms at the Owl's Nest is called the Captain's Room. With a king-size bed, a gas burning fireplace, and windows that provide an excellent view of the mountains, it was naturally my favorite, until I saw the other well-appointed rooms, then I couldn't decide. The Howell Room and Wicker Room both have gas burning fireplaces, antique and period furnishings and special views of the property. The Duck Room is decorated with rich dark greens that are set off by its wildlife prints. Its full bath features a claw-foot tub, and the room has twin beds that make a king-size bed on request.

---

**Owl's Nest Inn at Engadine**
**2630 Smokey Park Highway; Candler, NC 28715**
**(800) 665-8868; (704) 665-8325**
**Innkeepers: Mary & Jim Melaugh**
Rooms: 4; Private baths: 4; Rates: $$-$$$; children over 6
Affiliations: NCBBI, PAII, Asheville Chamber
Payment:    Amenities:

## Pisgah View Ranch
## Candler

It sometimes amazes me how you can miss important things in your own neighborhood. This summer we discovered that one of the best "getaways" in the mountains of North Carolina was only a few miles from our home at the base of the 5,749-foot Mount Pisgah. In 1790, Uriah Davis built a log cabin on a 2,000-acre land grant in its shadow. His great-great-great grandchildren run the Pisgah View Ranch on that property.

The tract of land, in the family since the adoption of the American Constitution, has been an important stopover for guests since Ella Davis opened a boarding house on the property in 1915. Railroad workers would make the long ride to her home by buckboard, arriving just in time for a late dinner of fried chicken, roast beef, or pork chops. Before Ella died, she divided the estate among her children. In the early 1940s, her daughter, Ruby Davis Cogburn together with her husband, Chester, purchased some of the land and opened the Pisgah View Ranch. Ruby lived and worked in her home only 100 feet from where she was born. During the off season, she and Chester traveled the world. Each spring, they would reopen their doors and people from all over the world would come to them. Ruby's legacy of "good food and plenty of it" along with comfortable lodgings, is now carried on by her son Max, her daughter Phyllis and Phyllis' husband Sam Parris. The cabin built by Uriah Davis is still located on the property where it was built and serves as museum operated by Max's wife, Mary, for visitors to the Pisgah View.

There is so much to do at Pisgah View Ranch that you have to plan on staying at least a couple of nights. It takes that long just to really savor the ambiance of the ranch. Of course, your day begins with checking into one of the many cottages or cabins located on the grounds. They vary from individual units complete with fireplace to duplex log cabins

and others such as the "Whippoorwill" with its own living room, two bedrooms, two baths and kitchenette.

While you're checking in, you might want to sign up for a horseback ride up the mountain. Your guide on these rides is an experienced wrangler, and knows much of the history of Pisgah View. I admit that I'm not really a horseman, yet the wrangler was able to find me a horse that was patient with all my stops for photographs. Rides of an hour or two are available, and they are the only thing that is not included in the daily rate.

Activities at the ranch include a large L-shaped heated pool, tennis courts, volleyball and shuffleboard and plenty of lawn games. There is nearly 1,700-acres for hiking and the kitchen will even prepare a picnic lunch for your excursions. However, be sure to be back in time for dinner. Three meals a day are served in the dining room, and each is served family style. While the fare changes from day to day, the cooks at the ranch set one of the best tables around. Their fried chicken and county ham dinners with cornbread stuffing and oatmeal pie are very popular with guests.

Evening brings nightly entertainment of country-western or bluegrass music, cloggers, square dancing. Family night, hosted by Max Cogburn is a treat for guests. His stories about the ranch are legendary. As you walk back to your cabin, you may discover, as we did, that the stars seem to shine brighter and the air smells a bit fresher than it did when you first arrived.

---

**Pisgah View Ranch**
**Rt. 1; Candler, NC 28715**
**(704) 667-9100**
**Innkeepers: Phyllis Parris & Max Cogburn**
24 cabins (41 rooms; 7 suites); Private baths: 48; Rates: $-$$
Affiliations: Asheville Chamber
Payment:   Amenities:

# The Sassy Goose
## Brevard (Cedar Mountain)

Just 12 miles south of Brevard is a small family resort known as the Sassy Goose. Located on fifty-four acres, Bob and Bette Vande Weghe created the perfect hideaway with something for everyone. You will discover a peace and tranquility that you seldom find anywhere.

Bob and Bette built the 2,000-square-foot lodge strictly for guests. Their home is a hundred feet or so away.

Containing only three bedrooms, the lodge also houses the library. Here guests will find not only books, but games, color TV and VCR, large wood-burning fireplace, and a guest refrigerator. The breakfast room, with its large windows and deck, looks out over the lake. They serve the continental style breakfast, consisting of juices, fruits, cereals, and breads here each morning.

In addition to the lodge, there are two log cabin suites, each about 400-square feet. They have outfitted each cabin with a queen-size bed and color TV. The mini-kitchenettes in the cabins offer a two-burner stove, microwave, refrigerator, and the necessary pots and pans. While both cabins have decks, one also has a fully screened porch.

The wooded acreage offers trails, walking paths, and plenty of room for child or adult to roam. One trail leads to a small waterfall. Another leads to a ¾-acre trout pond where you can feed the fish or catch and release. There is a six-acre lake where guests may swim, paddle a canoe, or take a ride on the electric battery-operated pontoon boat. I can't forget the Volley Ball/Badminton court, or the 30 by 50 foot barn. This structure is open to guests and offers table tennis and other games. There is also croquet, an all-weather tennis court and even a par two golf

course where you can practice your chip shots. Bob even provides the clubs. For more serious golfing, there is the Sherwood Forest Golf Course, a par three course, a few miles up the road. In addition, Connestee Falls offers a full 18-hole course.

While located in the country, The Sassy Goose is close to other area attractions. Caesar's Head State Park is six miles south, just across the South Carolina border. This is one of the "high" spots of the South Carolina up-country in beauty, elevation and visibility. On a clear day there is an excellent view of the mountains.

Pretty Place, an open air chapel constructed by the Civilian Conservation Corps during the depression, is also nearby. Located on the side of a mountain, Pretty Place provides a 20-mile view. It is a favorite place for weddings, meditation and reflection.

Down the road a piece and around the corner is Granny's Place restaurant. Open for breakfast and lunch, Granny's is a favorite for the locals. Friday nights, Granny's place also serves prime rib by reservation only. Up 276 is the Raintree Restaurant. We can both highly recommend their filet mignon.

The Sassy Goose provided Angel and me a much needed place to rest and relax.

---

**The Sassy Goose**
**P.O. Box 228; Reasonover Dr.; Cedar Mountain, NC 28718**
**(704) 966-9493**
**Innkeepers: Bob & Bette Vande Weghe**
Rooms: 3; Private Baths: 5; Cabin suites: 2; Rates: $$
Open May-November
Payment: 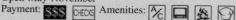  Amenities:

## The Dogwood Inn Bed & Breakfast
## Chimney Rock

Sitting in the shadow of Chimney Rock, on the bank of the Rocky Broad River, is the Dogwood Inn. The original inn was built in 1890 as a stagecoach stop between Asheville and Charlotte. North Carolina highway 64/74 was then called the Hickory Nut Gap Turnpike.

Through flood in 1916 and fire in 1930, the Logans ran the inn for three generations. One month after fire destroyed all of Chimney Rock Village, the Logans rebuilt the inn on the remaining foundations, identical to the original. Over the years, the inn went through other difficult periods. Finally, like all things of hidden value, the inn was rediscovered by Marsha Reynolds and her brother, Mark. By investing, with a lot of work, they are bringing the Inn back to its former glory.

Because the Inn is nestled in a natural thermal belt that runs through the area, visitors can enjoy the four porches, large yard and the sound of the rushing river year round. We enjoyed the sound of the river as we went to sleep. Our window gave us a great view in the morning as the sun came up on Chimney Rock.

Marsha and Mark serve a European style buffet each morning in the dining room or on the porch overlooking the Rocky Broad River and Chimney Rock. In addition to cereals, granola and yogurt there are fruits and juices and homebaked breads. While the entrées change from day to day, guests have a choice of two. One is always an egg dish, and the other is normally pancakes, waffles or French toast. Morning coffee and tea is always available before breakfast on the upstairs buffet.

Hickory Nut Gorge is just 14 miles long. It twists and turns with the river from Gerton, in Henderson County, to Lake Lure, in Rutherford County. On the north side of the Gorge is the 3,967-foot mountain,

Sugar Loaf. On the south side is Chimney Rock Park. Here you can take an elevator up twenty-six stories through the inside of the mountain to a 75-mile view of Hickory Nut Gorge and Rutherford County. Afterward, enjoy a walk to one of the highest waterfalls east of the Mississippi, Hickory Nut Falls, with a 404-foot drop.

Movie fans may think the waterfall looks familiar. That's because it was featured in *The Last Of The Mohicans* starring Daniel Day Lewis. The motion-picture industry discovered the gorge in 1915. Stars such as Douglas Fairbanks, Clark Gable, Mary Pickford and Gloria Swanson have all visited the area to make movies. *Dirty Dancing*, starring Patrick Swayze, featured Lake Lure.

With a drive through the area or a quick walk through Chimney Rock Village, you will quickly see why Marsha and Mark fell in love with the Dogwood Inn. The two-story inn provides a perfect setting for relaxing, or a starting place to explore the many shops, restaurants and attractions in the area. Down the road from the inn there is canoeing, horseback riding, golf, fishing, and miles of trails to explore.

---

**The Dogwood Inn Bed & Breakfast**
**P.O. Box 159; US 74 Hwy.; Chimney Rock, NC 28720**
**(800) 992-5557; (704) 625-4403; Fax: (704) 625-8825**
**Innkeepers: Marsha & Mark Reynolds**
Rooms: 10; Private Baths: 6; Shared Baths: 4; Rates: $$; children over 12
Affiliations: NCBBI, PAII
Payment: $$$ CHECKS    AMEX DISCOVER Amenities: A/C

# Highland Lake Inn
# Flat Rock

Remember going off to camp as a kid? I do! My days at camp were some of the best days of my life. Our stay at Highland Lake Inn reminded me of those days—fishing, swimming, canoeing in the lake, the aroma of wood smoke in the air. Highland Lake Inn is much more than a camp, yet it's neither a bed and breakfast nor is it a country inn in the traditional sense. Some would call it a resort. I call it a perfect getaway because it has the best that each has to offer.

Located just a few miles outside Hendersonville in Flat Rock, Highland Lake Inn is convenient to all of the attractions of the mountains. Down the street is the world-famous Flat Rock Theater, the State Theater of North Carolina and one of the top ten in the nation. During its 15-week season, the Vagabond Players work with famous guest actors, such as Kyle McLaughlin and Burt Reynolds, to present American classics, comedy, musicals and whodunits.

To the south is Connemara, the 240-acre farm where Carl Sandburg spent the last 22 years of his life. Sandburg—poet, author, lecturer and Pulitzer Prize winner, moved here in 1945 with his wife, three daughters, grand-children and his wife's herd of prize-winning Chikaming goats. Sandburg died in 1967, and Connemara became a National Historic Site the same year.

These are not the only points of interest available to visitors. Biltmore is a short drive away in Asheville, Chimney Rock to the east in Hickory Nut Gorge, and to the west is Transylvania County. With more than 150 in the county, it is known as the "home of the waterfalls."

There is much to do around Highland Lake Inn, but there is also much to do without ever leaving the 180-acre complex. Entrance to the inn is a narrow road just past the waterfall created by the dam. Drive up the lane

and you may see both children and adults dropping from the rope-swing into the cool waters of the 30-acre lake. Others may be swimming, canoeing or sunbathing. To your left, several horses stand ready to greet new visitors to the property. At the top of the hill is the lodge which has 20 rooms, each with private bath. Its spacious lobby, complete with fireplace, has an atmosphere that is both rustic and modern at the same time. Other accommodations at Highlands include several duplex cabins, each with private entrance, fireplace and private bath. There are also five cottages that range in size from two to four bedrooms. An elegant 16-room Inn with fireplace- and Jacuzzi-suites was added in 1996.

As you drive past the cabins, the Olympic sized swimming pool, tennis courts, basketball, horse shoes and volleyball nets all beckon you to come and play. Two miles of hiking trails, organic gardens, wildflower meadows, and the barn with its country critters, call to young and old.

What was once a boys' camp has been turned into a mountain paradise by Larc and Kerry Lindsey. However, the magic and intimacy of Highlands doesn't just involve play. It also includes one of the finest restaurants in the area. Larc, the inn's chef, turns his culinary skill to providing entrées of Scallopini of Lamb a la Edgar, Free Range Hen Rustica, roast pork loin or filet mignon. Again and again the kitchen at Highland Lake Inn has taken award after award for its excellent cuisine.

A bed and breakfast... a country inn... a resort—all of these. Highland Lake Inn is a haven for the stress-weary.

---

**Highland Lake Inn**
**P.O. Box 1026; Highland Lake Drive; Flat Rock, NC 28731**
**(800) 762-1376; (704) 693-3868; Fax: (704) 696-8951**
**Innkeepers: The Lindsey Family**
Rooms: 58; Private baths: 56; Suites: 6; Cottages: 6; Cabins: 10; Rates: $$-$$$
Payment: CHECKS MC VISA AMEX DISCOVER  Amenities: A/C 📺 🖥 🎿 👥 👪 ♿

## The Claddagh Inn
## Hendersonville

For nearly a century, the Claddagh Inn has been welcoming visitors to Hendersonville. If the walls could talk they would tell the stories of guests who came for a few days and took home memories of the Blue Ridge Mountains that would last a lifetime.

They would tell of Chimney Rock Park with its 75-mile view of the Blue Ridge Mountains. They might inform you of the land of the waterfalls where you will find more than 150, including Whitewater Falls (a 411-foot drop), the highest falls east of the Mississippi River.

I am sure the walls would remember the countless trips made by guests to Asheville to visit Biltmore Estate, or take a drive along the Blue Ridge Parkway.

Most of all they would tell of historic Hendersonville and Flat Rock; of Connemara, once home to Carl Sandburg and of the Flat Rock Playhouse, considered one of the top ten summer stock theaters in the county. They would also tell of Historic downtown Hendersonville, just a few blocks away, with its almost parklike setting, it quaint shops and antique stores.

Guests are still finding new things to do in the area and the walls of the Claddagh are hearing new stories. The walls are learning of dinners at restaurants such as Expressions and Huberts, two of the areas finest. After nearly a century, the Claddagh and its innkeepers are still helping guests have enjoyable memories of the days and nights they spent in the mountains.

The exact date the Inn was built is unknown. We do know it was built at the turn-of-the-century for W.A. Smith, an attorney and onetime mayor of Henderson County. Smith sold the home to Elsie Sindorf in 1906, and it was she who converted it into a boarding house. In 1985, Fred and Marie Carberry purchased the building, made major internal renovations, and opened it as Hendersonville's first bed and breakfast. It was the Carberrys who named it "The Claddagh."

"Claddagh" means loyalty, love and friendship; it is exemplified in the atmosphere of the B & B. At the time of our visit, Vickie and Dennis Pacilio were maintaining the traditions of the innkeepers before them. Now that the time has come for them to pass the keys to August and Geraldine Emanuele, they are passing on traditions as well. As of this writing, we have not had the opportunity to meet the new innkeepers. After conversing on the phone with them, we look forward to another stay in this beautiful bed and breakfast.

Built in the Classical Revival style, the green and yellow exterior with its large wraparound veranda invites you just to stop and "sit a spell." Through the front doors are oriental rugs, wood paneling, and an eclectic mix of antiques and period furnishings that provide a comfortable setting for a night's stay or an extended visit. Each of the 12 guest rooms and two suites has a private bathroom, TV and a telephone. Air-conditioning is also provided for individual room comfort.

Sue Kargl, a recent graduate of the National Center for Hospitality Studies, will be helping the new innkeepers by preparing hearty country-style breakfasts each morning for guests. Visitors can look forward to eggs (cooked any style you want), hash browns or southern-style grits, locally prepared ham, bacon or sausage along with fresh breads or homemade muffins.

Future plans for the Claddagh Inn include a Sunday brunch and formal high tea each weekday afternoon. Of course, the evening social hour with the innkeepers, other guests and a glass of sherry will remain a tradition for years to come.

---

**The Claddagh Inn**
**755 N. Main St.; Hendersonville, NC 28792**
**(800) 225-4700; (704) 697-7778; Fax: (704) 697-8664**
**Innkeepers: August & Geraldine Emanuele**
Rooms: 12; Private baths: 14; Suites: 2; Rates: $$
Affiliations: AAA, Hendersonville Chamber
Payment: $$$ CHECKS MC VISA AMEX DISCOVER Amenities: A/C 🖥 🌐

# Echo Mountain Inn
# Hendersonville (Laurel Park)

Echo Mountain Inn sits high above Hendersonville (2,120 feet) on Echo Mountain at an elevation of nearly 3,000 feet. The mountain provides some of the most impressive views in Western North Carolina. The view from the windows of Echo Mountain Inn is like looking at a model railroad from a third-story balcony. At night you have a feeling that you're actually looking at the sky, with millions of stars, instead of a city. The sky itself always looks brighter from the veranda of Echo Mountain Inn.

Here on top of the mountain, the temperatures are cooler during the summer than they are in the valley below. It may have been the temperatures on the mountain or the view that prompted a local doctor to build the large stone and native wood structure in 1896 as a summer home.

In the early 1920s, the property was purchased and turned into a private girls school. By 1929, the area around Hendersonville was already becoming a favorite tourist destination. Travelers would come from the lowlands of both North and South Carolina to escape the heat. The girls school was converted into an inn to accommodate the many visitors to the area. The cool temperatures high on the mountain made the Inn one of the most popular in the area, a natural getaway.

The main structure at Echo Mountain Inn houses the main dining room and 22 guest rooms. The rooms are decorated with an eclectic mix of antique and contemporary furnishings. The rooms provide cable television and individual phones. Most of the rooms have excellent views of the mountains, and many have wood-burning fireplaces.

Over the years the Inn has undergone numerous changes. In 1959, outbuildings were added to provide additional rooms for guests, several offering kitchenettes. A two-bedroom cottage includes two baths, living and dining rooms, and a full kitchen. Over the last few years, the Inn has un-

dergone additional renovations. On our last visit to the Inn, we found new carpet in both the lobby and the rooms, a small dance floor added to the dining room, and several of the rooms in the main building had been remodeled into mini-suites.

The "L" shaped dining room at Echo Mountain can easily accommodate 85 for dinner and is often used for special functions, meetings and wedding receptions. The windows offer spectacular views of the city below. Guests tend to linger over dinner as the lights of the city come on. One area of the dining room, with its large stone fireplace, is where the innkeepers serve continental breakfast each morning to inn guests. The dining room is open to both inn guests and the public for evening dinner and Sunday brunch.

Resting on three acres near the top of the mountain, Echo Mountain Inn offers guests convenient access to the city. However, there is a wonderful feeling of seclusion from the busy town below. Those who just want to unwind can take a dip in the swimming pool, play a game of shuffleboard, or relax on the covered porch with a good book from the Inn's library.

Only three miles from historic downtown Hendersonville, Echo Mountain Inn is close to area attractions such as the Carl Sandburg Home National Historic Site in Flat Rock. Also located there is the Flat Rock Playhouse, considered one of the ten best summer stock theaters in the country. Chimney Rock Park is only 15 miles east of Hendersonville. To the west is Transylvania County with its more than 150 waterfalls.

---

**Echo Mountain Inn**
**2849 Laurel Park Hwy. Hendersonville, NC 28739**
**(704) 693-9626**
**Innkeepers: Peter & Shirley DeMaras**
Rooms: 26; Private baths: 37; Suites: 8; Efficiencies: 3; Rates: $$-$$$$
Payment: $$$ CHECKS MC VISA DISCOVER  Amenities:

## Mountain Home Bed & Breakfast
## Hendersonville (Mountain Home)

A doctor commented after staying at Mountain Home, "Prescription: stay here for two nights, and you won't have to take any aspirin and call me in the morning."

This is a place to come in, sit on the porch, relax, and enjoy the amenities. No inn or bed and breakfast is alike. The thing that makes them different is the fact that they are a reflection of their innkeepers. Bob and Donna Marriott purchased Mountain Home because they really like people. They like making people feel special. They're not pushy about wanting to talk to you, but if you want to sit and visit, they're always available.

Their enjoyment in doing for their guests is part of what makes Mountain Home special. For example, Donna is a professional cake decorator and will make cakes for birthdays, anniversaries or romantic weekends and have it in the room when you get there. Wine or sparkling cider also can be in the room for special occasions. Just give them about a week's notice for these special services. They also can arrange with the local deli for picnic baskets. While at Mountain Home recently, I listened while Donna made dinner reservations for a guest who had planned a romantic weekend.

Mountain Home is five miles from downtown Hendersonville, six miles from the Asheville Airport and only 15 minutes from Biltmore Estate. Built on ground that used to be a stagecoach stop, the three-story English country style home is constructed of local stone and wood. While they do not specialize in the corporate trade as some bed and breakfasts do, it is well suited for the traveling business person. The seven guest rooms are well furnished. Each room (and bathroom) has a telephone.

Telecommunication lines for computer use are available if needed. Each room includes cable television, and a couple of the rooms have a whirlpool bath. There is also a guest kitchen available and a fireplace in the parlor.

For the traveling public, not only are the amenities enjoyable, but the full breakfast is also a treat. You will enjoy blueberry blintz soufflés, ham, peaches & cream French toast, scrambled egg casseroles, fresh muffins, and fruit juices.

For those interested in area attractions, be sure to drive to Flat Rock and visit Connemara. Carl Sandburg spent the last years of his life on this 280-acre working farm. This is where he wrote his only novel, *Remembrance Rock*. Also in Flat Rock is the state theater of North Carolina, the Flat Rock Playhouse. It is considered one of the ten best summer stock theaters in the country. Its Vagabond Players perform Broadway and London hits featuring comedy, American classics, musicals, farces, and whodunits.

At the edge of Hendersonville's Airport, the WNC Air Museum features restored and replica airplanes such as the 1942 Stearman and a 1942 Fairchild. Or take 5th Avenue West that becomes the Laurel Park Highway and dead-ends at Jump Off Rock. The scenic overlook has long been a favorite of visitors, residents, and lovers.

---

**Mountain Home Bed & Breakfast**
**P.O. Box 234; 10 Courtland Blvd.; Mountain Home, NC 28758**
**(800) 397-0066; (704) 697-9090**
**Innkeepers: Bob & Donna Marriott**
Rooms: 5; Private Baths: 6; Suites: 1; Rates: $$-$$$$; children over 10
Affiliations: NCBBI, NB&BA, AAA♦♦♦
Payment:     Amenities:

# The Waverly Inn
# Hendersonville

Opening its doors in 1898, The Waverly Inn has never closed. The nearly one-hundred-year tradition of care and attention to detail has become a hallmark of the Waverly. Today these qualities are carried on by John and Diane Sheiry and Diane's sister, Darla Olmstead.

John and Diane have between them more than thirty years' experience in the hotel and convention business. They came to Hendersonville and The Waverly to escape a life that kept John traveling most of the time. While they work harder now, as the Inn requires their constant attention, they can work together.

With the help of local contractors and a hotel renovation contractor from Atlanta, John and Diane have completely renovated the Waverly. The furnishings, wallpaper, and curtains, are the type of eclectic mix that you would have originally expected to find in the home. Nothing seems out of place.

With common rooms on each of the Inn's three floors, the 7,000-square-foot home provides plenty of room to socialize. Guests gather on one of the two verandas, the library or the Victorian parlor where the fireplace is the focal point on cool evenings.

Each morning, John prepares a full breakfast that may consist of hot cereals, eggs (cooked the way you like them), stone-ground grits (from a 100-year-old mill), home fries, or three-grain pancakes with *real* New Hampshire maple syrup. The local butcher shop grinds the Inn's sausage twice a week and provides fresh bacon as well. Breads are baked locally, and each day Darla prepares treats of banana-nut bread, real Toll House cookies, cinnamon bread or applesauce-oat bran muffins.

Grab 'em quick. While breakfast is all-you-can-eat, they bake the treats only once each day.

Be sure to ask about their weekend specials such as the Wine Lover's Weekend (held twice each year) and the Murder Mystery Weekend (held three times a year). The Vagabond Players of Flat Rock Playhouse conduct the Murder Mysteries at the Inn.

The Playhouse, located a few miles from the Inn in Flat Rock, is the state theater of North Carolina. It is considered one of the ten best summer stock theaters in the country. Its Vagabond Players perform Broadway and London hits featuring comedy, American classics, musicals, farces, and "whodunits."

A couple of blocks from The Waverly is Historic Main Street. It offers a parklike setting with attractive shops and excellent restaurants. The many craft and antique centers should be high on your agenda. Another area attraction is Connemara, the 280-acre homesite of Carl Sandburg. The Waverly is only a short drive from Chimney Rock Park, Pisgah National Forest, or Asheville's Biltmore Estate. John, Diane or Darla can provide you with ideas for day-trips or a romantic evening out.

**The Waverly Inn**
**783 N. Main St.; Hendersonville, NC 28792**
**(800) 537-8195; (704) 693-9193; Fax: (704) 692-1010**
**Innkeepers: John & Diane Sheiry**
Rooms: 14; Private Baths: 14; Suites: 1; Rates: $$-$$$$
Affiliations: NCBBI, IIA, PAII, Asheville Chamber, Hendersonville Chamber
Payment:  CHECKS  MC VISA AMEX DISCOVER Amenities:

# The Brick House
# Hot Springs

Now the Brick House isn't an inn, nor is it a bed and breakfast. It is my favorite getaway so I *had* to include it. This is where we go when we need to get away, where we went while this book was printed. When you stay, you have the full run of the house. Only one family (or group) stays in the house at a time.

It's like a trip to Grandma's. Upon arriving, you find a note on the refrigerator saying that she had to leave for a few days. Now you're to make yourselves feel at home.

The 75-year-old Brick House sits high on a hill above Spring Creek. On the 3½-acre grounds there are walking trails, picnic spots, horse shoes, and the goat pen (one goat named Spic, the other Span). At the creek there are several good fishing spots, a swimming hole and a waterfall.

The fully furnished house has five bedrooms that will sleep up to twenty people, two bathrooms, a large living room, dining room, and kitchen. You'll find three fireplaces, and three color TVs. There's no cable or antenna. There is a VCR however, and Frank and Donna will allow you to borrow movies from them, or you can rent them in town. There's a dishwasher, a microwave, and a gas grill on the porch. You'll find not only glasses, plates and silverware, but also all the necessary items to bake a cake, have a picnic, or prepare a romantic dinner. The house literally has everything you need except the meat, potatoes and vegetables.

Frank and Donna purchased the house in 1988 and took a year to clean, paint and fix up the place. The yard was in such bad shape that you couldn't even see the creek. They bought the place for their children to use when they came to town. It has evolved into a retreat for all of us.

Hot Springs used to be a thriving community. Six trains a day came to town. The springs themselves were the drawing card. Undoubtedly, since the beginning of time, the hot mineral springs have bubbled forth from the ground near the French Broad River. Yet, the earliest recorded date of their discovery is 1778 and since that time there have been three hotels built on the site.

The first hotel, the Warm Springs, was three stories tall and built of white brick. It was destroyed by fire in 1838. The second, the Patton, burned in 1884. The most famous of the three was the Mountain Park Hotel. Built in 1886 on a one hundred-acre tract, the Mountain Park's Gothic-style building had four corner towers and two hundred bedrooms. Entertainment included bowling, billiards, tennis, swimming, horseback riding, boating, and target shooting. The first golf course in North Carolina was also built here. They had an orchestra that played every evening in the ballroom.

They're all gone now, and Hot Springs' population adds up to about 500. After years of being closed, the Springs are again open. What attracts people to Hot Springs today? A whitewater ride down the French Broad River followed by a warm soak in the Hot Springs and a stay at the Brick House.

**The Brick House**
**P.O. Box 462; Hot Springs, NC 28743**
**(704) 622-3425**
**Innkeepers: Frank & Donna Fraquelli**
House: 1; Rooms: 11; Bedrooms: 5; Private Baths: 2; Rates: $$
Payment:  $$$ CHECKS Amenities: 🖥 ⛷

## Lodge on Lake Lure
## Lake Lure

*National Geographic* magazine calls Lake Lure "one of the 10 most beautiful man-made lakes in the world." The lake was formed by the 115-foot high, 600-foot dam across the Rocky Broad River. The 1,500-acre lake, located in a cross-shaped valley, has more than 27 miles of shoreline.

The lake was the brainchild of Dr. Lucius B. Morse. He wanted to create a lakeside resort complete with casino, polo fields, golf course and major hotels. The dam was completed in 1926, but the stock market crash of 1929 ended his dream.

The Inn, built in the style of a European hunting lodge, was built over-looking the lake in the 1930s Highway patrolmen used it as a recreation center. Legend has it that much of the original construction labor was provided by convicts.

While the outside is unimposing, the inside is very different. It has high, vaulted ceilings, hand-hewn beams, wormy-chestnut walls, and a massive stone fireplace so wide that a millstone is inlaid in its center. The real story of the Inn, however, is the view. From the stone porch or the tall windows across the breakfast sunroom, the view is nothing short of inspirational.

Robin Stanier always wanted an inn. Her previous job, selling oil-drilling equipment, took her to exotic places like London, Singapore, Mexico, Australia, and Venezuela. For years, she collected items from all over the world to decorate her inn. In 1989 her dream came true. Her husband Jack had been in steel sales and was an avid sailor. On the library mantelpiece is a picture of their 32' sailboat now renamed "Down Payment."

The Inn is not without boats, however. A sunset lake cruise on the pontoon boat should not be missed. There are also canoes and a johnboat. Swimming from the dock, lounging on the sundeck over the boathouse, or relaxing in the hammock on the veranda is also highly recommend.

Breakfast at the Lodge on Lake Lure is an event. There are homemade muffins, apple dumplings or fresh breads. During the week, you may find French toast, puff pancakes or banana-buckwheat pancakes. Sundays, they offer a special remembrance of New Orleans; eggs Benedict. Whatever the fare, breakfast is a treat.

For those who want to explore, Lake Lure sits at the edge of Hickory Nut Gorge. The gorge is 14 miles long, twisting and turning with the river from Gerton, in Henderson County, to Lake Lure, in Rutherford County. On the south side of the gorge is Chimney Rock Park. An elevator travels 26 stories inside the mountain taking you to Chimney Rock and a 75-mile view of Hickory Nut Gorge and Rutherford County. Be sure to take the trail to Hickory Nut Falls. It is one of the highest waterfalls east of the Mississippi River with a 404-foot drop.

The waterfall at Chimney Rock was featured in *Last Of The Mohicans* starring Daniel Day Lewis. Lake Lure was featured in *Dirty Dancing* starring Patrick Swayze. Be sure to take the pontoon boat ride with Lake Lure Tours. They can provide you more history and motion-picture trivia.

---

**Lodge on Lake Lure**
**P.O. Box 519, Charlotte Drive; Rt. 1, Box 529-A; Lake Lure, NC 28746**
**(800) 733-2785; (704) 625-2789; Fax: (704) 625-2421**
**Innkeepers: Jack & Robin Stanier**
Rooms: 10; Private Baths: 10; Suites: 2; Rates: $$-$$$
Affiliations: NCBBI, PAII
Payment:        Amenities:

# Earthshine Mountain Lodge
# Lake Toxaway

Adventure! Earthshine offers adventures from 0-10 (easy to strenuous). If the most adventurous thing you want to do is read a book in the hammock, great! However, if you want to challenge yourself and make your stay a hard-driving time you'll never forget, they've got that too.

Marion Boatwright and Kim Maurer wanted a place that would "give guests a fresh perspective on how we all relate to each other, and the natural world." By drawing on their experience in managing camps and conference centers, then adding their own vision and hard work, they have accomplished just that. On March 1, 1990, after months of planning, the lodge opened its doors.

The 70-acre Earthshine is located on a 100-year-old homestead. Having spent every weekend, holiday and vacation on a farm as I grew up, Earthshine has the feel of a trip to Grandma's. After supper, they invite you to go down and feed the animals or gather the eggs from the chickens. In the fall you can press apple cider. In the spring, help shear the sheep and do some spinning.

There's horseback riding that starts on the property and wanders into the Pisgah National Forest next door. Evenings offer Big Circle Mountain dances and sing-a-longs or Cherokee Indian ceremonies.

They offer something for everyone, such as the Adventure Club for children. Kids (ages five and above) can do camp-like activities such as dam building, gathering blackberries, learning about the farm animals or visiting the Cherokee village. There is the "High Ropes" course that entails getting out of your "comfort zone" and "challenging yourself way up in the trees." They bring you to a place that feels frightening,

yet is completely safe. It is a great vehicle for personal growth, expanding your perceived limits and working off a lot of adrenaline. Yet, in addition to all the activities, there is always time to be alone, or have family time.

Earthshine has really caught the spirit of the Appalachians and yet has gracious accommodations. Kim and Marion built the 6,000-square-foot log cabin lodge by hand in six months. The dining room, conference room, and eight guest rooms are located in the lodge. Each of the rooms has a private bath, a double bed (made of logs from Idaho) and a 'Little House on the Prairie' loft for the children. A three-room cottage is available for larger families.

The dining room serves award-winning meals. Under the American plan, Earthshine provides three meals a day. Breakfast favorites include pancakes and sausage, eggs and grits, French toast, as well as fresh fruits, juices, and homemade granola. Lunches might offer chicken, tortilla and fajitas or soup and sandwiches. Dinners are the specialty of the house with trout, duck, roast turkey, pork chops or grilled salmon steaks. I promise, whatever the day's menu might be, you won't go hungry.

At Earthshine, you must feel comfortable in a casual atmosphere that is committed to excellence. CNN, L.L. Bean, *Vacation Magazine*, *Southern Living*, *Touring America* and *Family Fun* have all recognized that Earthshine is special. I know you will too.

---

**Earthshine Mountain Lodge**
**Rt. 1, Box 216-C; Lake Toxaway, NC 28747**
**(704) 862-4207**
**Innkeepers: Kim Maurer & Marion Boatwright**
Rooms: 8; Private bath: 8; Cabins: 1; Rates: $$
Payment:     Amenities:

# The Greystone Inn
# Lake Toxaway

I had been told before our stay that defining The Greystone would be difficult; that it was more of a resort than an inn. I found that The Greystone really isn't hard to define. Just allow your thoughts to turn to the elegance of summer homes owned by the Rockefellers, Henry Ford or Lucy Armstrong-Moltz. Then try to imagine what it must have been like in the early 1900s to be their personal guest.

In the early 1900s, these and other notable people of the era came to Lake Toxaway to stay at the legendary Toxaway Inn. They were drawn to the beauty of the mountains and enjoyed the finest in European cuisine and service. Lucy Armstrong-Moltz once commented, "I've been around the world twice and discovered no place more beautiful or special. This, is the loveliest place on earth." Her love of the area prompted her to build a magnificent six-level, 16,000-square-foot Swiss chalet to be her summer home.

In 1916, an unusually rainy summer followed by a disastrous August hurricane, destroyed the dam and brought an end to an era. Yet Lucy Armstrong-Moltz stayed and made the chalet her permanent home. Forty-five years after the flood, a group of investors rebuilt the dam and redeveloped the property in the area. Some of the most expensive real estate in North Carolina is located around Lake Toxaway. In 1985, Tim and Boo Boo Lovelace purchased the Armstrong-Moltz mansion, elegantly renovated the estate, and opened The Greystone Inn. Today it is an award winning AAA, four-diamond inn with the amenities of a small private resort yet with the charm and intimacy you would expect when staying at a country inn.

The "Mansion" includes 19 guest rooms decorated with antique and period reproductions. There are canopied or brass beds, fireplaces, private patios and Jacuzzis. It was heaven to return after dinner and find the bed turned down, mints on the pillow, and a fire that the staff had built in the wood-burning fireplace.

In 1988, the Hillmont building was added to the complex. Each of its 12 spacious rooms features the same luxuries and more as the "Mansion." The Hillmont was built in the same architectural style and offers private balconies, gas fireplaces and Jacuzzis. Recently, the Lakeside Cottage, built for guests in 1919, was completely restored. It houses two luxuriant suites and Greystone's newest addition—the Spa. Here you will be pampered by the caring touch of The Greystone's professional staff. Angel and I took advantage of the Spa to unwind from nearly 9,000 miles of driving.

The Greystone operates under the Modified American Plan, which means breakfast and dinner are included in the daily fare. The breakfast menu offers everything from a variety of juices, fresh fruits and cereals to entrées of pancakes, omelets, Belgian waffles, and eggs Benedict. All entrées come with bacon, sausage, hash browns and/or grits and English muffins or toast.

Dinner at The Greystone is an event in the formal dining room (jackets required). Elegant six-course gourmet dinners offer an assorted menu. The evening we were there, they offered us a choice of New York Strip Steak Diane, Jamaican Angels (boneless breast of chicken and jumbo shrimp) or Trout "Pontchartrain."

Activities abound at The Greystone from idyllic rides on the electric canopied boat, to water skiing. Take a dip in the pool, play croquet, volleyball or other outdoor sports such as tennis and championship golf, or take one of the many guided hikes to spectacular waterfalls. Just be sure to allow time for the late afternoon champagne cruise on Lake Toxaway.

---

**Greystone Inn**
**Greystone Lane; Lake Toxaway, NC 28747**
**(800) 824-5766; (704) 966-4700; Fax: (704) 862-5689**
**Innkeepers: Tim & Boo Boo Lovelace**
Rooms: 32; Private baths: 32; Suites: 1; Rates: $$$$-$$$$$
Affiliations: IIA, SIA
Payment:    Amenities:

## Merry Heart Cabin
## Morganton (Nebo)

The Merry Heart Cabin is not really a bed & breakfast, although you can have breakfast delivered to your door in a picnic basket. Yet, Merry Heart is a true "get-away-from-it-all" and one of our favorite places. As such, it deserves to be included in this book.

Hand-hewn logs make up this late 1800's cabin. Its high cedar-beamed ceiling provides room for a sleeping loft. The floor, made of rustic brick, is highly polished. The cabin makes a perfect romantic hideaway. There is a queen-size bed in the loft and room for three to sleep downstairs.

A fully equipped kitchen provides all the basics from toaster and coffee maker, to pots, pans, and microwave. You'll find flour, baking soda, catsup, mustard and shortening. Everything necessary to prepare a breakfast, lunch or a full dinner except the meat and potatoes. On the porch is a charcoal grill and picnic table.

For warm days, the Cabin is air conditioned. The furnace is more than adequate on cool evenings, but the fireplace is much more enjoyable. Rocking chairs, a porch swing, and tucked just out of sight, a hot tub. All are there to help you relax.

While the number-one draw is the quiet time at Merry Heart, there are days of adventures at the Cabin. Cart rides and llama trekking are available. You may use the tubes and canoes for trips down the river, or you can fish. There is even a ski boat, complete with driver, if you want to go water skiing. A hiking trail leads to Shortoff Mountain and across the ridge to Table Rock and Hawksbill.

Located off I-40, about halfway between Asheville and Hickory, the Merry Heart Cabin is close to most of the major attractions in the western part of the state. However, Lake James is only five minutes away.

Be sure to stop at the nearby country store down the road from the Cabin for one of the best ice cream cones around. You also can pick up a few groceries for dinner or the makings of a picnic lunch at the convenience store.

Leslie and Connie Smart desire to offer an atmosphere of recreation. It doesn't matter whether you choose to spend time at their miniature animal petting farm, skiing, or just relaxing by the fireplace. The name 'Merry Heart' comes from the Bible's Book of Proverbs (17:22) "A *Merry Heart* doeth good like a medicine."

On the property, just over the hill, you'll find the miniature animal petting farm. It has miniature horses, dwarf goats, miniature donkeys, sheep, cows and pigs. This is a part of the Merry Heart Ministry. While Leslie is a trained counselor, Connie, and their daughters, Ashley and Kelly, visit retirement homes, the disabled, and the home-bound using "pet therapy." Their outreach also includes food collections for the less fortunate, and donation collections for the local Hospice.

The location of Merry Heart Mountain is ideal, with the perfect hosts to help you unwind.

---

**Merry Heart Cabin**
**1414 Merry Heart Lane; Rt. 2, Box 768; Nebo, NC 28761**
**(704) 584-6174**
**Innkeeper: Connie Smart**
Rooms: 3-room cabin; Private Baths: 1; Rates: $$
Payment: $$$ CHECKS  Amenities: A/C ▣ ▢ VCR ▨ ▨

# Pinebrae Manor Bed & Breakfast
## Rutherfordton

Of all the bed and breakfasts that we visited for this book, I knew the least about Pinebrae. It came highly recommended, but I didn't know what to expect. From the moment I pulled into the drive, I realized there was a grace and style that set it apart. The large Georgian-style home with its immaculate grounds reminded me of a planation home from the colonial period.

Built in the early 1900s as part of the county's facility for the indigent and elderly. The house was closed in the mid-1960s and Social Services used it until 1978 for offices. In 1981, a local builder purchased the house and after renovations were completed, he used it as his family home.

Early in 1991, Allen and Charlotte Perry purchased the 6,000-square-foot home and ten acres to turn it into a bed and breakfast home. Two porches with rocking chairs provide relaxed viewing of the beautiful wooded areas. Inside, the Perry's dedicated nearly 2,200 square feet to guests. Located on the second floor are the four guest rooms and the large gathering room that has a working fireplace and a fine library. A formal living room with piano and the dining room is on the main floor.

Charlotte and Allen have carefully decorated Pinebrae with Ethan Allen furniture, antiques and family heirlooms. The Carolina Room is large and, in addition to its private full bath, has a king bed, and fireplace. The Georgian Room, equally large, also offers a king bed and private shower-bath. The two remaining rooms, the Williamsburg and the Charleston, are comfortably-sized with double beds and share a large bath.

The full country breakfast served each morning in the dining room is a true "southern style" meal. You can look forward to sausage, bacon, or

ham, with eggs, grits and homemade biscuits. There is also fresh fruit, fruit juices, and cold cereal. Blueberry pancakes and gourmet breakfasts add variety for those staying several days!

Located near the center of Rutherford County, Pinebrae Manor is a short drive to areas such as Lake Lure and Chimney Rock Park. *National Geographic* magazine describes Lake Lure as one of the ten most beautiful man-made lakes in the world. Chimney Rock Park is a 1,000-acre commercial park open year round. You can take an elevator up through the mountain to the top of a 315-foot monolith that provides up to a 75-mile view.

North and northeast of Rutherfordton you can pan for gold. Gold mining was a major industry in the early 1800s. Rutherford County was the leading producer of gold in the country before the finds in California. They say there is still gold to be found. The Bechtler's Mint, where area gold was minted, is in Rutherfordton. Cleghorn, the former home and studio of painter John Pike, is south of Pinebrae. Pinebrae Manor has a golf package with Cleghorn Golf and Country Club. If you like country stores, be sure to visit the Washburn Store near Forest City. The Washburn family has owned and operated it since 1831.

**Pinebrae Manor Bed & Breakfast**
**Hwy. 108, RR 5, Box 479-A; Rutherfordton, NC 28139**
**(704) 286-1543; Fax: (704) 287-3755**
**Innkeepers: Allen & Charlotte Perry**
Rooms: 4; Private Baths: 2; Shared Baths: 1; Rates: $-$$
Affiliations: NCBBI
Payment:     Amenities:

# Ivy Terrace Bed & Breakfast Inn
# Saluda

Saluda's major claim to fame is the Saluda Grade. In the early 1800s Saluda was a crossroads. Two well-traveled paths, the Winding Stair Road and the Howard Gap Road, intersected here. Drovers brought their livestock herds across the mountains to the South Carolina markets.

Just after the Civil War, construction on the railroad began. The three-mile stretch from Saluda to Melrose Junction has a grade that varies from four to seven percent. The steepest standard-gauge railroad grade in the United States, crested at Saluda.

Here, in 1890, the Ivy Terrace was built as a summer home. Only seven miles north of Tryon (but 1,000 feet higher in elevation) Saluda was much cooler in the summer. Yet, since Saluda is at the very edge of the thermal belt that runs through the area, it provides mild winter weather.

The original house had only four rooms. In the 1930s the Clippard family added the second floor. During the 1930s and 1940s, the house was operated as a boarding house.

In 1991, Diane and Herbert McGuire purchased the property with the idea of making it a conference center for meetings. Extensive renovation slowed down the opening of the center. The need for local accommodations gave them the idea of adding the bed and breakfast. Today, the two complement each other.

The conference center is located just behind the house. It is about 500 square feet and will accommodate meetings for 3-15 people. It offers fax, computer hookups, overhead projectors and slide projectors.

Since most meetings are small and usually take place during the week, the eight-room bed and breakfast can easily accommodate travelers. With more

than 4,400 square feet in the house, there is plenty of room to move around without stepping on one another. Each of the comfortably-sized rooms has a private bath, a couple even have fireplaces. The Red Room on the first floor is fully handicap-accessible. This room also has private access to the garden.

Also on the main floor is the Beadboard Room. It has a queen-size pencil poster bed, corner fireplace and a private entrance from a wraparound porch. Just off the porch are the small garden pools. You can hear the gurgling as water flows from one pool to the next. The third room on the main floor is the Soldier Blue Room with a full-size acorn poster bed, and private, open porch.

The five other bedrooms are upstairs. Each is well decorated with period antiques and have access to the covered porch overlooking a waterfall set among the stone terraces and shaded gardens.

Breakfast is served each morning from 8:00-9:00 in the common dining room at individual tables, allowing you to eat at your own schedule. A typical breakfast might include apple cider or fresh orange juice, cheddar French toast with maple syrup, honey-marinated Canadian bacon, and sautéed apples.

While at the Ivy Terrace, be sure to take the short drive to Pearson Falls Park. The Tryon Garden Club owns and operates the park and maintains the riverside trails and picnic facilities. The 308-acre park is home to several waterfalls. While there is an admission charge, the price is low and well worth it.

---

**Ivy Terrace Bed & Breakfast Inn**
**Main Street; Hwy. 176; Saluda, NC 28773**
**(800) 749-9542; (704) 749-9542**
**Innkeepers: Diane & Herbert McGuire**
Rooms: 8; Private Baths: 8; Rates: $$-$$$
Affiliations: AB&BA, NB&BA, NCBBI, PAII
Payment:    Amenities:

# The Oaks
# Saluda

Saluda, with a population of just over 500, sits at the top of the steepest standard-gauge railroad grade in the United States. The problems of building the grade seemed insurmountable; unstable blasting powder, cuts filling in with water, and then the fills sinking. Finally the North Carolina legislature sent in convicts to help build the grade. On July 4, 1878, the first passenger train made the trip up the grade.

There was no Saluda when the railroad arrived, just a small town called Pace's Gap. For years it had been the intersection of two very important roads over the mountains. Drovers would bring their livestock across the mountain following either the Howard Gap Road or the Winding Stair Road to markets in South Carolina. With the coming of the railroad, the area grew and by 1881 a charter was drawn up creating the town of Saluda.

By the 1894, Saluda was a major community, and a local banker decided to build a home at the edge of town. This beautiful turreted home remained a private residence until around 1904 when it became a boarding house. By then Saluda had become a stop over for the railroad and a destination in itself. At one point there were 37 boarding houses in the community, one of which was The Oaks.

The Oaks remained a boarding house until the 1940s when the highway came and the importance of the railroad decreased. After the interstate was built a few miles outside town, and the railroad stopped its daily layovers, the community of Saluda returned to a sleepy little community. In the mid-1980s, Saluda's popularity as a getaway brought several bed and breakfasts to the community. In 1988, The Oaks opened its doors once more to guests coming to the mountains.

Today, innkeepers Crowley and Terry Murphy have created a lovely hideaway at The Oaks. Each of the four guest rooms includes a private bath,

color cable TV and distinctive decorating patterns. Your choices include the Red, Green, Blue or Gold rooms with a choice of full-size or queen-size beds. Common areas include a library with fireplace, a living room, a wraparound porch and a deck. A new addition is the carriage house with two sitting rooms, one downstairs and one upstairs. The carriage house also includes a full kitchen upstairs, a comfortable bedroom on the second floor and a bath and a half.

A fabulous full breakfast is served family-style in the gracious dining room. Favorite menus include a three-cheese crustless quiche, sauteed ham with tomatoes, onions and green peppers or French toast with almonds and apricot purée, sausage and fresh fruit compote.

While in the area, be sure to visit the variety of shops along the railroad tracks in Saluda and then take the drive down the mountain toward Tryon. One of our favorite places in this part of the Blue Ridge is the private park managed by the Tryon Garden Club. There is a small fee to enter Pearson Falls Park but it is well worth the price. This 250-acre park has an abundance of wildflowers, and both hiking and bird-watching are favorite pastimes.

Farther down the road, the community of Tryon offers opportunities for some of the finest antiquing in the area. We enjoy going to the last theater in North Carolina that still has a carbon-arc projector.

**The Oaks**
**Rt. 1, Box 10; Saluda, NC 28773**
**(800) 893-6097; (704) 749-9613; Fax: (704) 749-9613**
**Innkeepers: Crowley & Terry Murphy**
Rooms: 4; Private baths: 4; Guest houses: 1; Rates: $$-$$$
Affiliations: NCBBI, AAA
Payment: $$$ CHECKS MC VISA  Amenities: ☐ ☒ ☺

# The Orchard Inn
# Saluda

I learned quickly that the real owner of the Orchard Inn is Lucy, the black labrador retriever. She graciously permits Newell and Veronica (Ronnie) Doty to act as hosts and innkeepers. She performs the important tasks such as welcoming guests to the inn or showing them around the 12 acres. One of her favorite duties is introducing guests to the 12-foot-wide porch with rockers and swings. She knows that, in addition to fine food and comfortable rooms, the major point of emphasis at the Orchard Inn is peace and quiet.

Newell came to Saluda and the Orchard Inn in 1993, after years as an executive in the insurance business. Ronnie had worked as a school guidance counselor. The dream of owning a bed and breakfast had been with them for years. The problem was finding the right location. At 2,600 feet, on a mountain just above the famous Saluda Grade, they discovered the Orchard Inn.

The Saluda Grade, built just after the Civil War, is the steepest standard-gauge railroad grade in the United States. The three-mile stretch from Melrose Junction to Saluda has a grade that varies from four to seven percent.

The original lodge building was 40 by 60 foot and built in 1926. The Brotherhood of Railway Clerks built it to be a summer retreat for clerks and their families. From 1964 until 1981, the building was used as a restaurant under three different names and managements. In 1981, Ken Hough and his wife purchased the building, made major renovations and opened the Orchard Inn.

Under the management of the Hough's, the Inn developed a fine reputation as both inn and *the* place for evening dinner. Having recently

been a guest for breakfast and dinner, I can say that Ronnie and Newell are maintaining tradition and reputation.

Entering off the wide porch through the double doors, one of your first experiences at the Inn is the large yet comfortable living room. Antiques and original art adorn the room, and Oriental rugs are placed on well-polished hardwood floors. A highlight is the fieldstone fireplace. The large common area provides room to socialize, yet there are small, quiet places as well. An alcove serves as a well-stocked library. Across the back of the Inn, overlooking the peaks of the Warrior Mountains, the porch is the dining room for both breakfast and dinner.

The room rate includes a full breakfast. Reservations for dinner are required by Inn guests as well as the public. Dinner at the Orchard, like everything else, is meant to be a leisurely experience.

The eclectic furnishings of the nine guest rooms (each with private bath) reflect the mood of the Orchard Inn. Homemade quilts, handwoven rag rugs, and brass or iron beds, make a perfect mix. The Boxwood and Twin Poplar Cottages have been recently remodeled to include fireplaces, whirlpool tubs and decks. Paulownia Cottage is larger with a king-size bed, sitting area and deck that boasts the best mountain view in Polk County.

The 1926 building was meant to be a retreat. Today, it truly is.

---

**The Orchard Inn**
P.O. Box 725; Saluda, NC 28773
(800) 581-3800; (704) 749-5471; Fax: (704) 749-9805
**Innkeepers: Veronica & Newell Doty**
Rooms: 9; Private Baths: 9; Suites: 3; Rates: $$$-$$$$
Affiliations: PAII, IIA
Payment:    Amenities:

## Mimosa Inn
## Tryon

For more than 200 years, hospitality has been the byword at the Mimosa Inn. The original building, burned in 1917, was first a plantation house. As time went on, it became a stagecoach stop on the first trading route through the territory. Finally, it was converted into a 60-plus room inn.

The 10,000-square-foot building that is now the Mimosa Inn was originally the recreation hall for the first inn. The parquet flooring in the main parlor is from the inn's bowling alley.

After the fire in 1917, the building was remodeled. It served as the inn and restaurant until it was purchased for use as a private home in 1977. Sandi and Jay Franks purchased the three-acre site 12 years later, in 1989, to reopen the Mimosa.

Today the Inn's nine rooms provide a welcome retreat for guests. The large common room on the main floor, decorated with antiques and reproductions, offers comfortable surroundings in which to relax. On cool evenings, guests curl up in front of the large fireplace with hot chocolate, tea or coffee. The baby grand adds to the ambiance of the room. When the weather is warm, the tree-shaded stone patio with outdoor fireplace is another favorite gathering place for guests. On the second floor, another common room provides television, a library, and a guest kitchen for preparing late night snacks.

The 24 by 40 foot formal dining room looks out on the large front lawn and, in the distance, the Blue Ridge Mountains. In addition to being the breakfast room, the dining room is often the site of area business meetings, cocktail parties, and weddings. When the weather is pleasant, Sandi serves breakfast outside on the veranda. Breakfast favorites include Sandi's French

toast with strawberries. Other dishes might be breakfast casseroles, fruit, muffins, or coffee cake. She works hard to make sure that guests who stay for several days always have something different.

Located on the southern edge of the Blue Ridge Mountains, the Mimosa usually experiences cooler summer temperatures than the lowlands. Yet, being in the thermal belt, winters are normally mild.

While the mild temperatures have always been a drawing card of the Mimosa, there is much to do in the area. A short drive from the Mimosa is where you'll find Shunkawakan Falls. The falls originally fell more than 500 feet, making it one of the highest water falls in Eastern United States. Recent blasting for road construction has broken it into two sections. Ask Sandi for directions to this and Pearson's Falls, a private 308-acre park just north of Tryon.

The Polk County Historical Museum, located in the old Southern Railroad Depot, is also worth visiting. For evening entertainment, you might visit the Tryon Theater that was originally built in 1939 as a vaudeville theater. Today, it operates with the only carbon-arc projectors in the state.

One of the major points of interest in the area is the Foothills Equestrian Nature Center (FENCE). This is the sight of Spring and Fall Steeplechase, and home of the Carolina Carriage Club. The unique facility has miles of wooded hiking and walking trails.

**Mimosa Inn**
**One Mimosa Lane; Tryon, NC 28782**
**(704) 859-7688**
**Innkeepers: Jay & Sandi Franks**
Rooms: 9; Private Baths: 9; Rates: $$; children over 6
Payment:   Amenities:

# Pine Crest Inn
# Tryon

Since the turn of the century, visitors have discovered that Tryon is a perfect getaway year round. Located in a "thermal belt," the gentle foothills of the Blue Ridge Mountains enjoy cool summers and warm winters.

In 1918, Carter Brown, a hotel owner from Michigan, created a charmingly rustic private retreat called Pine Crest for family, friends and fellow equestrians. In the 1920s, Brown played a major role in establishing the Tryon Riding and Hunt Club. It made the area a leading equestrian center. Fox hunting is a Tryon tradition and the famous Block House Steeplechase is held each spring.

Visitors are still coming to the foothills of Tryon for the mild temperature, steeplechase, fox hunting and to stay at the world-class Pine Crest Inn. Carter Brown would be very pleased with the extensive renovations and restoration that innkeepers Jeremy and Jennifer Wainwright have made to the inn. The Wainwrights, originally from Great Britain, have created a retreat with the feel of an English country inn. The decor is rich in hunter greens and burgundies with rich leather chairs, beautiful upholstered furnishings, stone fireplaces and hardwood floors. The wide porches, tranquil garden, immaculately kept lawns and wooded grounds all add to the flavor of the inn.

Thirty-two air-conditioned rooms, most with fireplaces, can be found in the main lodge and cottages scattered around the nine acres of Pine Crest. Each room or suite offers private bath and includes telephone, cable television and VCR. An extensive collection of video tapes is available in the lobby. While we had the opportunity to see many of the rooms at Pine Crest, our personal favorites were the "Woodcutters" and the 200-year-old "Swayback" cottages. Both remind us of cottages nestled in an English village.

Dining at the Pine Crest is a treat not to be missed. Begin with a trip to the Fox and Hounds Bar with its full beverage service in an intimate setting that is complete with a gas fireplace. Then enjoy elegant cuisine in a charming colonial-style dining room. From Pork Tenderloin Cassis and Maryland Crab Cakes to Roast Duck Bigarade or Rack of Lamb, the Pine Crest dining room offers guests the finest meals in the area. For inn guests, morning choices include a complimentary continental plus breakfast or you can order from a full menu of eggs, waffles, bacon, sausage or ham.

Located at the base of the Blue Ridge Mountains, activities abound around Pine Crest. Four golf courses, the Links O' Tryon, Red Fox Country Club, Tryon Country Club and the Cliffs at Glassy are all within an easy drive and open to guests at the inn. Sight-seeing: waterfalls, hiking, horseback riding and canoeing can also be found in the area. Tryon is one of the best communities in Western North Carolina for antiquing and our favorite movie theater is located near downtown. The Tryon theater is the last in the state to use the old carbon-arc projector.

Railroad buffs will enjoy the drive up the mountain to Saluda. Saluda sits at the top of the steepest standard-gauge railroad grade in the United States. The three miles from Melrose Junction to Saluda varies in grade from four to seven percent with more than fifty curves along the way. Just before Saluda, Pearson Falls Park, a private park managed by the Tryon Garden Club, has an abundance of wildflowers. Bird-watching and hiking are favorite pastimes in this beautiful park, and the falls themselves are well worth the small entry fee.

**Pine Crest Inn**
**200 Pine Crest Lane; Tryon, NC 28782**
**(800) 633-3001; (704) 859-9135**
**Innkeepers: Jeremy & Jennifer Wainwright**
Rooms: 23; Private baths: 32; Suites: 9; Rates: $$$-$$$$$
Affiliations: IIA, AAA, Mobil
Payment:    AMEX 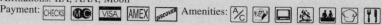 Amenities:

## Dry Ridge Inn
## Weaverville

The history of Weaverville has revolved around the Dry Ridge Inn for almost 150 years. Dry Ridge was built in 1849 as a parsonage for the Salem Campground. This was a religious revival camping area that was incorporated in 1832.

Out of the Great Revival of the early nineteenth century, campgrounds were created across the south. Antebellum Carolinians came from all over to attend these camp meetings. The meetings were not only a time of spiritual renewal, but were also a popular recreational outlet for rural and urban Carolinians.

When the Civil War came, the parsonage took on a new role in the community as a hospital. Confederate soldiers from all over the area were brought to Dry Ridge. Conditions during the war were terrible and pneumonia was almost always fatal. The high altitude, pleasant weather, and spacious surrounding made Dry Ridge a perfect place to recover from an illness that killed almost as many men as rifle fire.

In 1888, C. C. Brown purchased the parsonage. Brown had eight children; the Dry Ridge provide much-needed room. Brown remodeled the home and it remained in the family until 1958. One of his children, Fred, became mayor of Weaverville.

Paul and Mary Lou Gibson came to the Dry Ridge in 1992. He turned his talents from corporate finance to cooking, cleaning, and the day-to-day running of the inn.

Mary Lou's talent is on the third floor. A cathedral ceiling and skylight provide a perfect gallery for her art. Her monotypes and water media works have brought her nationwide fame. In addition to being included in many juried exhibitions, she held many of her own exhibitions in Wisconsin and

New York from 1984-90. While the Inn is open year round, you may see Mary Lou's art only by appointment.

Sometimes when you visit an inn, you almost wonder if you should sit on the chairs. Yet, here, there is more of a feeling of coming home. Paul and Mary Lou decorated the country farmhouse with an eclectic mix of American and European antiques. From the large porch across the front of the house with its rockers and the piano in the front parlor to the hot tub and well stocked guest refrigerator, you know you are welcome. The stage has been set by Paul and Mary Lou. Now all you have to do is relax and enjoy.

While Weaverville is close to Asheville (only ten minutes away), it offers a nice blend of small town friendliness and relaxed atmosphere. If you wish to explore the area, you're only a short drive from the Zebulon B. Vance Homestead off Reems Creek Road. This is a fully restored late-eighteenth century farmstead that was the home of North Carolina senator and Civil War Governor, Zebulon B. Vance. In less than 20 minutes you can be at Biltmore Estate, the Antique Car Museum, or Pack Place in downtown Asheville.

At the end of the day, return to Weaverville for dinner at the Four-Cent Cotton Cafe or the Weaverville Milling Company (my favorite). A few minutes later, the pleasant surroundings of Dry Ridge will welcome you home.

---

**Dry Ridge Inn**
**26 Brown St.; Weaverville, NC 28787**
**(800) 839-3899; (704) 658-3899**
**Innkeepers: Paul & Mary Lou Gibson**
Rooms: 7; Private Baths: 7; Rates: $$
Affiliations: NCBBI, PAII
Payment:        Amenities:

# Weaverville Featherbed & Breakfast
## Weaverville

In all the years that we have traveled in Western North Carolina, I have never seen a home in the Asheville area that has a better view of the mountains than the Weaverville Featherbed & Breakfast.

The communities of Asheville and Weaverville are on a large plateau surrounded by mountains. The average elevation on the plateau is 2,700 feet. Since the Weaverville Featherbed & Breakfast is located high on a ridge at about 3,000 feet, the house sits above everything else. As a result, on a clear day you can see to the North Carolina/Tennessee border to the northwest. Look to the southwest and you will see Mount Pisgah (5,721 feet) on the Buncombe/Haywood County line, more than 30 miles away.

Innkeepers Sharon Ballas and Shelley Burtt (a mother/daughter team) will tell you that what they bought was the view, and that the 100-year-old house was thrown in for free. From the hard work they have to put into the house after years of neglect, "free" might not be the right word!

The house was built near the end of the nineteenth century as a homestead sitting on a 300-acre farm. In the early 1920s, the house was purchased by the Methodist Missionary Alliance Church, renamed the Bethel Home, and turned into a sanitarium. In the twenties, tuberculosis was a major illness and many believed that the clean air of the mountains would help to cure them. During this time, Asheville and the surrounding communities of Black Mountain and Weaverville became internationally known for their sanitariums. Dr. Casto, a prominent physician, ran the Bethel Home for more than 20 years.

After the Bethel Home stopped operating, gaps exist in the history of the house. Sharon knows that for a time it was operated as a boarding house, and at one point was completely abandoned. Finally a real estate developer purchased the home, moved it higher up on the ridge, and then lost interest

in renovating it as his family home. Over the next four years, this 100-year-old Queen Anne sat vacant, was vandalized and its future looked grim. But there are still heroes. Sharon and her daughter, both realtors, were looking for a major life change. South Florida no longer held the promise it once held for them, so they began a quest to find the right location for a bed and breakfast. It required only one look at the view from the porch to know they had found their dream, and that the grand old Queen Anne still had life and laughter in her.

After the contract crews finished with the "behind the scenes" wiring, plumbing, roofing and general repair, the race was on as Sharon and Shelley painted, decorated, and furnished the 6,000-square-foot home. Nearly 80 windows had to be fixed, scraped, and painted, as did the entire outside of the house. They finally opened one room in Spring 1994. Over the course of the summer, they finished the last of the repairs and opened an additional 5 rooms to guests.

From the deep featherbeds to the hearty mountain-style country breakfast, the Weaverville Featherbed & Breakfast is waiting be a part of your memories of a visit to the mountains. Located only a few miles from Asheville, all of the attractions of the mountains are an easy drive away. However, the feeling of Weaverville is what attracts so many: it still has the atmosphere of small town living. It's safe to walk on the streets at night, people stop and say hello, business people in the shops and restaurants are honestly happy to see you, and guests leave only after making reservations to return.

---

**Weaverville Featherbed & Breakfast**
**3 Le Perrion Drive; Weaverville, NC 28787**
**(704) 645-7594; Fax: (704) 658-3905**
**Innkeepers: Sharon Ballas & Shelley Burtt**
Rooms: 3; Private baths: 6; Suites: 3; Rates: $$-$$$
Affiliations: AAA
Payment:       Amenities:

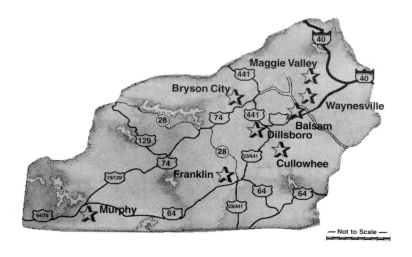

# Southern
# Mountains

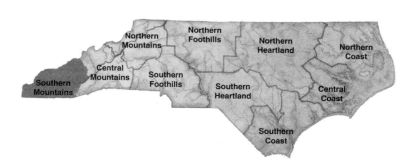

## Balsam Mountain Inn
## Balsam

Before driving up to the Inn, stop for a moment where the Balsam Mountain Depot once was located. Imagine what it must have been like in the early 1900s. There would have been folks on the platform waiting for a carriage to take them up the hill to the Inn: families from all over the eastern seaboard who had come to mountains for pleasure, and salesmen who had come to peddle their merchandise. You can almost hear the sounds of the Southern Railway locomotive as it waited at the highest railway station east of the Rocky Mountains.

Several years ago the trains stopped coming, the depot was moved and, for a while, the Balsam Mountain Springs Hotel (as it was once called) was abandoned. When Merrily Teasley came to the area, she knew the time had come for the Inn to recapture its former glory. In just one year she was able to bring the Inn back to life. She meticulously followed the guidelines set by the U.S. Department of Interior for the restoration of historic buildings. Today the Inn has earned a place on the National Register of Historic Places.

Brothers-in-law Joseph Kenney and Walter Christy from Athens, Georgia, began construction of a two-story hotel in 1905. It wasn't until they had the basic frame completed that they discovered that one could not see the roof of the Inn from the train depot at the bottom of the hill. They modified the plans, added a third floor, and produced a Neo-Classical Victorian structure with a two-tier porch stretching across the entire front of the building. Construction was completed in 1908.

Today, Merrily has finished the restoration of the 42,000- square-foot Balsam Mountain Inn. She has opened the restaurant, installed an elevator to the third floor, and furnished the 50 guest rooms with period antiques.

Located just one mile from the Blue Ridge Parkway, the Inn sits on 26 acres of forest and meadow high on top of a ridge. It's only 35 miles east to Asheville or 30 miles west to the Great Smoky Mountains National Park. If you're looking for something to do while at the Inn, visit the Oconaluftee Indian Village in Cherokee, pan for precious stones at the Gold Mine just south of Dillsboro or take a ride back in time on the Great Smoky Mountains Railway. There are whitewater rafting, canoeing, and horseback riding in the summer and skiing in winter. Some folks will enjoy the quaint shops and antique dealers found in the small communities of Dillsboro, Hazelwood, and Waynesville. Others will appreciate a hike around the property past natural springs and then being able to sit in a comfortable rocker on the porch with a tall glass of ice tea. Forget your book? The Inn's library contains more than 2,000 volumes from which to choose. There are games to play, and scrumptious meals to enjoy.

Breakfast is included in your daily fare. Lunch and dinner are available in the Inn's dining room at an additional charge. Breakfast varies each day, and entrees may include egg soufflé, an omelet, or French toast accompanied by bacon, muffins, coffee and juices. For lunch, a garden salad, roast beef or turkey and cranberry sandwich can be ordered from the menu. Dinners bring prime rib, mountain trout, lamb chops or salmon filets to the table, all prepared to Merrily's exacting standards.

Thanks to Merrily and her fine staff, the Balsam Mountain Inn has not only reclaimed its glory, but perhaps even surpassed it. If you are looking for just the right place to relax in the mountains, the Balsam Mountain Inn is it.

---

**Balsam Mountain Inn**
**P.O. Box 40; Seven Springs Drive; Balsam, NC 28707**
**(704) 456-9498; Fax: (704) 456-9298**
**Innkeeper: Merrily Teasley**
Rooms: 47; Private baths: 50; Suites: 3; Rates: $$-$$$
Affiliations: Mobil, AB&BA, PAII
Payment: $$$ CHECKS MC VISA DISCOVER Amenities:

# Hemlock Inn
# Bryson City

Visitors come from all over with the same purpose; to watch the "Big Screen" from the porch at Hemlock Inn. The rocking chairs provide a front seat to the ever-changing vista of the three valleys to the Frye Mountains across the way. The scene changes with the weather, the season, and the time of day. The clouds, the shadows, the flights of birds, even the sounds change.

Built in 1952, the Hemlock Inn was originally part of a mountain homestead. The idea was to provide a natural retreat on the mountain. The Shells, John and Ella Jo, purchased the Inn in 1968. They decided to keep it just the way it was. Since 1988, their daughter, Elaine, and son-in-law, Morris White, have maintained the tradition "To give their guests a change of scene and a change of pace. To share the beauty and peace, and to know that the guest's holiday has been restful, relaxing and happy."

Guests? Strangers? Both may be the wrong term. I quickly learned that all who stay at the Hemlock feel more like family. I met one family that has been coming to the Inn every summer for 18 years, another since 1969.

Breakfast is the great icebreaker at the Inn. (Dinner too, since it's included in the rate.) By the time the breakfast bell rings at 8:30 a.m., most guests have already watched the sun come up over the mountains from the porch. Breakfast is served in the main lodge at round wooden tables, each with its own Lazy Susan. A gentle nudge with a finger, and a full breakfast is before you. Eggs, country ham, bacon, and homemade biscuits (accompanied by local honey and homemade jams and jellies), are all part of the morning menu.

"Breakfast Talk" turns to plans for the day. Located only three miles from the Deep Creek entrance to the Great Smoky Mountains, there is plenty to do. Streams for wading, tubing and fishing. Mountain rivers for

whitewater rafting. Trails for exploring. The town of Bryson City offers shops from antique to arts and crafts for you to explore. Our *personal* favorite way to spend a day is a ride on the Great Smoky Mountains Railway. You may take trips to Dillsboro or the Nantahala Gorge.

There are more than 553 square miles of federal land in Swain County. Over 40% of the Great Smoky Mountains National Park is within the county's borders. The Nantahala National Forest, and more than half of the 30-mile long, 10,530-acre Fontana Lake are within minutes of the Inn. To the north is the Cherokee Indian Reservation, the largest Indian reservation in the east. Of its 50,000 acres, 29,000 acres are within the county.

With all there is to do in the area, you can see why talk at the breakfast table turns to plans for the day. By evening dinner (the bell rings at 6:00) everyone has worked up an appetite for roast beef and mashed potatoes, or country fried steak with baked potatoes. Another evening, dinner might be country ham or fried chicken. The all-you-can-eat fare (prepared by highly experienced mountain cooks) is a perfect way to round out the day. Through the evening, guests return to the porch for the final show of the day. The shadows created as the sun goes down act as a grand finale before retiring to comfortable rooms or cabins.

---

**Hemlock Inn**
**P.O. Drawer EE; Bryson City, NC 28713**
**(704) 488-2885**
**Innkeepers: Morris & Elaine White**
Rooms: 19; Private Baths: 19; Cottages: 3; Rates: $$$-$$$$
Affiliations: IIA
Payment:  Amenities:

# Nantahala Village
# Bryson City

More than 48 years ago (1948) when the Great Smoky Mountains National Park was new, this mountain lodge was built of native stone and wormy chestnut. It was built deep in the Nantahala Gorge, before there was even electricity in the area. Today the Inn consists of more than 200 acres, 14 rooms in the main lodge and 42 secluded cabins.

In 1991, John Burton and Jan Letendre purchased the Village. They have made major improvements to the property, and have renewed the spirit of the Village. The Village has now received the Family Resorts of the Year Award twice from *Family Circle* readers.

John, a member of the 1972 U.S. Olympic Team as a canoeist, first came to the area in 1959 to paddle the Nantahala River. After graduating from University of North Carolina at Chapel Hill in 1975, he became president of the Nantahala Outdoor Center. He held this position for 16 years. Jan, a certified public accountant, worked at the Outdoor Center from the early 1980s until just before she and John purchased the Village. It was their combined experience at the Outdoor Center that prepared them for running the Nantahala Village.

The Inn operates under a European format with no meals included, but there is a restaurant on site. We were very pleased with each of our meals, and we both can highly recommend the Village Rib Eye. They marinated it in a special blend of spices and topped with lemon-parsley butter. Julia Hunt, also a former employee of the Outdoor Center, was hired to manage the food service operations. The restaurant seats just under 100, and the banquet room seats 70. In addition to serving three meals a day, they also do parties and weddings. They hold six to eight dinner concerts annually, featuring the Asheville Symphony.

Activities at the Village include everything from ping pong and billiards to a large swimming pool. There is tennis, volleyball and shuffleboard. For the more daring, there is biking, hiking and horseback riding. There are stables on the property leased to Harold and Virgie Loftis. Guided trips range from an hour to all day. You can arrange for overnight trips as well.

Across the road from the Village is the Great Smokies Rafting Company, a part of the Nantahala Outdoor Center. The Center's main location is a few miles down the road. Even if you're not adventurous enough to go whitewater rafting, a trip to the Center is worthwhile. Here, deep in the very bottom of the gorge, the views are as incredible as the beauty of the river.

To the north of the Village is Bryson City and Cherokee, both with entrances to the Great Smoky Mountains National Park. In Bryson City you can take a ride on the Great Smoky Mountains Railway. From town, it goes back to the gorge or to Dillsboro. There are hundreds of adventures to be found in the area. The Nantahala Village serves as a great vacation base.

**Nantahala Village**
**9400 Hwy. 19 W.; Bryson City, NC 28713**
**(800) 438-1507; (704) 488-2826**
**Innkeepers: John Burton & Jan Letendre**
Rooms: 14; Private Baths: 59; Cabins: 45; Rates: $-$$$$
Payment:      Amenities:

## West Oak Bed & Breakfast
## Bryson City

Not all plans in business go the way you want them. Sometimes that leads to disaster, and sometimes the result is better than the original idea. This is the case at West Oak Bed & Breakfast.

Mercedith Bacon wanted to start a tourist service. The idea was to build a headquarters, buy a bus and provide tours of the western part of the state. After buying the bus, she quickly realized that she couldn't handle it in the mountains. She modified her plan, purchased a 19-passenger bus and, again, ran into problems. This time with liability insurance. The project died. Now she had the problem of what to do with the building she had purchased.

With her husband, she had traveled extensively in Europe and stayed in many bed and breakfasts. Bryson City was a perfect location, so she converted her building into a bed and breakfast. The idea was such a success that, soon after she started it, she had to add two more rooms downstairs. Then, because of demands for space, she started using the log cabin next to her home. After her husband died in 1990, she opened a wing of her home for guests. Now the West Oak Bed & Breakfast includes a total of ten rooms in three separate buildings. Guest room furnishings and amenities vary. There are singles, doubles and suites. There is telephone and color television. No matter which you choose, a full country breakfast is always included.

When Angel and I stayed at the West Oak, Mercedith was again in the process of a major renovation. By now, those two rooms are complete and look similar to the rooms above.

Located in Swain County, Bryson City is the county seat and the major point of commerce. The railroad arrived in 1884 in the mountains and

with it came the loggers. Sawmills sprang up and woodworking plants were built. The first hotel was built after the railroad arrived. It wasn't until 1914 that the first car appeared in the city. As the roads were built over the mountains, more and more cars showed up. By 1927, Congress authorized the creation of the Great Smoky Mountains National Park. Shortly afterward, land acquisitions began. By 1940, the Park, containing more than 500,000 acres, was dedicated.

Today, much of the land around Bryson City is federal land. The national park, a national forest and the largest Indian reservation in the east are all within an easy drive of Bryson City. Visitors come to rest, enjoy the mountain beauty, and explore both shopping and countryside. They come to ride on the Great Smoky Mountains Railway as well as the whitewater. Some want to learn of their heritage, or discover the heritage of the Cherokee at the Oconaluftee Indian Village and the outdoor drama *Unto These Hills* in Cherokee, NC.

Whatever the reason you go to Bryson City, there is one place you should not miss, the Bryson City Island Park. A 120-foot suspended footbridge takes you to a seven-acre island. Here, at the edge of Bryson City, is Angel's and my favorite picnic spot. The picnic area, fishing, trails, and river access for canoes and kayaks, makes it a perfect spot to unwind.

---

**West Oak Bed & Breakfast**
**948 Richmond St.; Bryson City, NC 28713**
**(704) 488-2438**
**Innkeeper: Mercedith Bacon**
Rooms: 10; Private Baths: 10; Rates: $$
Payment:     Amenities:

# Cullowhee Bed & Breakfast
# Cullowhee

Charles and Janet Moore put a lot of care into opening their bed and breakfast. They began with a swing through Georgia and North Carolina staying at a variety of bed and breakfasts and inns to decide exactly what they wanted, and most importantly, what guests wanted in a bed and breakfast.

One of their most important criteria was a location that would be convenient to major points of interest in the mountains, yet located away from the hustle of the city. They also wanted a bed and breakfast with a good reputation that was already in operation. After a visit to Cullowhee, they knew they had found the ideal accommodation.

Near the banks of the Tuckasegee River they found a traditional style, two-story home sitting in the center of five acres of pines, oaks and maples. With four comfortable rooms, three of which have private porches overlooking the expansive lawn, and a large granite patio across the back of the house, Charles and Janet have created a very intimate bed and breakfast. The nearly 4,000 square feet of space provides guests enough room to move around comfortably without the feeling generally associated with a small bed and breakfast. However, the house is small enough that Charles and Janet can give more personal attention to the needs of their guests. That attention to detail shows in the flower arrangements that Janet adds to the rooms for special occasions. She also allows guests to pick the best time for the traditional country breakfast that she serves family style each morning in the dining room or on the patio. By special arrangement, breakfast can even be served on your own private porch.

The community of Cullowhee is best known as the home of Western Carolina University. This school, which was founded in 1889 for mountain children, has grown into a center for arts and culture in the area with about 7,000 students currently enrolled.

The long history of the Tuckasegee River basin can be seen in the prehistoric hieroglyphics on Judaculla Rock, located between Cullowhee and Cashiers. These hieroglyphics give testament to the people who have been attracted to the area for thousands of years.

The area was also a major Cherokee community long before the first Europeans arrived. Hernando DeSoto is the first recorded European to visit the area around 1540. It took another 300 years before the first settlers moved into the area. You will find much of this history on display at the Mountain Heritage Center located on the campus of Western Carolina University. For visitors to the area, the Center with its museum is an important stop in beginning to appreciate the mountains. In addition, the Center has a number of programs that are designed to help preserve and promote the area's unique heritage. One of its most popular programs is the Mountain Heritage Day, a festival of mountain music, arts and crafts that attracts thousands of people each year.

With Dillsboro only a short drive away, a trip on the Great Smoky Mountains Railway is another way to enjoy the area. Each day froom May to October, excursion trains, pulled by either diesel or steam locomotive, depart the Dillsboro depot to take you through the river valley to Bryson City and back. Along the way you will see where the train wreck in *The Fugitive* was filmed. Here also is the 836-foot-long Cowee Tunnel driven through solid rock by convict labor. A new attraction in Dillsboro is the Historic Railway Museum that offers more than 3,000 articles of railroad memorabilia and a large model railroad within a 5,000-square-foot building.

---

**Cullowhee Bed & Breakfast**
**150 Ledbetter Rd.; Cullowhee, NC 28723**
**(704) 293-5447**
**Innkeepers: Charles & Janet Moore**
Rooms: 4; Private baths: 4; Rates: $$
Affiliations: NCBBI, PAII
Payment: 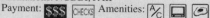 Amenities:

## Applegate Inn Bed & Breakfast
## Dillsboro

There's more to the Applegate Inn than its location. I will admit that location is one of its best drawing cards. On one side of Scott's Creek it's quiet and peaceful. Yet take a 125-yard walk, cross a footbridge, and you are at the depot of the Great Smoky Mountains Railway. Cross the tracks and you're in downtown Dillsboro, a quaint village of antique dealers, specialty stores, and artists' working studios.

This is where Judy and Emil Milkey have created a mountain getaway. It's spotlessly clean and comfortable. The Milkeys love people and it shows. The large living room, complete with fireplace, is warm and inviting. They have attractively furnished each of the four guest rooms. The Creekside Room has a queen bed and is decorated in the French Provincial style. The Valentine Room, with Victorian furnishings, has a queen-size sleigh bed and overlooks the goldfish pond. In addition, there are two efficiency units available for extended stays or guests with families.

Since Judy loves to cook, breakfast is a treat. Naturally, with a name like Applegate, you can expect to find apple pancakes, apple fritters, apple muffins, and apple breakfast sandwiches. Of course, there are also Belgian waffles, eggs, sausage and bacon. The eggs are a bit different as they contain two secret ingredients. Guests have to guess what they are.

While Judy loves to cook, she hates rules. As a result, there aren't many at the Inn. Just relax and have a good a time. The front porch is a guest favorite. Here you can watch the mallards or the fireflies. If you love trains, like I do, then watching the train is a great way to spend some time. Mystery lovers should be sure to ask about Judy's Murder Mys-

tery Weekends. While you're there, introduce yourself to the toy poodles and the talking parrot.

On the opposite side of the creek is the new Historic Railway Museum. The 5,000-square-foot museum houses more than 3,000 articles of railroad memorabilia. The collection covers more than 140 years of railroad history. For model railroad enthusiasts, one of the largest model railroads in Western North Carolina is on display. Other items include hundreds of antique models trains, brakeman's lanterns, and bronze bells.

Filmmakers used the Great Smoky Mountains Railway in the making of *The Fugitive*, starring Harrison Ford. Lewis Grizzard said, "After seeing *The Fugitive*, all other train wrecks, real or staged, will forever pale in comparison." It took two months to create the set, four days to shoot the entire sequence, but only sixty seconds for the crash. When you ride the train from Dillsboro, you can see where it all took place. In addition, you'll ride through the Cowee Tunnel. Built by convict labor, legend has it that 19 men (who died in the Tuckasegee River shackled together) haunt the tunnel.

Dillsboro got its start when William Dills built the Riverwood Shops in 1882. The new Riverwood Shops, located across the Tuckasegee River and above the Applegate, feature work of local artisans and are worth the visit.

**Applegate Inn Bed & Breakfast**
**P.O. Box 567; 163 Hemlock St.; Dillsboro, NC 28725**
**(704) 586-2397**
**Innkeepers: Judy & Emil Milkey**
Rooms: 4; Private Baths: 3; Shared Baths: 1; Efficiencies: 3; Rates: $$
Affiliations: AAA, NB&BA, PAII, Jackson Co. Chamber
Payment:     Amenities:

# The Jarrett House
# Dillsboro

For more than a hundred years the Jarrett House has opened its doors to travelers from all over the world. Its hospitality and good food are a Western North Carolina tradition.

When the railroad came to the area in 1882, all that existed in Dillsboro were a few shops built by the town's founder, William Allen Dills. Today, these shops are known as the Riverwood Shops. Two years after the railroad arrived, Dills built a hotel and named both it and the mountain it faced for his youngest daughter, Beulah. The hotel quickly became the official dining place for passengers and railroad employees. For years, the number of passengers who would be dining was telegraphed ahead each day from the train depot in Balsam.

In 1894, Dills sold his hotel to R. Frank Jarrett of Franklin. Jarrett could not have picked a better time to buy the inn. It was a time when people were flocking to the mountains to visit mineral springs for the restorative powers they were purported to have. When Jarrett discovered that a sulfur spring was located at the back of the hotel, he renamed the inn Jarrett Springs Hotel. To capitalize further on the springs, he built a summer house around the spring with seats for guests.

Jarrett had many other interests, including writing poems and songs, so he left the day-to-day operation of Jarrett Springs to his wife "Miss Sallie." It was she, not the spring, who brought fame to the hotel because she set one of the finest tables in the mountains. Folks would spend an entire day traveling to Dillsboro just to eat one of her meals. Fried ham, redeye gravy, and hot buttermilk biscuits were all served family-style. Food was offered up in such quantity that if any guest ever had to ask for more, the meal was on the house.

The Jarretts ran the inn until Frank's death in 1950. Over the years, several different owners ran the operation, and each maintained the reputation for

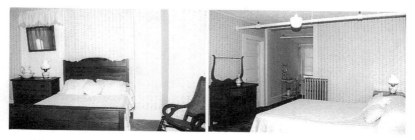

good food and southern hospitality. When Jim Hartbarger and his wife, Jean, acquired the inn in 1975, they were committed to keep the traditions alive. Today, the Jarrett House is family business with sons, Buzz and Scott along with their wives, Mary and Sharon carrying on the traditions.

Over the years they have carefully restored the Jarrett House and added southern fried chicken, fresh mountain trout, and baked ham to the daily menu. However, true hospitality, as well as the famous mountain cured ham, is still a part of the daily fare.

It was the railroad that changed Dillsboro's humble beginnings. By 1888, the town had become an important community. Two sawmills with their own lumberyards, several mines, and six general stores served the people of the river valley. The mills are gone now, and the population is only 150, but Dillsboro has become a haven for artists and craftsmen. Each year, thousands of visitors come to visit more than 50 shops and galleries in the community. They also come to ride the Great Smoky Mountains Railway and to raft down the Tuckasegee River.

During the season, the Great Smoky Mountains Railway takes visitors through the river valley to Bryson City. Whether you take a half-day ride in an open car or take a dinner excursion in one of the the air-conditioned cars, the railroad is still the perfect way to experience the beauty of the mountains. At the end of the day, the folks at the Jarrett House are there to make you feel at home. Comfortable rooms, each decorated with period antiques of walnut and oak, take you back to a time when the world was just a little less frantic.

---

**The Jarrett House**
**P.O. Box 219; Dillsboro, NC 28725**
**(800) 972-5623; (704) 586-0265**
**Innkeepers: Jim & Jean Hartbarger**
Rooms: 18; Private baths: 18; Shared baths: 4; Suites: 3; Rates: $$; children over 12
Affiliations: PAII, SIA
Payment: $$$ CHECKS  Amenities: A/C 🖥 🍽 ♿

## Olde Towne Inn-Bed & Breakfast
## Dillsboro

Local residents call Jackson County the "Great Variety Show." Visitors to the area quickly learn that the county has indeed earned the title. Within the county's 499 square miles you will find spectacular scenery, important historical locations and a large part of the Cherokee Indian Reservation.

Two of the first residents along the banks of Scott Creek were G.L. and M.E. Snider who constructed a farm house in 1878 on the river road leading from Sylva, just two miles away. Soon, others were drawn to this pretty river valley. In 1882, William Dills built what are today known as the Riverwood Shops. This was the beginning of Dillsboro. The railroad arrived in 1882, and the first hotel was constructed in 1884. By 1888, the town had become an important community with lumberyards, sawmills, mines, and six general stores. Today the population of Dillsboro is less than 150, but it has become a haven for artists and artisans. The 50+ shops and galleries in the community, along with the Great Smoky Mountains Railway, draw thousands of visitors each year to ride the excursion trains, raft down the Tuckasegee River, and to visit the variety of shops.

Over the years the Snider farmhouse changed hands many times. For many years in the early 1900s it was the home of Parsons Kincaid, a railroad station agent. In the 1970s it was a doctor's home and office; in the early 1980s, a rooming house. In August of 1989, Olde Towne Inn-Bed & Breakfast opened and the farmhouse has welcomed guests year round ever since. The labor of love that went into the creation of the Olde Towne Inn is visible in every room. Antique claw-foot tubs, carefully chosen antiques, country crafts, floral prints and the delightful smells of home-baked breads take you back in time to a late 1800's

farmhouse. The historic house is nestled against the side of a mountain. The three charming guest rooms are upstairs where the guests can sit on the balcony and look down upon the town of Dillsboro or gaze at mountains in every direction. Since the community of Dillsboro grew up around the home, today what was once a country farmhouse is located on the main street of Dillsboro. Every shop, cafe and restaurant are within an easy walk of your front door. Even the depot for the Great Smoky Mountain Railway is only one block away.

Each day during the season, the railroad takes you to Bryson City and back again through small communities in the river valley and past the most beautiful scenery in the mountains. From simple half-day trips to dinner excursions and even combination rail/rafting trips, the Great Smoky Mountain Railway is a perfect way to experience both the color and flavor of the mountains. Tours of the Tuckasegee River, Nantahala Gorge, Valley River and Red Marble Gap are all available. There are excursions by both diesel and steam locomotive. The Tuckasegee River tour will take you past the spot where the train wreck in *The Fugitive* was filmed and through the 836-foot-long Cowee Tunnel. A new attraction, the Historic Railway Museum, offers more than 3,000 articles of railroad memorabilia and one of the largest operating model railroads in North Carolina—all within a 5,000-square-foot building.

**Olde Towne Inn-Bed & Breakfast**
**P.O. Box 485; 300 Hayood Rd.; Dillsboro, NC 28725**
**(704) 586-3461**
**Innkeepers: Gretchen & Dave Dilks**
Rooms: 3; Private baths: 3; Rates: $$; children over 10
Affiliations: Jackson Co. Chamber, Dillsboro Merchant's Assoc.
Payment:  Amenities:

# Buttonwood Inn
# Franklin

Liz Oehser came to the mountains in 1984 to get away from the Florida heat. On a cul-de-sac, tucked away among tall pines, dogwood and rhododendron, she found the Buttonwood Inn. The Inn sits between the 5th and 7th greens of the Franklin Golf Course.

The original house was built in the late 1920s as a summer cottage. Another wing was added in 1957. In 1980, major renovations turned the cottage into a bed and breakfast.

Built of white pine, with a batten board exterior, the Inn is unpretentious until you walk inside. The first items to receive your attention are the rustic antiques and hand-crafted collectibles. From the white pine walls to the polished hardwood floors, Liz has decorated the inn with an eclectic mix of antiques that fit together perfectly. There is a feeling of home about the place. The air smells pleasant. You'll find yourself going from room to room to look at the miniatures, or looking at cross-stitching, decorated baskets, and asking about various pieces such as the church pew, or the sled. At one time, Liz spent more time making hand-crafted items herself. Now the Inn requires most of her time.

Two of the four rooms are names for their styles: the Dresden-Amish Room and the Country Room. Sister's Room is named because, well, when Liz's sister comes to visit, that's where she always stays. Each of the beds are covered with homemade family quilts. The rooms are large enough to be comfortable, and one has a small kitchen area for guests who stay a bit longer.

There must be something about the crisp mountain air that whets one's appetite. Her full breakfast offers goodies such as stuffed French toast, egg soufflés, Dutch babies with baked peaches, scones with homemade

lemon butter, or sausage-apple rings and strawberry omelets. It's a good thing that she likes to cook.

With all there is to do in the area, staying at the Buttonwood Inn is easy to do. Located next to a 9-hole golf course, many guests find their thoughts turn to the fairways. For an 18-hole course, Mill Creek Country Club is down the road.

For others, gem mining takes priority. Macon County is rich in gems and minerals and is a favorite spot for rock hounds. The famous Cowee Valley north of Franklin lures thousands each year to its ruby mines, which still yield valuable stones to lucky "miners." The Franklin Gem and Mineral Society operates an outstanding small museum in the old Macon County jail.

Franklin lies between two popular scenic gorges, the Cullasaja and the Nantahala, both noted for their wild grandeur. As a result many who come to the area are interested in following the waters as they create magnificent spills. There is the Lower Falls with a drop of 250 feet. There is also Dry Falls, a favorite with visitors who enjoy walking behind the roaring water.

Whatever your taste, Franklin has a friendly atmosphere and a casual life-style. It offers a smorgasbord of outdoor activities, from wilderness camping to golfing. Yet, it also offers some of the finest antique shopping in the western part of the state.

---

**Buttonwood Inn**
**50 Admiral Drive; Franklin, NC 28734**
**(704) 369-8985**
**Innkeepers: Liz Oehser**
Rooms: 4; Private Baths: 2; Shared Baths: 2; Rates: $$
Affiliations: NCBBI
Payment: $$$ CHECKS Amenities: 🖉

## The Franklin Terrace
## Franklin

Your journey into the past, when southern hospitality was at its best, begins as you turn into the circular drive. The wide porches of the Plantation-style two-story bed and breakfast act as a time machine taking you to easy days of peace and relaxation. Upon entering the Terrace, you find a beautifully decorated parlor and large guest rooms filled with period antiques.

Franklin is the first North Carolina town on the US 441-N corridor, en route to the Great Smoky Mountains. It's a small town with a friendly atmosphere and a casual life-style. You are offered a smorgasbord of outdoor activities, from wilderness camping to golf. It lies between two popular scenic gorges, the Cullasaja and the Nantahala, both noted for their wild grandeur. In its rush downhill through its ancient canyon, the Cullasaja River it creates the Lower Falls, with a drop of 250 feet, and the Dry Falls. Dry Falls is a favorite with visitors who enjoy the walk behind the roaring water. The scenery is accessible thanks to the winding US 64, which hugs close to the wall of the gorge on its climb from Franklin to Highlands.

The region is one of great unspoiled beauty. Nearly half of Macon County, of which Franklin is the county seat, lies within the Nantahala National Forest. Rugged mountain ranges rise to a series of peaks more than 5,000 feet above the valley of the Little Tennessee River.

The natural resources of the region are not limited to the mountain scenery and wildlife. The area is also rich in gems and minerals, and is a favorite spot for rock hounds. The famous Cowee Valley, north of Franklin, lures thousands each year to its ruby mines, which still yield valuable stones to lucky "miners."

Within walking distance of the Terrace is an outstanding small museum in the old Macon County jail. The museum is operated by the Franklin Gem and Mineral Society. Among the displays is a 49-pound corundum crystal, taken from a local mine in 1888. Also within walking distance you will find gem shops, antiques, and galleries.

Built as a school in 1887, the Franklin Terrace is listed on the National Register of Historic Places. In 1989, Helen Henson purchased the Terrace at auction by accident. She was asked to give the opening bid. During the auction Helen continued to raise her bid. Thinking that she would make only one more bid to help raise the price of the property, she found that she was the highest bidder. The only problem was that the furniture for the Terrace had been sold already during the auction.

While refurnishing the Terrace, Helen discovered a love of antiques that shows in every room. Antiques are even available for sale in the main-floor gift shop along with area crafts and gifts.

The continental-plus breakfast is served in a bright and cheerful room with windows facing south and east. When the weather is pleasant you can even enjoy your breakfast on the screen porch. Breakfast generally includes six different types of fruit, cereal, home baked muffins, breads and croissants.

---

**The Franklin Terrace**
**67 Harrison Ave.; Franklin, NC 28734**
**(800) 633-2431; (704) 524-7907**
**Innkeepers: Helen Henson**
Rooms: 9; Private bath: 9; Cottages: 1; Rates: $$; Children over 3
Open April 1-November 15
Payment:     Amenities:

## Smokey Shadows Lodge
## Maggie Valley

Maggie Valley is a three-mile strip at the base of the Balsam Mountains, whose peaks reach up to 6,000 feet. The community was named for the daughter of its first postmaster.

High above Maggie Valley, Smokey Shadows Lodge sits at an elevation of 4,500. It was built in 1953 of native stone and hand-hewn chestnut logs. The logs came from a grist mill that was moved when they created the Great Smoky Mountains National Park. Inside the lodge, the exposed beams and wormy chestnut walls dominate. The great room has a massive stone fireplace and time-polished hardwood floors. The entire place is spotlessly clean.

The lodge is "country" in its furnishings from the crocheted table cloths in the dining room to the wood and leather locks on the doors. There are handmade quilts and pillows, antique photos, kerosene lamps and candles. The 12 guests rooms, while small, are comfortable and have private bath. Two cabins: Shadow Shack (sleeps two) and Shinn Dig (sleeps six) are available for those needing a bit more room. Downstairs, a favorite with youngsters, is "the stable" capable of sleeping eight.

The porch, running the full length of the lodge, is filled with rocking chairs. An old porch swing has a prominent location. The view from the porch is inviting. Many people come to the porch in slippers and bath robes with cups of tea or coffee to watch the sun come up.

Some dreams take time. Owning Smokey Shadows was a childhood dream for Ginger Shinn. She and her mother stayed at the lodge when they came to visit relatives in Maggie Valley. Years later, Ginger convinced her husband, Bud, that they should buy the lodge. Their first attempt fell through when someone else purchased the lodge. They

waited six years for the lodge to come back on the market. Finally, in 1983, the dream came true.

While many come to stay at the inn, others come for the "country gourmet dinners" that Ginger serves. While the room rates do not include dinner, the price is nominal for both room and meal. Weddings, family reunions, and company functions have all taken place at Smokey Shadows. It was even featured in a movie, *Fire On The Mountain*.

There is no television in the rooms, nor telephone, but you won't miss them. There are so many other activities to enjoy. In addition to nature trails, just up the road is the Cataloochee Ski area. Horseback riding and golf is also available in the area. Down the mountain you will find the entrance to Ghost Town in the Sky theme park, Soco Zoo, and the Stompin' Grounds with its professional clogging teams. Waynesville, with its quaint shops and galleries, is only a 15-minute drive away.

If you *really* get the desire to wander, The Great Smoky Mountains National Park is only ten miles away. The more than 500,000 acres offer adventures that will last a lifetime. Hiking trails, waterfalls, pioneer villages, horseback riding and some of the highest peaks east of the Mississippi River all help to captivate the visitor.

---

**Smokey Shadows Lodge**
**P.O. Box 444; Fie Top Rd.; Maggie Valley, NC 28751**
**(704) 926-0001**
**Innkeepers: Bud & Ginger Shinn**
Rooms: 12; Private Baths: 14; Cabins: 2; Rates: $-$$; children over 5
Affiliations: Haywood Co. Chamber
Payment:  CHECKS  VISA  Amenities:

## Huntington Hall Bed & Breakfast
## Murphy

Located in the farthest western county of Cherokee, Murphy is nearer to the capitals of seven other states than it is to its own—Raleigh. Murphy is only a two hour drive from Atlanta, Chattanooga, and Asheville. The Nantahala River is only 20 miles to the east and the Ocoee River, site of the 1996 Olympics kayaking and canoeing events, is to the west.

In the valley created by the Valley and Hiawassee Rivers, a settlement once called Huntington grew and prospered. It wasn't until years later that the community took the name of Murphy. One of Murphy's earliest residents, J.H. Dillard, a successful lawyer, mayor and twice elected to the North Carolina House of Representatives, and his wife, Dixie, built a beautiful home at the corner of Valley River Avenue and Dillard Street that was a focal point in the community. More than one hundred years later, the two-story house is once again an important residence in Murphy as the home of Bob and Katie DeLong.

Bob had 19 years of experience in the hotel industry and Katie worked in corporate America. Both wanted to do something more important. They made an offer on the house after their first visit. After months of work to reopen fireplaces and refinish flooring, they completely restored this 1881 country Victorian home. Each of the five guest rooms is charming with a personality of its own. Decorating schemes match the mood of the rooms with their old pine heartwood floors and tall windows. They also added much appreciated amenities like individual heating and air conditioning units, private baths and color cable television. Afternoon refreshments, turn down service, and homemade chocolate truffles on your pillow complete the picture of hospitality.

"Service" is the byword at Huntington Hall, and I believe breakfast proves that best. You can't sit at the breakfast table and count calories,

although they can handle special requests with advanced notice. Mornings bring a different entree and a variety of goodies to the table each day. You might discover your plate filled with crepes with ginger, peach and apricot sauce or gingerbread or banana pancakes with fruit, coconut and walnuts topped with ice cream and syrup. Other special treats include stuffed French toast with cream cheese and strawberry preserves, or filled with sausage and muenster cheese.

Over the years, we have spent a lot of time in Murphy. The country side is rich in its diversity, the people of the valley hospitable, and the climate comfortable most of the year. The Great Smoky Mountain Railway has excursions from Andrews, the Nantahala Gorge and Bryson City as well as from their home depot in Dillsboro an hour to the northeast. The area is perfect for whitewater rafting, canoeing, fishing and hiking. The Tusquittee Pioneer Village, is located just 15 miles east of Murphy.

The Pioneer Village, a homegrown museum, consists of 18 buildings, the oldest of which was built in 1832. The village contains all of the things you would have found in a small mountain community just before the turn of the century; a syrup mill, blacksmith shop, school and church. Thousands of pioneer artifacts fill every nook and cranny.

A short distance from Murphy is the Joyce Kilmer Forest - the only virgin forest east of the Mississippi River. The John C. Campbell Folk School at Brasstown is only six or seven miles away.

---

**Huntington Hall Bed & Breakfast**
**500 Valley River Ave.; Murphy, NC 28906**
**(800) 824-6189; (704) 837-9567; Fax: (704) 837-2527**
**Innkeepers: Bob & Kate DeLong**
Rooms: 5; Private baths: 5; Rates: $$
Affiliations: NCBBI, PAII, AAA
Payment:      Amenities:

## Stone Manor Inn Bed & Breakfast
## Murphy

Bed and breakfasts come in all sizes. That is what makes them unique. The Stone Manor Inn is one of the smallest bed and breakfasts in which we stayed.

Something else that makes bed and breakfasts distinctive is the innkeeper. They are a reflection of the personality, taste and interests of the owner. In this case, there's only one prerequisite to enjoying a stay at the Stone Manor. You must enjoy being mothered, especially at breakfast. Sue (Mama Sue) is going to make sure that everything is just right.

Two years before Sue Sechler opened rooms upstairs, she opened Mama's Sue's Kountry Kitchen downstairs. She loves people and the intimacy of a small B & B. She also loves the comfortable surroundings of a small restaurant, so she decided to combine the three. It works.

The historic landmark that Sue chose for the Stone Manor was built in 1949 by Dr. Victor F. Taylor. Dr. Taylor (assisted by "Mac" McCarter and a few others) personally hauled the blue marble from Tennessee. Other trips were made to Georgia for pink marble and to Marble, NC for the gray and white marble. They built the entire house of marble.

Sue purchased the building in December of 1990. After renovation, she opened the doors to Mama Sue's Kountry Kitchen in the fall of 1991. The bed and breakfast opened in October of 1993.

Breakfast is included with your stay and served in Mama Sue's Kountry Kitchen. (The prices are so reasonable that even if you paid for breakfast, it would still be a bargain.) Breakfast is what *I* would consider a traditional country meal. From the menu you can choose bacon, sausage, or Kountry Ham, eggs (any style), grits and homefries. There are

also pancakes, and French toast, or oatmeal with brown sugar, raisins or cinnamon. While lunch is not included, the menu is more than suitable, and very well priced. Mama Sue serves dinner Friday and Saturday nights only. Her motto for the Kitchen is "You go away properly stuffed and wearing a smile because you didn't have to pay too much."

Murphy is a nice quiet town to visit. Angel and I go there every chance we get. It is one of the oldest settlements in the state. Hernando deSoto visited the Cherokee village of Guasili in 1540. Nearly three centuries later, an Indian trading post was established on a site that would become Murphy. The Cherokee County Historical Museum can help provide history of the area, including the Cherokee's removal along the Trail of Tears.

Just 18 miles south of Murphy is Fields of the Wood, a 200-acre Biblical theme park. The John C. Campbell Folk School is located in Brasstown. Part of the Nantahala National Forest and more than 8,700 acres of wilderness lakes are in the county. The Murphy area is more than just mountains, lakes and rivers. It's fairs and festivals, such as America's oldest wagon train, bringing thousands together for a time of sharing. It is also real friendly people.

**Stone Manor Inn Bed & Breakfast**
**505 Peachtree St.; Murphy, NC 28906**
**(704) 837-8676**
**Innkeeper: Sue Sechler**
Rooms: 4; Private Baths: 4; Rates: $$; children over 3
Payment:     Amenities:

## Grandview Lodge
## Waynesville

For any business, the real test is time. Few inns have remained as long as the Grandview Lodge. For the last 50 years, the Inn has been a haven for travelers to the southern mountains of North Carolina. It has a well-deserved reputation for good food and quality lodging.

Located on 2½ acres just outside Waynesville, the Grandview Lodge began as a large farmhouse built in the 1890s. Its role as a farmhouse changed in the 1930s when a family from upstate New York purchased the house and made it their midpoint stop between New York and Florida.

In the early 40s, new owners decided to remodel the house and make it an inn. They added rooms, prepared dinner for their guests and began a tradition for others to follow and upon which to improve. In the 60s, the Inn changed hands to the second set of innkeepers who also made additions and changes. Like the original innkeepers, they stayed for 20 years.

For years, Stan and Linda Arnold had been talking about escaping corporate life, starting their own inn, and making a new life for themselves. The story goes that Stan, a corporate manager, finally came home from work one day in 1986 and said, "I've had it. Let's do it or stop talking about it." They have now been innkeepers of the Grandview Lodge for ten years.

The Arnolds have made many improvements over the years both to the building and to the already fine reputation of the Grandview Lodge.

The three buildings of the Inn house nine rooms, each with private bath, cable TV, and two beds. The antique furnishings are "comfortable and functional" without being the least pretentious. We appreciated the furnishings that are pleasant to the eye, without worrying about whether or not it was safe to sit down. In the main lodge, three of the guest rooms include gas-burning fireplaces. All of the rooms have queen- or king-size beds. The two suites at the

Grandview are great for extended stays; they are more like mini-apartments with their own kitchens. The common area, located in the main house, is complete with TV, VCR, piano, games and good books to make you feel right at home. Patches and Boots (the two resident cats) can help you wander the grounds.

Now, I have to tell you that for all of the amenities at the Grandview Lodge and for the special care the innkeepers provide, the real story of the Inn is the dining room. This is Linda's domain and her meals are truly fit for a king or queen.

Operating as a traditional inn, breakfast and dinner are included in the daily rate. During a short stay in Connecticut, Linda, a home economist, attended the Culinary Institute of America at Hyde Park and took the regional American Cooking Course. The meals are not exotic and are usually planned around the harvest of locally grown vegetables and fruits. Breads, muffins, biscuits as well as jellies, jams and relishes are all homemade. Mornings may bring locally produced sausage or bacon, apple oatmeal muffins or blueberry muffins, grits or potatoes, whole grain pancakes, scrambled eggs, or waffles with apple cider syrup. There is also fresh fruit, hot and cold cereals, juices, teas and coffee.

The dining room is open to non-resident guests by advanced reservation. When dinner comes, be prepared to feast on entrees of lemon chicken, pork chops, pork roast, beef burgundy, or oven fried chicken all served with garden fresh vegetables, homemade breads, and wonderful desserts. A favorite dessert at the Inn is Linda's "Chocoholic Tart" with two kinds of chocolate plus chocolate liqueur.

**Grandview Lodge**
**809 Valley View Circle Rd.; Waynesville, NC 28786**
**(800) 255-7826; (704) 456-5212; Fax: (704) 452-5432**
**Innkeepers: Stan & Linda Arnold**
Rooms: 9; Private baths: 9; Suites: 2; Rates: $$-$$$
Affiliations: Mobil, Haywood Co. Chamber, Smoky Mtn. Host
Payment:  Amenities:

## The Swag Country Inn
## Waynesville

We had no idea what to expect when we first went to the Swag. It came highly recommended. Dinner, I was told, was prepared by a chef from the Culinary Institute of America. We knew there would be bath robes, hairdryers, a refrigerator, and even a coffee grinder and maker in our room. That's all we knew, though. By the end of our stay, I knew that we had found a first-class inn.

The first part of the adventure began with a six-mile drive up a narrow blacktop road taking us up nearly 2,000 feet in elevation. I thought I was almost there when the last sign pointed to a gravel drive. The adventure was just beginning. The last 2.5 miles of gravel road takes you another thousand feet up to an elevation of 5,000.

The ridge was cleared more than seventy years ago. It took Dan and Deener Matthews' vision to see its potential. There was no road then, only a steep trail. It took three bulldozers, a dynamite crew and 150 trucks (each carrying 17 tons of gravel) to build a road. In 1971, five abandoned log and stone structures from Tennessee and North Carolina were taken apart and hauled up the mountain. Next came the task of putting them back together to make the main lodge of the Swag. The oldest structure used was built in 1795. The living room is constructed of logs from an old church from Hancock County, TN.

They didn't plan to open an inn. It just turned out that way. The World's Fair came to Knoxville and they opened the doors for one season. At the end of the summer, so many people wanted to come back that Deener didn't have the heart to tell them "no." That was in 1982. Deener runs the inn 5 1/2 months a year. The other 6½ months she lives in Manhattan where Dan is rector of the Trinity Church, Wall Street, in the city of New York.

Each of the thirteen rooms and three cabins is different, yet comfortable, and decorated with style. Many rooms have fireplaces or wood-burning stoves. Most have queen-size beds and all have private baths, several with steam showers and jacuzzis.

The Chestnut Lodge houses an excellent library. In the basement is a regulation-size racquetball court and a redwood sauna. In the main lodge, the living room with cathedral ceiling is a focal point of the Inn.

There is plenty to do at the Swag. You can begin your day reading the 8-page FAX edition of *The New York Times* that they deliver to your door. Then take a trip to the dining room for a breakfast of cinnamon apples, or have an oatmeal sundae. With notice, they will pack a lunch for you. Now you can begin a day's outing.

Walk out the door. Twenty steps takes you to the Swag's private entrance to the Great Smoky Mountains National Park. With over a mile of the Park bordering the Swag, and over 500,000 acres to explore, you should be hungry for the four-course dinner that Deener and the chef have prepared for you at the day's end.

**The Swag Country Inn**
**Rt 2, Box 280-A; Hemphill Rd.; Waynesville, NC 28786**
**(800) 789-7672; (704) 926-0430; Fax: (704) 926-2036**
**Innkeepers: Deener Matthews**
Rooms: 14; Private Baths: 17; Cabins: 3; Rates: $$$$-$$$$$; children over 7
Affiliations: PAII, IIA, NCHMA, AHMA, Open May-October
Payment:      Amenities:

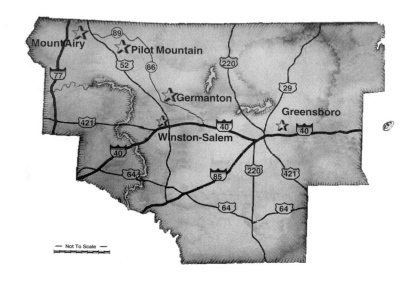

# Northern
# Foothills

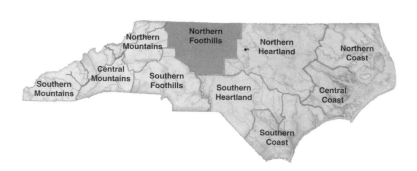

## MeadowHaven Bed & Breakfast
## Germanton

The Fains' call their bed and breakfast "A Contemporary Country Retreat."...and they're right. This is where innkeepers go to relax. The "retreat," located on twenty-five acres, provides a little bit of everything.

There's a guest pantry in the Main House with complimentary snacks and beverages available 24 hours a day. The 18 by 32 foot indoor pool is heated year-round. Multicolored parrots and lovebirds surround the pool. There is a large outdoor hot tub. The game room contains a pool table, ping-pong, cards, and board games. In addition to the acreage, which offers plenty of room to move around, there is a stocked pond where you can fish (catch and release), and horseshoe pits. The large common room has a fireplace, reading materials, and a video tape library. Soft music is piped from a built-in stereo system.

The original chalet-style home was built in 1976. The woodwork throughout most of the house is hand-stained California driftwood. Skylights, stained glass, custom painting and stenciling add to the unique decor. A large sun deck overlooks the pond and Sauratown Mountain.

Sam and Darlene purchased the property in April of 1992. Before opening in December, 1992, they landscaped the property, added bathrooms and completely redecorated the house. New additions include fully-equipped log cabins at the back of the property and a glass-enclosed breakfast room in the Main House. This is where Sam serves his country breakfast at individual tables each with mountain views.

They have done a wonderful job with MeadowHaven. Each of the rooms is comfortable and very well decorated. We stayed in the Master Bedroom. It, like the other rooms, has phone, color TV and VCR. It also

contains a two-person whirlpool bath, and a separate custom steam shower/sauna. Other in-room extras include hooded terry bathrobes, hairdryers, and toiletries. Furnishings are an eclectic mix—from wicker and bamboo to antiques and brass or iron canopy beds. You also will find many items from the Bob Timberlake Collection.

Darlene is a native of Stokes County and lived on the property with her brother (who designed and built the house) and his family. A former conference center manager, Darlene now works in her family's construction business.  Sam is from the Flat Rock area just south of Hendersonville. His great-grandparents ran a boarding house in the Flat Rock area. Running a B & B is apparently "in his genes." Sam acts as Host and Chef. He was an assistant breakfast chef at a large hotel prior to preparing breakfast at MeadowHaven. His breakfasts are a real treat. Magic is another of Sam's specialties. You will find his magic memorabilia in the game room.

There is much to do in the area. Tour the art gallery, winery, and fresco in the small Moravian village of Germanton. Golf at Hemlock or Stonewall golf courses. Go horseback riding at Mountain View Stables. There are miles of bike paths. Ten minutes north of MeadowHaven are the 6,340 acres of Hanging Rock State Park where you can picnic or hike. The Dan River winds through Stokes County and offers canoeing or tubing. To the west is Pilot Mountain, a 1,400-foot quartzite monadnock. Winston-Salem and historic Old Salem are 16 miles south of the inn. The regional jetport is forty-five minutes away in Greensboro.

*NA*

**MeadowHaven Bed & Breakfast**
**P.O. Box 222; Hwy. 8; Germanton, NC 27019**
**(910) 593-3996**
**Innkeepers: Samuel & Darlene Fain**
Rooms: 3; Private Baths: 3; Cabins: 4; Rates: $$-$$$$; children over 13
Affiliations: PAII
Payment:       Amenities:

## Greenwood Bed & Breakfast
## Greensboro

While I have lived in North Carolina for a long time, I never really thought of Greensboro as a destination. To me it was a pass-through community on my way to and from another area of the state. My feelings changed with our stay at the Greenwood Bed & Breakfast. We were amazed at how much there was to do in the city of Greensboro. In addition, it's centrally located for trips to Winston-Salem, High Point, Burlington and Asheboro.

Innkeepers Mike and Vanda Terrell at the Greenwood Bed & Breakfast were exemplary hosts for our explorations of the community. While they have lived in Greensboro only a few years, they have learned the area and can help with suggestions for shopping, restaurants, and visiting points of interest in the community.

The Greenwood, only a few blocks from downtown Greensboro, is located in the Fisher Park Historic District. This area was one of Greensboro's first planned neighborhoods. The development in this area began in 1919, making the Greenwood (circa 1910) one of the oldest houses in the district. Its design is unique as very few Victorian "stick style" homes were built after the 1890s. Yet the architect used the best features of angular lines, asymmetrical style and multiple gables to create a very elegant home. To this the Terrells have added an eclectic mix of traditional and period antiques to make it both comfortable and practical as a bed and breakfast.

As the guest rooms are on the second floor, the Greenwood has an unusual feature of a fully equipped second floor guest kitchen. In addition to the guest refrigerator, we especially appreciated the bowl of goodies that Vanda keeps in each room. After exploring Greensboro, I was ready for a late night treat. The second floor also has its own guest parlor complete with cable television and VCR.

The park, directly across the street from the Greenwood, acts as an extension of the front yard, and offers pleasant surroundings for an early morning walk be-

fore breakfast. Vanda's generous breakfast prepared us for a day of exploring all that Greensboro has to offer. While her offerings vary from day to day, there is always coffee, teas, and fresh squeezed orange juice. Casseroles, peaches and cream French toast, apple cinnamon waffles or gingerbread pancakes are only a few of the house favorites.

Activities in Greensboro range from shopping in a restored century-old cotton mill, to the Walkway of History. Theatrical productions in Greensboro out-number any other community in the state. There are the Barn Dinner Theatre, the Livestock Players Musical Theater at the Carolina Theatre, Razz-Ma-Tazz Musical Revue Company, and the Greensboro Children's Theatre. Each weekend some of the nation's funniest comedians appear at the Comedy Zone.

In addition to historic districts like Old Greensborough, the area has several major historic sites like the Blandwood Mansion and Carriage House. At Tannenbaum Park you will find the Colonial Heritage Center and Hoskins House. Near downtown is the Greensboro Historical Museum and it's just a short drive to the Chinqua-Penn and Mendenhall Plantations or the Old Mill of Guilford. For sports enthusiasts, Greensboro is also the host of the Richard Petty Museum. Here, too, is the Greensboro Coliseum Complex, one of the largest and most diversified entertainment, civic and sports facilities in the Southeast.

Still looking for something to do? Try the Natural Science Center of Greensboro, the 18 miles of HO- and N-scale model railroads at the Carolina Model Railroaders, or enjoy more than 200 acres of walking trails at Guilford Courthouse National Military Park, the oldest military park in the country.

---

**Greenwood Bed & Breakfast**
**205 N. Park Drive; Greensboro, NC 27401**
**(800) 535-9363; (910) 274-6350; Fax: (910) 274-9943**
**Innkeepers: Mike & Vanda Terrell**
Rooms: 4; Private baths: 4; Rates: $$
Affiliations: NCBBI, PAII, AAA
Payment:  Amenities:

# The Merritt House Bed & Breakfast
## Mount Airy

Pat and Richard Mangels always wanted a historic home. While their son was in college, they stayed in their first bed and breakfast...and loved it. They enjoyed it so much they started looking for a way to combine their interests. After looking at many locations, they chose the Merritt House after just one visit.

William E. Merritt moved to Mount Airy in 1888. Here, he established a brickyard to supply bricks for his hardware store and new home. He completed the house in 1901. Built in the Queen Anne style, popular at the time, the large house has 12 rooms.

The four guest bedrooms are large, with the Country Room being the largest. As its name implies, this room is decorated in a country style. It is complete with armoire, four-poster bed, spinning wheel and nick-knacks.

The Elizabeth Room, located on the first floor, is named for the last child of the Merritt family who lived in the house. The colors and furniture are similar to what had been in the home during her time. The 11-foot ceiling and original plaster molding give this room a very Victorian feel.

Most of the items in Victoria's Room belonged to either Pat's mother or grandmother. Her grandmother was wardrobe mistress for Ringling Brothers Circus and made the first drapes for the Radio City Music Hall in New York City.

The hunter green and burgundy colors of Richard's Room make it very masculine. It is decorated with firemen's memorabilia and the walls adorned with pictures and models of fire engines.

Mount Airy is a great place for a bed and breakfast. Mount Airy, the boyhood home of Andy Griffith, was used as the base for the fictional television town "Mayberry." Many sites throughout the town are reminiscent of the popular TV series. There's Floyd's City Barber Shop, with owner Russell Hiatt, who has been cutting hair at this location for more than 48 years. The Snappy Lunch, home of the famous pork chop sandwich, is the oldest eating establishment in Mount Airy. The downtown area is a National Register Historic District. Here you will find many shops, restaurants, and other buildings in a turn-of-the-century atmosphere. In addition, there are more than 34 historic structures or locations around the community.

While most of us will remember Mount Airy because of Andy Griffith, the world's largest open-faced granite quarry is also here. I was amazed to find that I had visited buildings and historic sites in other towns made of Mount Airy granite. You may have even walked on the world-famous stone. Let me name just a few: the Capitol Building in Harrisburg, Pennsylvania; the Wright Brother's Memorial in Kill Devil Hills, North Carolina; the Dilworth Plaza in Philadelphia; the curb along Pennsylvania Avenue in Washington, D.C.

Griffith and granite are not the only reasons to come to Mount Airy. The Blue Ridge Parkway, Pilot Mountain State Park and Hanging Rock State Park are all within easy drives of Mount Airy and the Merritt House.

---

**The Merritt House Bed & Breakfast**
**618 N. Main St.; Mount Airy, NC 27030**
**(800) 290-6290; (910) 786-2174**
**Innkeepers: Pat & Rich Mangels**
Rooms: 4; Private Baths: 4; Rates: $$
Affiliations: NCBBI
Payment:     Amenities:

# Pine Ridge Inn
# Mount Airy

Like many Americans, I grew up watching the Andy Griffith show. The citizens of Mayberry seemed like an extension of my own family. As the years passed, I learned that there are few communities in the world where all of the people are as friendly as they were portrayed on television; that is, until I had the opportunity to visit Andy's hometown of Mount Airy when we worked on the first edition of this book. We decided then that we would return to the area as often as possible. To paraphrase my grandfather, the people there are "down right hospitable."

While working on the second edition of *North Carolina Getaways*, we again had the opportunity to visit the area when we stayed at the Pine Ridge Inn. Even though we had heard good things about the Inn, we were quite unprepared for its elegance.

Once the home of textile baron John Springthorpe, the 9,600-square-foot Inn has been carefully decorated throughout. The 20 by 30 foot great room, like other rooms in the Inn, is decorated with museum-quality antiques. In one corner sits a 100-year-old Steinway Grand Piano that was custom-built for Mary Curtis, founder of the Curtis Institute of Music in Philadelphia. The great room, library and dining room all feature woodburning fireplaces. The library, with color TV and VCR and hundreds of books, makes a great place to while away the hours.

Each of the six guest rooms has been carefully decorated with antiques and reproductions. Each has a large private bathroom complete with shower/tub combination, hair dryers and plush bathrobes. All of the rooms include cable TVs, phones, and ample chairs and elbowroom for relaxing. The different rooms offer a collection of brass or canopied beds from twin- to queen- and king-size.

While the Inn is very elegant, there is still the feeling that you can prop your feet up with a good book. You may want to take a walk around the

eight acres, or take a dip in the large swimming pool. The screened gazebo houses a hot tub and sauna and is complete with a bar for social or family functions.

New to the Inn since our stay is dining service. Chef Tyler Sloan has recently joined the staff. A graduate of the Culinary Institute of America, Tyler has experience as both innkeeper and chef.

A full breakfast is included for inn guests; however, the dining room is also open to the general public for breakfast, lunch and dinner. The breakfast menu offers such choices as eggs (any style) with bacon, sausage or country ham or Western omelets. Daily specials are also available. The lunch menu varies from shrimp Florentine and chef salads to a variety of sandwiches including Reuben, grilled pork, grilled teriyaki chicken.

The dinner menus at the Pine Ridge Inn varies each day, but a sampling includes sautéed trout with a sauce of white wine, grapes, green onion, tomato and butter, or filet mignon—rubbed with garlic and cracked peppercorns.

The area around the Pine Ridge Inn is rich in things to do. The Blue Ridge Parkway is less than 15 miles to the east. Here you can follow the Parkway south and west to the Great Smoky Mountains National Park or north to the Shenandoah National Park. A few miles to the east is Mt. Airy, with its quaint shops, outlet malls, and numerous historic sites. To the south, less than an hour's drive, is Winston-Salem with museums, art galleries and Old Salem.

---

**Pine Ridge Inn**
**2893 W. Pine St.; Mount Airy, NC 27030**
**(910) 789-5034; Fax: (910) 786-9039**
**Innkeepers: Ellen & Manford Haxton**
Rooms: 6; Private baths: 6; Rates: $$-$$$
Affiliations: NCBBI, AB&BA, AAA, Mobil
Payment:      Amenities:

## Scenic Overlook Bed & Breakfast
## Pilot Mountain

Beginning a bed and breakfast requires a dream and a willingness to share it with other people. At Scenic Overlook the vision didn't start with an old house that needed restoring, but an incredible view of Pilot Mountain. Here on 37-acres, Gayle and Alan Steinbicker have built not just a bed and breakfast, but a romantic retreat. Their goal: that you "enjoy a oneness" with nature and with your partner.

Each of the three floors covers about 2,900 square feet. With nearly 9,000 square feet of space, they could have opened a bed and breakfast with eight or nine rooms. Instead, they chose to have three spacious guest suites in addition to a smaller guest room.

All of the rooms offer a view of Pilot Mountain and the six-acre lake. The lake is stocked with fish (catch and release only) and there are walking trails in addition to the exercise room and gift shop on the premises.

Each suite has a gas fireplaces (two are framed with hand-carved mahogany) complementing the impressive decor. The well-furnished suites also include coffee maker, refrigerator, microwave, TV and VCR. The bathrooms are large and feature whirlpool tubs (with beautiful wooded views) and separate showers. Each bath is perfectly appointed right down to the hairdryers.

A full breakfast is served in the dining room overlooking the lake and Pilot Mountain. Weather permitting, Gayle will serve it on the deck that runs the length of the house.

Scenic Overlook is located only two minutes from Pilot Mountain State Park (it's practically in their backyard). "The Pilot" is a quartzite monadnock (a rock that has resisted the elements for millions of years

while the erosion has worn away the rest of the area). The Big Pinnacle rises 1,400 feet above the valley floor with the knob extending more than 200 feet from its base. Pilot Mountain is not part of the Blue Ridge Mountains, but part of the Sauratown Mountains. At the park you will find hiking, picnicking, nature study and climbing. The wonders of the Blue Ridge can be discovered on the Parkway, thirty minutes to the northwest.

To the north just 15 miles is Mount Airy, the boyhood home of Andy Griffith and the fictional town of "Mayberry." Numerous sites throughout the town are reminiscent of the popular television series. In addition, there are more than 34 historic structures or locations around the community. The community of Pilot Mountain is the fictional town of "Mount Pilot" from the Andy Griffith Show.

Just 20 minutes to the south is Winston-Salem. Here you will find a blend of old and new. Old Salem, founded by the Moravians in 1766, provides a glimpse of the past. ScienceWorks with planetarium, exhibits on space, the human body, and an environmental park, takes you into the future.

Historic Rockford is another interesting place to visit. This was the original Surry County seat. The one-lane bridge across the Yadkin River is almost worth the trip in itself, but the General Store is the real treasure in Rockford.

**Scenic Overlook Bed & Breakfast**
**144 Scenic Overlook Lane; Pinnacle, NC 27043**
**(910) 368-9591**
**Innkeepers: Gayle & Alan Steinbicker**
Rooms: 1; Private Baths: 4; Suites: 3; Rates: $$-$$; adults only
Payment:  Amenities:

R. Carriker Photography © 1994

## Brookstown Inn
## Winston-Salem

The Brookstown Inn has the distinction of having received the four diamond award from AAA. While larger than we typically think of a bed and breakfast (with forty rooms and thirty-one suites) its style, ambiance and historical significance guaranteed its inclusion.

The structure was built in 1835 to be the first cotton mill in the state. In 1856 the cotton mill was refitted to become the Wachovia Flour Mill. In 1880, a large addition was made and the factory became the first to have electricity in the south. Before WWI, the building was again converted to a cotton mill and remained as such until after the war. Almost lost to the wrecking crew in the 1970s, the old textile mill found new life as a result of being listed on the National Register of Historic Places. In 1984, after extensive renovation, the Brookstown Inn opened rooms in the oldest part of the factory.

Today, the Brookstown is decorated with an eclectic blend of the seventeenth- and eighteenth-century furnishings. You will find antiques and reproductions of Scottish, English, Irish and Colonial America. They have covered the floors with Romanian Kilim rugs and guest rooms feature custom-made quilts from the Appalachian Mountains. There is antique porcelain in an early North Carolina cupboard, along with handwoven baskets, pewter and silk flowers. Throughout the Inn you will find exposed brick, beam and rafter. Together, they blend to create a very pleasant atmosphere for work or play.

The breakfast room, with brick floors, offers one of the most complete continental breakfasts we enjoyed while writing this book. You will find sausage biscuits, fresh fruits, and dry cereals. There are Moravian buns and cakes as well as other fresh breads, plus coffee, tea and a variety of juices.

R. Carriker Photography © 1994

Each of the rooms is large, with many windows to provide plenty of light. You would never think that you are in a factory that was more than 150 years old. Individually-controlled heating and air conditioning, cable TV, turndown service and plush towels are all a part of the service of the Brookstown. From the moment you enter the Inn, there is a feeling that this is what travelers experienced decades ago at finer hotels.

Located near both downtown Winston-Salem and Old Salem, the Inn becomes a perfect rest stop for both tourists and business travelers. They can provide facilities for meetings, weddings and other social functions.

Darryl's Restaurant is in the complex, but not owned by the Brookstown. However, I *can* recommend lunch and dinner. The food and service are *more* than acceptable.

Winston-Salem is an interesting blend of small-town friendliness and metropolitan attractions, activities and shopping. One of the largest malls in North Carolina is the Hanes. However, my favorite shopping area is the Reynolda Village with its small specialty shops and restaurants. If you're looking for something to do, I recommend starting with Old Salem. It's only a few blocks away from the Brookstown Inn and provides you with the history of the town.

---

**Brookstown Inn**
**200 Brookstown Ave.; Winston-Salem, NC 27101**
**(800) 845-4262; (910) 725-1120; Fax: (910) 773-0147**
**Innkeeper: Deborah Bumgardner**
Rooms: 40; Private Baths: 71; Suites: 31; Rates: $$$-$$$$
Affiliations: NCHMA
Payment:        Amenities:

# The Henry F. Shaffner House
## Winston-Salem

It required two years, from 1905 to 1907, to build the Shaffner home. The Queen Anne-style house was unique for its time as each room had its own fireplace and gas fixtures for lighting. Yet, the house had central heat and was wired for electricity. The house was built for Henry F. Shaffner, a prominent Winston-Salem businessman, and cofounder of the Wachovia Loan and Trust Company, in 1893. At the time of his death in 1941, he was Chairman of the Board of Wachovia Bank & Trust Company. His wife remained in the home until 1949.

In 1990, just months before it was to be destroyed, local businessman Henry Falls and his wife, Betty, purchased the house. They were determined to save it from the wrecking ball. Henry and Betty wanted to restore the home to its original grandeur. The job of restoring the structure took longer than it did to build it. It required two years for one man to strip all the paint off the wood.

Each room has been completely restored to reflect the period of the house. The interior of the house has tiger oak woodwork which has been painstakingly refinished. Brass fixtures were cleaned, repaired and replaced, when necessary. Nine ornate fireplaces have been fully restored. They laid plush carpeting and brought the hardwood flooring back to a high luster.

The front parlor, with its baby grand piano, is a favorite gathering place for guests. The second floor library and reading room attracts guests who prefer peace and quiet. During warm summer evenings, guests also gather in the sun room to enjoy complimentary wine and cheese and be cooled by an antique ceiling fan.

History of Winston-Salem is reflected in the Shaffner House. There is a carved wooden mantle in the dining room with a silver plate bearing

the dates 1766-1907. The mantle is from the first house built in the area. The dates reflect its construction and the year it was destroyed. The gabled roof was originally covered with cedar until a nearby fire in 1920. Shaffner and his son used buckets of water to extinguish cinders that were falling on the roof. Shortly after, the cedar was replaced with copper shingles that are still in place today.

Each of the six large rooms and two suites is well appointed with antiques and reproductions. Upholstery and fabrics used in the rooms are a reflection of the period in which the house was built. Central air-conditioning, luxurious robes and towels, telephones and cable TV are only a part of the amenities in each room.

The continental-plus breakfast is served each morning in the dining room at individual tables for two. Waffles, quiche, fruit and muffins are a part of breakfast. In addition, breads, cereals, granola, coffee, teas, and juices are available.

Downtown and Old Salem are within easy walking distance of the Shaffner House. Arrangements can be made to have a horse-drawn carriage pick you up for a ride through Old Salem. We found the staff of the Shaffner to be well versed in Winston-Salem history, dining choices and places of interest.

*30" from Greensboro*
*unmarried pm 16/25*

**The Henry F. Shaffner House**
**150 S. Marshall St.; Winston-Salem, NC 27101**
**(800) 952-2256; (910) 777-0052; Fax: (910) 777-1188**
**Innkeeper: Betty Falls**
Rooms: 6; Private Baths: 8; Suites: 2; Rates: $$-$$$$
Affiliations: NCBBI
Payment: $$$ CHECKS MC VISA 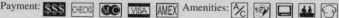AMEX Amenities:

## Lady Anne's Victorian Bed & Breakfast
## Winston-Salem

Sometimes we forget the work that goes into opening and running a bed and breakfast. It took three years of renovation (and cutting through bureaucratic red tape) to open the doors of the Lady Anne.

Shelley Kirley, a recreation therapist, became interested in bed and breakfasts while in California's Napa Valley. Her interest took her to Winston-Salem and a house built in 1890 for a tobacco manufacturer, L.L Lunn. Kirley and Steve Wishon worked side by side to bring the Lady Anne back to life. Today, the house is on the National Register of Historic Places and is a fine example of the Queen Anne style.

Lady Anne is decorated with stained glass windows and fine antiques from the turn of the century that reflect the Victorian age. While only minutes from the central business area of downtown Winston-Salem, it's easy to forget the rush once you enter Lady Anne. Shelley works hard to make sure that everything is in place, whether it's for a romantic getaway or a special occasion. Business travelers also find that its location makes the trip to Winston-Salem more comfortable.

Rates are surprisingly low for the quality of hospitality, breakfast, accommodations and amenities you receive. Each of the rooms are bright, well-decorated and include a private bathroom, phone and cable TV. Some rooms include two-person showers, whirlpool baths, VCR, stereos, mini refrigerators and coffee makers. Other rooms offer private porches or balconies.

Shelley might offer you French toast, waffles, or omelets for breakfast along with homemade breads, bagels and muffins. You'll find fresh fruits, dumplings, juices as well as gourmet coffees and teas. She serves all this to you in the formal dining room or on the front porch.

There is so much to do in Winston-Salem that you should plan to stay several days. If you enjoy history, the Moravian town from the eighteenth-century of Old Salem will enthrall your every sense. The tone of an organ from the eighteenth century, tobacco drying, meat cooking slowly in a cast iron pot over a hickory log fire. Fresh bread, cookies baked in an oven that was first used in the late 1700s. These are only a few examples of all the sensations you will experience.

You also should take a tour of the Museum of Early Southern Decorative Arts (MESDA), located in Old Salem. Nineteen period rooms and six galleries include furniture, paintings and ceramics. Other collections show textiles and silver.

Time did not permit us to visit every point of interest in the area. However, here are some that I can recommend: The Nature Science Center, The Reynolda House, Bethabara Park and Tanglewood Park. The Science Center includes a tidal pool, planetarium and more than thirty acres with picnic sites, trails and farm animals. The Reynolda House Museum of American Art is a marvel in architecture built for R.J. Reynolds in 1917. It contains art from O'Keefe, Lawrence, and Remington to name a few. Bethabara Park's 80 acres feature a 1753 Moravian wilderness settlement. Tanglewood Park's 1,000 acres include golf, tennis, horseback riding, hay rides, bicycle rental, nature trails and gardens.

*closed*

**Lady Anne's Victorian Bed & Breakfast**
**612 Summit St.; Winston-Salem, NC 27101**
**(910) 724-1074**
**Innkeepers: Shelley Kirley**
Rooms: 2; Private Baths: 2; Suites: 3; Rates: $$-$$$; children over 12
Affiliations: NB&BA, Winston-Salem B&B Assoc.
Payment: $$$ MC VISA AMEX  Amenities: A/C 🖥 ♟ ✍

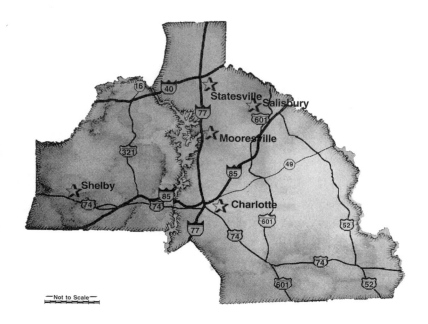

Not to Scale

# Southern Foothills

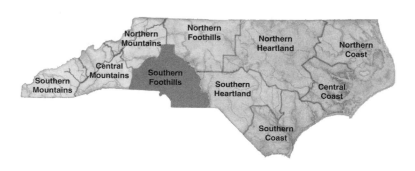

# The Inn Uptown Charlotte

Charlotte is one of our favorite places to visit. Being the largest city in North Carolina, it always has something to offer. Yet, with more than two dozen trips to the area, we had never found a place we liked to stay…until we discovered the Inn Uptown.

The location is great. Only two blocks from Discovery Place, and three from the main business district. Yet, the inn is so quiet that even on a Friday night, we were never bothered by the noises of the city.

Built in the Chateauesque style in 1890 by Edgar Andrews, the house was one of the first in Charlotte built as a speculative venture. Based loosely on the chateaus of France, the style is rare in the south. Another example, although one that exceeds the French style it copied, is the Biltmore Estate in Asheville. An interesting fact: this house was completed two years before the Biltmore.

Historically known as the Bagley-Mullen House, it was owned by only two families from 1890 until 1947. Elizabeth (Betty) Rich, who also owns the Heritage House Bed & Breakfast in Topeka, Kansas, discovered the property one Sunday afternoon in 1992. While the property had been used as office space for years, she knew that it would make a perfect bed and breakfast. Her son, Stephen, acquired the building. After extensive renovating, the Inn Uptown opened in June of 1992.

Within the three-story brick house you will find six beautifully-furnished rooms. During the week the rooms are ideally suited for the corporate traveler. Each room offers cable TV, writing desk, and phone (complete with modem capability). Fax and copier service are available and the inn has facilities for small meetings.

When the weekend arrives, the general feeling of the inn changes. There is a feeling of romance in the air. Four of the rooms have whirlpool baths, and four have fireplaces. Two of the rooms can become a suite, when needed. The most popular room is the Tower Room. You access its whirlpool bath by climbing a spiral staircase. There is nightly turn-down service and for special occasions wine, champagne and custom gift baskets are available.

Baked items are a specialty at the Inn Uptown with goodies such as chocolate butterballs or the "worlds's best cookie" in the room at night. Breakfast can bring Mississippi spice muffins, coffee cakes, blueberry coffee cake or fruit breads. The Uptown's full breakfast also features Betty's oatmeal pancakes and specialty casseroles including Peg's sausage pie or Galveston Brunch. There's bacon or sausage, fresh fruit, juices, coffee and teas.

After breakfast, a day of exploring might take you to Discovery Place with its rain forest, science circus, aquariums, OMNIMAX theater and planetarium. You might visit the Mint Museum, North Carolina's first art museum, featuring American, European, African and pre-Colombian art. Another favorite stop for us is Paramount's Carowinds. This 91-acre theme park straddles the North and South Carolina borders. Just south of Carowinds is New Heritage USA with one of the larger water parks in the Southeast.

**The Inn Uptown**
**129 N. Poplar St.; Charlotte, NC 28202**
**(800) 959-1990; (704) 342-2800; Fax: (704) 342-2222**
**Innkeeper: Elizabeth J. Rich**
Rooms: 6; Private Baths: 6; Rates: $$-$$$; children over 6
Affiliations: NCBBI, PAII
Payment:  Amenities:

# Spring Run Bed & Breakfast
# Mooresville

They spent six years collecting antiques to furnish the dream home they would build on Lake Norman. One month after completion of the house, Wayne and Mary Farley opened the doors to share their dream with others.

The three-story brick home contains over 4,000 square feet of space. Nearly 2,000 feet of that is dedicated to guests. There are two guest bedrooms each with private bath, a private guest living room and dining room. Rooms include queen-size beds, ceiling fans, intercoms, air conditioning and cable TV with several free movie channels. Another room acts as a gift shop, exercise room and game room. In this room you will find Mary's own brand of soaps, shampoos and lotions. "Spring Run Soap" is known throughout North Carolina.

They decorated the 17-room house with antiques, many of which Wayne restored or refinished. The solid mahogany front door is one of the first you will discover. Other items include an altar topped with marble and made into a bar, a 1905 Ferris wheel seat and a 1886 peanut roaster. The wall screen in the guest's living room came from Japan and is over 200 years old. In the formal guest dining room, the stained glass came from a church in Canada and is almost 200 years old. The Rose Medallion collection of china and porcelain in this room is also nearly 200 years old. In the shared guest/family room, you'll find a 1960 jukebox (complete with original songs from 1954-63), toy Ferris wheels and a 1940 gumball machine. As if that wasn't already perfect, there is also a fireplace, television and VCR.

Breakfast at Spring Run is a treat because Mary is an excellent cook. While many of her recipes come from a 70-year-old collection that belongs to Wayne's grandmother, she has also created special items for guests. The most famous recipe is her Banana Cream Shells, recently chosen as a finalist in a cooking contest which included all the southern states. You may be

fortunate enough to try it when she serves her three-course breakfast. Other treats include a pineapple shell filled with in-season fruits, heart shaped cinnamon french toast or Belgian waffles and either bacon or sausage.

The one-acre site occupied by Spring Run is on Lake Norman, the largest man-made lake in North Carolina. It has 520 miles of shoreline and more than 32,500 acres of water. Boating on the lake can be a ride in the Farley's paddle boat or on the Catawba Queen. This replica of a Mississippi riverboat offers sight-seeing and dinner cruises. Fishing can be as simple as from the Spring Run pier, or entering the weekly bass contest in the area. In both cases, you need to bring your fishing gear.

Things to do abound in the area. There's golf at the Mallard Head Golf Course. Duke Power State Park, with over 1,362 acres of land, offers fishing, picnicking, swimming and hiking. Canoe and rowboat rentals are available. Two of our favorite outings included a trip to the Lazy 5 Ranch and to Murray's Mill. The former is home to 400 animals from six continents. Your 3½ mile safari drive will give you the opportunity to see water buffalo, antelope, American bison, and even a rare African onyx, all from the safety of your car. Murray's Mill is a working grist mill and across the street from it is one of the best general stores in North Carolina.

---

**Spring Run Bed & Breakfast**
**172 Spring Run Drive; Mooresville, NC 28115**
**(704) 664-6686**
**Innkeeper: Mary Farley**
Rooms: 2; Private Baths: 2; Rates: $$; children over 10
Affiliations: AAA♦♦♦, North Mecklenburg Chamber, South Iredell Chamber
Payment: $$$ CHECKS MC VISA Amenities:

# Rowan Oak House
# Salisbury

Just three blocks from the turn-of-the-century business district of Salisbury, Les and Barbara Coombs have created an atmosphere for romance. They started with a beautiful Queen Anne home built in 1901 by Milton Brown for his bride, Fannie. To this they have added their own personal touches: antique furnishings, tantalizing breakfasts, and the warmth that comes from their own 35-year love affair. Barbara describes their as "one person in two skins."

Located in the West Square historic district, the Rowan Oak House features a wraparound porch, a magnificent carved oak door, seven columned fireplaces with intricate woodcarving, and stained and leaded glass throughout. Remarkably, the original electric and gas light fixtures remain. In the formal dining room, original French tapestry wallpaper graces the walls.

Guest rooms are large and beautifully furnished with period antiques. From the king-size four poster bed to high-backed mahogany antique beds, the furnishings for each room are in impeccable taste. One over-sized bathroom features a double Jacuzzi and a working gas fireplace. Another bath boasts a green marble shower for two.

Each morning the Coombs serve a lavish breakfast on 50-year-old Lenox china with sterling silver and tinted Depression glass. Barbara makes sure that variety is a part of the magic of breakfast. She serves items such as banana nut muffins, shrimp with hollandaise sauce, cheese and sausage casseroles or "featherbed eggs"—a layered casserole of scrambled eggs, flour tortillas, mushrooms and cheese served with homemade salsa.

For years, Barbara and Les had been living the stress-filled lives that demanding careers in corporate management and banking can bring. They longed for something that would permit them to work together and at the same time offer a place of sanctuary for tension-filled travelers. The Rowan Oak House was the culmination of a three-year search.

Project-minded and detail-oriented, together they have a vision for the house: to make Rowan Oak a premier bed and breakfast in North Carolina. They have already developed a reputation for running a haven for the romantic, and still they are able to cater to the needs of the traveling business professional. Murder Mystery weekends are a specialty of the house.

Historic preservation is an important part of Salisbury, a fact that becomes quite evident as you approach Rowan Oak House. The entire community seems to work together to make guests at the Rowan Oak feel welcome. The staff at the Visitors Bureau were very helpful in suggesting just the right places in the area for us to visit.

Maps to the 30-square-block area, consisting of historic Downtown Salisbury and the West Square, are available. The tree-lined streets showcase a collection of 19th and early 20th century homes. The Salisbury Station (built in 1907) and O.O. Rufty's General Store, reflect the period when the Rowan Oak was built.

Other major attractions in the area include the North Carolina Transportation Museum at Historic Spencer Shops, the Josephus Hall House built in the 1820s, and the Old Stone House (1766). The Rowan Museum is located in Salisbury in a 1819 Federal townhouse that was built by Jacob Stirewalt. Here you will find period rooms, antique furnishings, and artifacts dating back to the early 1800s.

Just 14 miles west of Salisbury, the Lazy 5 Ranch features a unique drive through an animal park with more than 450 exotic animals from around the world. The richest gold mining area east of the Mississippi was located at Gold Hill and today, the Historic Gold Hill Park and museum bring the era to life.

**Rowan Oak House**
**208 S. Fulton Street; Salisbury, NC 28144**
**(800) 786-0437; (704) 633-2086**
**Innkeepers: Leslie & Barbara Coombs**
Rooms: 4; Private baths: 4; Rates: $$-$$$; children over 10
Affiliations: NCBBI, AAA◆◆◆
Payment:     VISA Amenities:

## The Inn at Webbley
## Shelby

Approaching the front entrance on the circular driveway, you are trans-ported back in time to when Webbley was the home of the most powerful political organization in the history of North Carolina. The "Shelby Dynasty," produced every governor of North Carolina from the late 1920s to the late 1940s.

This grand 1852 home has been owned by two North Carolina Governors, a Lt. Governor, a U.S. Senator and Congressman, a U.S. Ambassador to the Court of St. James, and by an Undersecretary of the U.S. Treasury. Every single Governor of North Carolina since 1900 has been in this stately old mansion at least once.

The list of political leaders who have visited Webbley is not limited to the North Carolina boundaries. Nationally renowned figures such as Franklin D. Roosevelt, Harry S. Truman, Lady Bird Johnson, and Margaret Truman, have been guests at this historic home.

Over the years actors and entertainers Jack Benny, Ava Gardner, Andy Griffith, and Joan Crawford have been honored guests. Floyd Patterson was a visitor during his reign as World Heavyweight Boxing Champion. More recently, Webbley has hosted the likes of Whitney Houston.

The National Register of Historic Places has identified Webbley as one of the most distinguished private residences in North Carolina. The current owners of Webbley have received many awards for their loving and outstanding restoration of the home, including the Gertrude S. Carraway Award from Preservation/North Carolina.

This unique bed & breakfast inn has five bedrooms and several large common areas including twin parlors, a formal dining room and a bright and cheerful breakfast area. Each bedroom has its own unique decor including antiques, hardwood floors, Oriental rugs, designer fabrics and museum-quality window treatments and drapings.

The front porches, with their turn-of-the-century rocking chairs, are inviting and relaxing. The sense of grace and style inside the Inn finds its way outside to the formal rose garden, the brick walking paths, and the expansive brick courtyard surrounding the rear entrance.

Innkeepers, O. Max Gardner III (Governor Gardner's grandson), and his lovely wife, Victoria provide the finest in Southern hospitality. Max and Vickie's goal is to make every guest feel like a part of their extended family that goes back seven generations at Webbley. The care and attention for their guests is reflected in the special amenities they provide such as in-room phones, cable TV and plush bathrobes. For business travelers there is a fax machine and modem connections for personal computers. Guests are also encouraged to visit and relax at the Parlour Bar, which offers fine spirits and light fare daily from 5 to 10 p.m.

Breakfast at Webbley is an experience you will long remember. Vickie prepares and serves a gourmet breakfast each morning. Some of her specialties include Basque-style eggs piperade, overnight French toast, farm fresh dill eggs in crepes, Bismarck pancakes, smoked salmon or eggs Benedict, along with seasonal juices, freshly ground coffee, and an assortment of homemade breads.

Whether you're looking for a romantic getaway, a special "Murder Mystery Weekend," or an executive retreat, the Webbley is always a perfect choice. If you are like this visitor and author, your stay at Webbley will become a cherished memory.

---

**The Inn at Webbley**
**P.O. Box 1000; 403 S. Washington St.; Shelby, NC 28151**
**(800) 852-2346; (704) 481-1403; Fax: (704) 487-0619**
**Innkeepers: O. Max Gardner III & Victoria Harwell-Gardner**
Rooms: 5; Private Baths: 5; Rates: $$$; children over 16
Affiliations: NCBBI, PAII, AAA◆◆◆◆
Payment:     Amenities: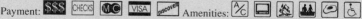

# Madelyn's Bed & Breakfast
## Statesville

Statesville sits at the crossroads of I-40 (running east and west) and I-77 (traveling north and south). Though it is at the crossroads, it is a pleasant, peaceful community. Both Charlotte, to the south and Winston-Salem, to the northeast, are only 45 miles away.

Here, Madelyn Hill (1994 president of the North Carolina Bed & Breakfast and Inns association) operates what was the first B & B in the county. The house, built in 1949, is only a few blocks from downtown Statesville. Like most of Statesville, the neighborhood is attractive, quiet and close to everything. Mitchell Community College is just up the road. It contains more than 170 structures, some dating back to the mid 1800s. One of Statesville's historic districts begins two doors away.

Do you remember the song *Hang Down Your Head, Tom Dooley*? The song recalls the story of Tom Dula. Zebulon Vance, Civil War Governor of North Carolina and Madelyn's great-great uncle, was Tom's lawyer. Actress Virginia Mayo was born here in Statesville as well as Kit Carson, the famous Indian scout. Kit was born in the county on Christmas Eve, 1809.

Each of the three guest rooms at Madelyn's, like the common rooms, is decorated with an eclectic mix of traditional and country. The rooms are large, pleasant and comfortable. Guests gather in the living room where VCR, cable television and fireplace are available.

Evening dining, such as Mayo's Italian Restaurant, the Black Angus or the Vance Hotel, is within walking distance. You can work off breakfast or dinner on the two-mile exercise walking course two blocks away from Madelyn's.

Breakfast is the real treat here. Broiled grapefruit, gingerbread pan-cakes garnished with almonds, strawberries and butter-pecan ice cream. A sausage cup with sausage, scrambled eggs and salsa, topped with cheddar cheese and then broiled. Baked apples and cranberries, blueberry muffins, stuffed French toast. These all find their way to the formal dining table.

In addition to being a good cook and hostess, Madelyn is chair-person of the Statesville area volunteer tourism board. She provides a wealth of knowledge about the area and all there is to do. Ask about a day-trip to Love Valley, a little "western" town just 20 to 25 minutes away. Rodeos and dances at the Silver Spur Saloon or horseback riding are a way of life here. On the Surry-Yadkin County line is a small Amish community. Fort Dobbs is north of Statesville. The fort, constructed in 1755, was built to protect settlers during the French and Indian War. Also to the north is the Arts and Science Center.

As you plan your day, you might want to consider a drive to the Lazy 5 Ranch to the southeast of Statesville. Here, from the safety of your car, you can see and feed more than 400 animals from six continents. Your safari on the 3½ mile drive will give you the opportunity to see water buffalo, antelope, American bison, and even a rare African oryx.

---

**Madelyn's Bed & Breakfast**
**514 Carrol St.; Statesville, NC 28677**
**(704) 872-3973**
**Innkeepers: Madelyn & John Hill**
Rooms: 3; Private Baths: 3; Rates: $$; children over 12
Affiliations: NCBBI, AAA◆◆◆
Payment: $$$ CHECKS MC VISA Amenities:

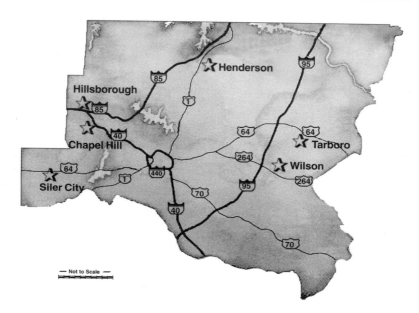

# Northern
# Heartland

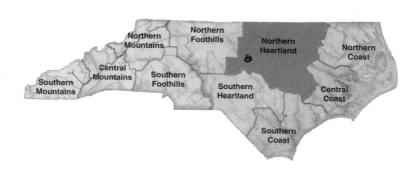

# The Inn At Bingham School
# Chapel Hill

Christina has always wanted to be an innkeeper. She grew up next door to a bed and breakfast, and her best friend's mother was an innkeeper. It took a few years, and a trip to more than 15 bed and breakfasts and inns in North Carolina and Virginia to find their ideal inn. I must admit, I think their selection was perfect.

With the countless activities in the area, the Inn At Bingham School makes a good base for the vacationer who wants to visit the area. Also for the business traveler its location couldn't be better situated. It's only 11 miles from Chapel Hill and less than a 30-minute drive to Raleigh, Durham, Burlington and the Research Triangle Park. Greensboro and Winston-Salem can be reached in less than an hour.

While location was also important to Christina and Francois, I think it was the history that meant the most. Bingham School opened in 1845 and served as a preparatory school for young men interested in going on to the University of North Carolina at Chapel Hill. During the twenty years the school was at his location, it was the most expensive boys school in the nation. While the school is no longer standing, the headmaster's home is now the Inn at Bingham School.

The oldest part of the inn was built in 1790. In 1801, a second house was built next door, and in 1835 the two were tied together. Even with its impressive history, at one time the house sat empty for nearly fifty years. Bob and Jane Kelly discovered the home in the 1980s and completed extensive restoration of the home. For the first time in its history, the house had electricity and indoor plumbing. Their restoration efforts won the Gertrude S. Kerry award for Historic Preservation.

Four of the five rooms at Bingham School are within the main house. The fifth is a suite located in what was once the Milkhouse. The

Milkhouse makes a perfect hideaway for honeymooners or a romantic getaway. With its own sitting room, whirlpool tub and three walls of full-length windows, the Milkhouse has a unique blend of antique and modern. It even has its own private parking area to add to the feeling of seclusion. Rooms in the main house feature hardwood floors, area rugs, and are furnished with period antiques.

The dining room, with its original "milk paint" ceiling, wrought iron chandelier, and crocheted tablecloth, makes an ideal setting for breakfast or one of Christina's romantic dinners. Christina's breakfast might include pear-almond waffles, lemon waffles with blueberry topping, or chocolate croissants. There is always homemade bread, fresh squeezed orange juice, as well as fresh seasonal fruit, coffee and a variety of gourmet teas. With a few days notice, Christina can prepare gourmet picnic baskets or one of her romantic dinners.

Location is also a highlight of the Inn At Bingham School. Down the road is the UNC at Chapel Hill, the nation's first state university (1789). The community of Chapel Hill has been nicknamed the "Southern Part of Heaven" and has existed since 1793. The two other major communities in Orange County include Carrboro and Hillsborough. Historic Hillsborough is sometime referred to as a museum without walls because of its historic district of more than 100 late eighteenth and early nineteenth century structures.

---

**The Inn at Bingham School**
**P.O. Box 267; NC 54 at Mebane Oaks Road; Chapel Hill, NC 27514**
**(800) 566-5583; (919) 563-5583; Fax: (919) 563-9826**
**Innkeepers: Francois & Christina Deprez**
Rooms: 5; Private baths: 5; Suites: 1; Rates: $$-$$$
Affiliations: NCBBI, PAII
Payment:  Amenities:

# La Grange Plantation Inn
## Henderson

La Grange Plantation Inn is the oldest home that we visited while writing this book. The oldest part of the house was built in 1770 by Colonel Hare. In 1825, the Hare family sold the property to Colonel William Robards. Then, in 1849, Robards' son-in-law, Stephen Royster, purchased the 5,000-acre plantation from the Colonel's estate. From 1825 until Dick and Jean Cornell purchased the property, it was owned by the same family. Dick and Jean bought the property from the Royster family in May of 1985 in a sale arranged by Preservation North Carolina.

The floor bounced, there were enormous cracks in the plaster, the brick hearths and chimneys had settled and the windows no longer fit the casements. As the property was on the National Register of Historic Places, the work had to meet Department of Interior guidelines. Months of planning, with the help of an architectural conservator and an area contractor, paid off. The stone foundation was stabilized, the restoration was completed and, by the fall of 1986, La Grange Plantation Inn opened its doors with limited facilities. In 1989 the Cornells received an award from the National Trust for Historic Preservation for their efforts.

Together, Jean and Dick painted, sanded, refinished and decorated the Greek Revival-style home. Jean designed and created different window treatments for each room. You can find English and American antiques and period reproductions throughout the house. Jean, who is English, refers to the style as "English Country." I would call it informal elegance.

Since the home did not have plumbing, a room on the second floor was redesigned to create three separate bathrooms. Directly below it, a second room allowed them to add two more. Now, each of the five guest rooms have very large, modern facilities. They provide plush terry bathrobes for the short walk across the landing from your room. Modern heat-

ing and air-conditioning has been added, permitting each guest to control the temperature of his room.

Each of the five guest rooms is large and comfortably furnished. Turn-down service and treats on your pillow add to the ambiance. Since both Angel and I read a great deal, we appreciated reading lights that were at just the right height.

They added a separate building, creating a large kitchen and dining room. An awning-covered breezeway connects the two buildings. As guests enjoy their breakfast they may be fortunate enough to watch a variety of birds at the feeders enjoying *their* breakfast. Just beyond the bird feeders are the pool and the new greenhouse.

The food at La Grange Plantation Inn is outstanding with a full gourmet breakfast. Coffee and tea await the early riser. Then you go on to soufflés, crépes or casseroles. Homemade breads both sweet and un-sweet, fresh fruits, juices, and cereals round out the meal.

There is plenty to do at the inn: swim in the pool, or play games, horse-shoes or croquet. With eight acres of wooded lands, bird watching is a favorite. So is fishing from the shores in the 50,000-acre Kerr Lake. Seven parks are around the lake, as are two commercial marinas offering everything from a fishing guide to boat rentals. Seventeen boat ramps provide access to the lake.

*closed*

---

**La Grange Plantation Inn**
**Rt. 3, Box 610; Nutbush Road; Henderson, NC 27536**
**(919) 438-2421**
**Innkeepers: Jean & Dick Cornell**
Rooms: 5; Private Baths: 5; Rates: $$; adults only
Affiliations: NCBBI
Payment:      Amenities:

# The Hillsborough House Inn
# Hillsborough

One of the reasons I love bed and breakfasts is that many are located in historical structures. Seldom, though, do I find one that has been in the family for as long as the Hillsborough House. Known locally as the Webb-Matheson House, Webbs have been living here for nearly 140 years.

For Katherine and her husband, R. Beverly (Bev) Webb, the decision to keep the home in the family and turn it into a bed and breakfast meant quite a change in their lives. While Bev grew up in Hillsborough, his family had made their home in Charlotte for the last 25 years.

Renovation of the house to make it a bed and breakfast and yet being sensitive to the historic significance of the home would require not only a major financial outlay, but incredible attention to detail. Bev, an attorney, had been chairman of the Charlotte Historic Properties Commission and president of the statewide Preservation/North Carolina. With his interest in historic preservation and Katherine's eye for detail as a designer and artist, they were both well prepared for the task.

Located on 6½-acres in the historic district of Hillsborough, the original structure was built in 1790. At that time the home consisted of just a couple of rooms on the main level, and a second floor sleeping room. Over the years the home has been added to many times. The additions, including an 80-foot-wide Corinthian-columned front porch, have given the home a surprising symmetry. For the Webbs to create a bed and breakfast, it would mean adding again to the home.

Work began on the oldest section of the house in 1990, with Katherine spending several days a week in Hillsborough assisting with renovation and planning the decorating. A new wing for the family quarters as well as a new kitchen, laundry and office all had to be added. The separate "summer kitchen," the oldest standing brick structure in Hillsborough

(1790s), was turned into a delightful three room suite perfect for romantic getaways.

Decorating with a blend of antique and contemporary fabrics, furnishings and art, the home is comfortable and each guest room has its own distinct personality. The rooms offer private baths, and king, queen or twin beds. There's a sitting area in each room and a variety of views from each room. Elizabeth's room with its old-glass double windows provides a view of the surrounding woods and Annie's room offers the fishpond. From the covered porches (off the west parlor, Joe's Room and Miss Eliza's Room), to the gardens, the walking trails over the property and the 1950's swimming pool, Katherine and Bev have created a haven for the traveler.

It was history that brought us to Hillsborough. More than 100 late 18th and early 19th century buildings in and around Hillsborough are listed in the National Register of Historic Places. During the Colonial and Revolutionary periods it was the center of political activity in the state. Yet we found that Hillsborough was more than just history. It's a flourishing community at the edge of the greater Triangle Area. It sits at the junction of Interstates 40 and 85. The cities of Durham and Chapel Hill are only 20 minutes away and Raleigh is within a 30-mile drive. The variety of restaurants offering delights from barbecue to candlelight dinners, along with quaint shops, antique shops and historic attractions make Hillsborough a destination with something for everyone.

**The Hillsborough House Inn**
**P.O. Box 880; 209 E. Tryon St.; Hillsborough, NC 27278**
**(800) 616-1660; (919) 644-1600; Fax: (919) 644-1600**
**Innkeepers: Katherine & Bev Webb**
Rooms: 5; Private baths: 5; Suites: 1; Rates: $$-$$$$; children over 10
Affiliations: NCBBI, AAA, PAII
Payment:     Amenities:

# Bed & Breakfast at Laurel Ridge
## Siler City

We fell in love with Laurel Ridge as we drove down the long winding driveway. Our destination was a post and beam country home nestled in a grove of mountain laurel. Having been on the road for days, finding a haven like Laurel Ridge was just what the doctor ordered.

In 1984, area craftsmen built the country home on a ridge above the Rocky River. David Simmons and Lisa Reynolds turned the home into a bed and breakfast in 1992. When they purchased the home in 1990 they knew it would serve the needs of their guests perfectly. Their 26 acres of land offer peace and quiet, making Laurel Ridge a great getaway for couples. Located in the heart of the state, they created a perfect base for business travelers to Greensboro and Raleigh/Durham and families visiting central North Carolina.

Situated away from the road, high on a ridge, the feeling of being in the mountains prevailed. The deer feeding in the pasture, and our hike along the wooded nature trails by the river enhanced this sensation. As you take the trail, be sure to stop at the gazebo that David built high above the river. One of the most romantic spots that we have seen exists here.

Decorated eclectically, Laurel Ridge is comfortable without being pretentious. You are encouraged to sit back and relax. The Rose suite on the second floor includes a queen-size canopied bed, a Jacuzzi for two and its own balcony overlooking the river. With nearly 500 square feet of space, this room makes a great retreat for an extended stay. A new addition at Laurel Ridge, the Carolina Cottage, features French doors that lead out to a 200-square-foot screened porch overlooking a wonderful view down to the river, a Jacuzzi and a queen-size bed. David and Lisa have designed the cottage to be completely wheelchair accessible, including the shower.

Breakfast at Laurel Ridge is an experience as David is truly a world class chef. In 1992, at the International Culinary Olympics in Frankfurt, Germany, he was a member of a culinary team that won gold and silver medals for their creations. With poppyseed pancakes, soufflés, and basil and pumpkin pancakes, seeing how David won his medals was easy. Many herbs and seasonings that David uses for breakfast come from the wonderful English country garden they created.

When the time comes to explore the area, you will find much to do. Chatham County has many artists and artisans offering everything from abstract sculpture, custom-designed iron- and metalwork and hand-painted floorcloths to original hand-crafted fine jewelry and wood-fired, salt-glazed stoneware. The gentle, rolling country roads are perfect for biking. The many antique shops offer furniture, quilts, toys and collectibles.

One of our favorite stops in the area is the world-famous North Carolina Zoological Park found only 30 miles from Laurel Ridge. This park is the world's largest natural habitat zoo. Natural barriers replace the bars allowing you to watch animals in their natural habitats. You can also take a stroll through the famous glass-domed aviary/rain forest where you can walk among the birds flying freely in a lush indoor wooded environment. Just beyond the zoo is the village of Seagrove that boasts one of the largest groups of working potters in the U.S. They continue the centuries'-old tradition of turning and burning pots. High Point, the home of the international furniture mart and huge showrooms that take days to tour, is just 40 minutes from Laurel Ridge. *N. A.*

**Bed & Breakfast at Laurel Ridge**
**3188 Siler City—Snow Camp Road; Siler City, NC 27344**
**(800) 742-6049; (919) 742-6049**
**Innkeepers: David Simmons & Lisa Reynolds**
Rooms: 2; Private baths: 4; Suites: 1; Cottages: 1; Rates: $$-$$$
Affiliations: PAII, NCBBI
Payment: $$$ CHECKS    Amenities:

# Lady Ann of Historic Tarboro
## Tarboro

A trip to Tarboro is kind of like taking a trip in a time machine. Many southern towns have seen the wrecking ball destroy the historic buildings and neighborhoods. Some have seen them fall from decay. Tarboro is an exception, it still holds it charm.

Incorporated in 1760, Tarboro's 16-acre Town Common is still the heart of the city. A 45-block residential historic district is one of the largest in the state. It is within this historic district that Linda Ann Tharrington started the Lady Ann of Tarboro.

Built in 1887, the Italianate style of the Lady Ann is unusual because the style passed from fashion by the 1880s. You would expect to find most buildings of this style in the northeast or in San Francisco. The Civil War Reconstruction and the 1870 depression led to very little new construction in the south during the popularity of this style.

Orrin Williams was a native of Tarboro and had been a Captain in the Confederate Army. During construction of the house, Captain Williams designed downspouts of copper to run through the posts of the house. Under the house, the water passed through a filtration system and from there into a cistern adjacent to a deep well. Whenever there was a period of drought or a water shortage and everyone else's water ran dry, people could always come to his house for water. Naturally, these were the same people who thought he was crazy when he started building the system.

Williams and his second wife had several daughters who grew up in the house. The property remained in the family for three generations until it was sold to Mrs. Moseley in 1945. Linda purchased the home from Mrs. Moseley in 1991 and began extensive renovating. She opened the bed and breakfast in December of that year.

Today the house has been restored to the way it would have looked in 1887. Linda did extensive research on even the color scheme of the outside, using the turn-of-the-century colors as a basis for her color scheme rather than the dark earth tones of the original palette. The three guest rooms also reflect Linda's research. For example, The Rose Room, located at the head of the walnut serpentine staircase, reminds you of an English rose garden. The room has a queen-size mahogany pencil bed crowned with a hand-tied cotton-net canopy.

Linda, a school teacher, was born in Tarboro, and manages the Lady Ann with the help of her two sons. Thomas, the oldest, is twelve, and Edwin is ten. They help with yard work and housework. On weekends, when Linda serves a full breakfast, they even help with the cooking. You'll find quiches or Eggs Monterey casseroles, fresh fruits, almond-raspberry muffins, homemade sourdough bread and gourmet coffees, all served in the formal dining room.

A block away from the Lady Ann is a national award-winning museum. The Blount-Bridgers House is an early Federal style home furnished with period antiques, many of them original to the house. This house, built in 1808, is a perfect starting point to explore the many historic sites in Tarboro. However, you may want to join Linda (or one of the boys) for an enjoyable round of golf at Hilma Country Club, the oldest golf course in North Carolina.

---

**Lady Ann of Historic Tarboro**
**1205 Main St.; Tarboro, NC 27886**
**(919) 641-1438**
**Innkeeper: Linda A. Tharrington**
Rooms: 3; Private Baths: 1; Shared Baths: 1; Rates: $-$$
Affiliations: Tarboro-Edgecombe Chamber
Payment: $$$ [CHECKS]  Amenities: [A/C] [🖥] [🏕] [🖇] [🌀]

## The Main Street Inn
## Tarboro

The Raleigh News and Observer once reported "The age of Victoria lives on in the historic Main Street Inn." It's true. This historic Italianate inn has been carefully and lovingly restored to reflect the period.

Built in 1885, and purchased shortly after that by W. H. Powell, the home has been a focal point of the community for more than 100 years. Mr. Powell was the president of Carolina Telephone and Telegraph. For this reason, the home was one of the first in the area to have a telephone. As president of the phone company, Mr. Powell was very influential in the community. His home was often the site of meetings and social gatherings. In time the house passed on to his daughter and her husband. It remained in the family until 1984.

Mr. Powell's daughter, Elizabeth, married Bill Marla, the superintendent of schools. Again, the house was a gathering point for area residents. Bill would sit on the porch and tell stories, his wife would bake, and the front porch would often fill with young people. In fact, the 100-year-old swing on the front porch was known as the "courting swing." Years later, the newspaper carried a story about the house and the swing. A young man read the article, clipped it from the paper and held onto it for more than five years. He thought the idea so romantic that he wanted to propose to his fiancee on that swing. He had his opportunity after Karen and Paul Andrus purchased the property and started the Main Street Inn.

Karen and Paul bought the property in 1989, and opened the bed and breakfast the same year. They completed extensive renovation to the house and decorated it with "walnut beds, marble top dressers, Oriental rugs and lace-filled windows." Each of the three guest rooms and one suite is large and comfortable, with a private bath. The suite has private phone and TV. It includes a sitting room, completely furnished

kitchen, dining area, bedroom and laundry area. It is perfect for families by the night or the week, or business executives who require a longer stay.

Karen serves afternoon tea and other delicacies either on the expansive fifteen-columned porch (complete with circular pergola) or in the formal sitting room. The porch with its swing and rockers is a perfect place to enjoy evening or morning coffee.

Karen's full breakfast is served in the formal dining room. She offers such fare as fresh fruits, home baked treats, stuffed French toast, and a variety of egg dishes. Juices, gourmet coffees, and teas complement the meal.

Tarboro is a charming community 75 miles northeast of Raleigh, the state capital. The 11,000 residents have worked hard to maintain their heritage. A 45-block historic residential area includes homes built in the Colonial, Antebellum and Victorian era. The 16-acre Town Common was established in 1760. Other historic structures include the Blount-Bridgers House built in 1808, and what is now the Pender Museum, built in 1810. To help maintain the city's cultural past, the downtown area is undergoing a $20 million historic restoration and revitalization project.

**The Main Street Inn**
**912 Main St.; Tarboro, NC 27886**
**(919) 823-2560**
**Innkeepers: Karen & Paul Andrus**
Rooms: 3; Private Baths: 3; Suites: 1; Rates: $$; children over 8
Affiliations: NCBBI
Payment:  Amenities:

# Miss Betty's Bed & Breakfast Inn
# Wilson

Miss Betty's sits on an acre and a half of land in the downtown historic district of Wilson. It is two miles from the largest antique market in eastern North Carolina and only six miles from I-95. Often selected as one of the best places to stay in the south, our stay was pleasant, the hosts warm and friendly, and the food excellent.

When Betty and Fred Spitz started Miss Betty's, the only building on the property they used was the Davis-Whitehead-Harriss House. It was constructed in 1858 as a one-story building. In 1872, it was expanded to include a second floor and remodeled in the Italianate style. After a complete renovation, the house was placed on the National Register of Historic Places. It is also a part of the Historic Downtown Wilson walking tour. The Spitz's purchased the house in 1989. Miss Betty's has now expanded to include three additional buildings. However, *this* house still includes their living quarters, four guest rooms and the formal dining room.

In 1990, a second building was moved two blocks to the property and completely restored. This cottage, which boasts a handsome cross gable, was built early in 1900, on what is now Barton College campus. A favorite with business travelers, it includes three rooms, a suite, and a sitting room.

Two separate buildings already on the premises were connected together to create the third building. Our room was one of the two king suites located here. Like all the rooms at Miss Betty's, we had a private bathroom, cable TV with remote control, and private telephone. Each room offers individual controls for heating and air conditioning. Our king bed was one of the most comfortable of our entire trip.

The fourth building, a Queen-Anne style home built in 1911, has been moved to the property, and is now undergoing renovation. This building will not actually be a part of the bed and breakfast. With four suites, kitchen, laundry

room and parlor, it will provide a sanctuary for the business executive during an extended stay, or on being transferred to Wilson.

Breakfast is served in the formal dining room of the main house. Miss Betty, dressed in Victorian-era apparel, prepares breakfast. Fred acts as host and server. While breakfast changes daily, the morning we were there, we enjoyed locally-made sausage and bacon, eggs, grits, homemade blueberry muffins, fresh fruits, fruit juices and, of course, coffee, tea, and milk. A variety of cereals was also available.

Miss Betty's truly recaptures the elegance and style of the Victorian era. Each of the homes is elegant and beautifully furnished with period antiques purchased locally in the "Antique Capital of North Carolina."

Local trips could include antiquing, touring the historic district or a stop at the unique science museum. It is downtown in Wilson's former post office and courthouse. As Wilson is "America's Largest Tobacco Market," a visit to the tobacco auctions is very interesting. Just south of Wilson, in Kenly, is the Tobacco Farm Life Museum. It houses artifacts from all aspects of farm life.

No trip to Wilson, however, would be complete without trying eastern North Carolina barbecue. There are several places in the area that Fred and Betty might suggest for lunch. *Our* lunch included a trip to Parker's for some of the best barbecue in the area.

*full*

**Miss Betty's Bed & Breakfast Inn**
**600 W. Nash St.; Wilson, NC 27893**
**(800) 258-2058; (919) 243-4447**
**Innkeepers: Betty & Fred Spitz**
Rooms: 7; Private Baths: 7; Suites: 3; Rates: $$; adults only
Affiliations: AB&BA, NCBBI, AAA, Mobil
Payment:      Amenities:

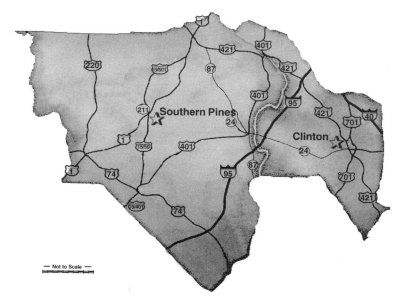

Not to Scale

# Southern
# Heartland

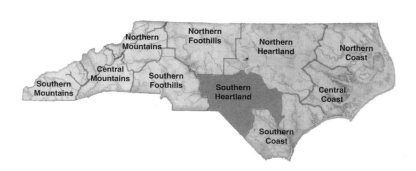

# The Shield House & Courthouse Inns
## Clinton

The Shield House and the Courthouse are actually two separate bed and breakfast inns located a block from one another. They operate individually, yet they're run by sisters: Anita Green at the Shield House Inn, and Juanita McLamb at the Courthouse Inn.

The features and amenities of the two bed and breakfasts are the same. Each offers a private bath, cable TV and air-conditioning. They have in-room phones, each with a private phone number. There are writing desks in the rooms as well. Soft drinks are available at all times. Microwave and microwavable popcorn is also available. The Courthouse Inn also has refrigerators in the rooms. Each of the bed and breakfasts is decorated with antiques.

Breakfast at the two bed and breakfasts is continental in style, offering coffee and teas, fruit juices, dry cereals, bagels, English muffins, and sweet breads. Breakfast is included in all room rates, but not with the two suites.

The Shield House Inn was built in 1916 for timber businessman Robert E. Herring. Mr. Herring designed this Early Classic Revival style house himself. If you enjoy architecture, the house offers a unique blend of styles. It features a large portico with four massive columns. The top part of these columns, known as capitals, are Corinthian. The columns on the large wrap-around porch have capitals in the Ionic style. The entryway is surrounded by beveled glass and opens into a large foyer. The six guest rooms are spacious and decorated with Victorian furniture.

The Courthouse Inn was built in 1818 as the county courthouse. Here we see more of a blend of the Early Classic Revival and Greek Revival styles. It was the first building in Clinton to have electricity. Originally located on the town square, it sold for $90 in 1904 and was moved to its present

location. They moved it by jacking it up and placing it on logs. The building was then pulled by a team of 20 mules to move it one block. In 1990, Juanita purchased it with the intentions of making it a bed and breakfast with nine guest rooms. Extensive remodeling was done at that time. However, many original features remain in the Inn today such as the wooden tongue-in-groove ceiling in the foyer and the hand-hewn front door.

Just 10 miles from I-40 and 30 miles from I-95, Clinton is the oldest and largest city in Sampson County. Raleigh is 60 miles to the north, and Wilmington is 60 miles southeast. Fayetteville and Goldsboro are both about 45 miles away.

Two points of interest in the area are major battlefields, Moores Creek National Battlefield and Bentonville Battleground. Moores Creek is administered by the National Park Service. On February 27, 1776, Royal Authority ended in North Carolina and helped to bring a vote for independence. North Carolina was the first colony to vote for it. At Bentonville, the last major confederate offensive of the Civil War was fought. Nearly 60,000 Federal troops under Sherman, and more than 30,000 Confederates under General Johnston, fought North Carolina's largest battle.

Whether you're in the Clinton area for business, a special occasion, or just relaxing, you'll find either of these two bed and breakfasts will meet your needs.

*C.H : 11/20*
*open o available*

**The Shield House & Courthouse Inns**
**216 Sampson St.; Clinton, NC 28328**
**(800) 462-9817; (910) 592-2634**
**Innkeepers: Juanita McLamb & Anita Green**
Rooms: 15; Private Baths: 15; Suites: 2; Rates: $$
Affiliations: NCBBI, NCHMA, Clinton Area Chamber
Payment:  Amenities:

## Knollwood House
## Southern Pines

Dick and Mimi Beatty spent two years searching for the perfect location to open a bed and breakfast. When they found Knollwood, the search was over. This English style manor house, located on five acres of dogwoods, azaleas, longleaf pine, and magnolia trees, overlooks the 14th and 15th fairways of the Mid-Pines Golf Course.

Knollwood was built in 1925 for a prominent Philadelphia family. Later, the Commandant of Fort Bragg lived in the house. Glenn Miller performed on the Knollwood lawn after a concert at the army base. Legendary golf players Ben Hogan and Walter Hagen were also guests in the Commander's home. When Bill Burke won the U.S. Open in 1931, the celebration took place at Knollwood.

The Knollwood became Dick and Mimi's on Thanksgiving Day, 1991. They put in four months of hard work to prepare the house to receive guests. Rewiring, refinishing, and landscaping all had to be done. Paints and fabrics had to be chosen. Eighteenth and nineteenth century antiques that the Beattys had collected and inherited were brought to Knollwood. Tapestries, a brick entryway, and the crystal chandelier add to the elegance that is Knollwood.

Dick runs the bed and breakfast while Mimi works in Chapel Hill. Turndown service, complete with bedtime treats, is only a part of the special amenities he provides. He makes sure that each of the two rooms and two suites has freshly-starched sheets and that the bathroom towels are changed three times a day. Need reservations for dinner, tee-times planned or information about the area? Just let them know a bit in advance.

Cocktails and a selection of hors d'oeuvres are served in the formal living room from 5:30-7:00 p.m. Cocktail hour is a time to get to know

the guests. The Beattys share their knowledge of the area and what it has to offer. Guests also have the opportunity to learn about their hosts. Dick's background includes being an officer at the Manhattan-based advertising agency, Ogilvy and Mather. Mimi is Director of Special Events for the Kenan Flagler School of Business in Chapel Hill. While New York City had always been their base, over the years they have lived in Connecticut, Chicago, Los Angeles and Germany. They have much to offer because of their interest in decorating, antiques, gourmet dining and entertaining.

Served in the beautifully decorated dining room, Mimi's breakfasts are positively an inspiration. Guest's favorites include a Viennese bread pudding served with a light puree of strawberries, raspberries and fresh-squeezed orange juice. Another favorite is her soufflés.

I would recommend Knollwood House to the discriminating traveler. The house is a joy to explore and the grounds immaculate. Dick and Mimi are excellent hosts.

The area offers much to see and do. If golf is your interest, there are thirty-four courses within a 20-mile radius. There are also art galleries, the North Carolina Symphony (which makes several appearances annually) and steeplechase. The climate is ideal for a visit anytime of the year.

*1⁵ from C. W.*

---

**Knollwood House**
**1495 W. Connecticut Ave.; Southern Pine, NC 28387**
**(910) 692-9390**
**Innkeepers: Dick & Mimi Beatty**
Rooms: 2; Private Baths: 2; Suites: 2; Rates: $$-$$$; children over 10
Affiliations: NCBBI
Payment: $$$ CHECKS VISA  Amenities: A/C

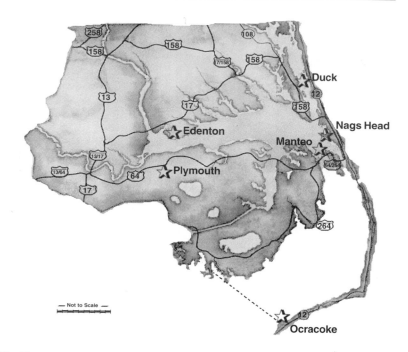

# Northern
# Coast

# The Sanderling Inn Resort
# Duck

The Sanderling isn't your typical bed and breakfast, nor is it a country inn in the traditional sense. While this may seem to be a contradiction, it is both. The Sanderling was started as a small twenty-six room inn by a Winston-Salem executive in 1985. The goal was to provide a family place much like the inns and resorts of the 1930s. A place where you could relax and enjoy one another without the hustle and bustle you normally find on the Outer Banks. Here you will find children carrying sand buckets instead of boom boxes. Adults often curl up with a good book in a rocking chair on private porches.

Part of the ambiance of the Sanderling is created by the management and staff who are considerate and hospitable. The amenities are the very best. From the imported soaps and plush monogrammed bath robes, to the beautifully decorated rooms and comfortable wicker/rattan furnishings, there is a sense of style about the Sanderling.

While the Sanderling has grown to seventy-seven rooms and ten suites, the atmosphere hasn't changed. Today the Sanderling is a full-fledged resort complete with tennis courts, platform tennis, indoor and outdoor swimming pool, a fully equipped health club, a massage room, and a swim spa. The Sanderling can accommodate meetings or special events from small gatherings to large groups of 125 people.

Stretching from ocean to sound, three miles of empty beaches are available to guests. The 3,400-acre Audubon Sanctuary lies next door assuring the guests that the Sanderling will always remain the way it is. The village of Duck, five miles south of the Inn, is

made up of quaint shops. It is without the commercialism found in the rest of the Outer Banks.

Sand dunes block most of the ocean view from the first floor. The best views are from rooms on the second floor. We had the good fortune to be in one of the loft suites. It had a complete kitchen, dining area, sitting area and half bath on the first floor. The second level contained the king bed and full bath.

Breakfast at the Sanderling is continental in style. However, there is a full-service restaurant on site that serves breakfast, lunch, dinner and Sunday brunch. The award-winning restaurant is in a life-saving station built in 1899. The structure, on the National Register of Historic Places, has been fully restored and contains many nautical antiques. While dinner specialties include seafood, they also offer duck and lamb. My personal favorite was the Black Angus Striploin with Jack Daniels gravy.

Although you can be in Nags Heads to the south in just twenty minutes, a drive north to Currituck Beach Lighthouse is a must. The Lighthouse was first lighted on December 1, 1875. Built of brick and reaching 158 feet into the air, it still provides a beacon to ships hugging the barrier islands. Flashing every 20 seconds, its signal light can be seen for 18 nautical miles. On the drive to the lighthouse you may be fortunate enough to see the wild horses that are descendants of the Spanish Mustang. They are all that remain of the Lost Colony.

---

**The Sanderling Inn Resort**
**1461 Duck Road; Duck, NC 27949**
**(800) 701-4111; (919) 261-4111; Fax: (919) 261-1638**
**Innkeeper: Tina Berger**
Rooms: 77; Private Baths: 87; Suites: 10; Rates: $$$-$$$$$
Payment: MC VISA AMEX DISCOVER Amenities: A/C 🖊 💻 VCR 🧺 🍽 ♿

# The Lords Proprietors' Inn
# Edenton

Edenton has often been called one of the prettiest towns in the South. "An idyllic atmosphere that includes not only the fabric and scale of the past, but also much of its leisurely charm," so states *The National Register of Historic Places.*

Edenton was one of the colonial capitals of North Carolina, and more than three centuries of history grace its tree-lined streets. Arch and Jane Edwards moved their family there from Washington, D.C. After purchasing and restoring Mount Auburn (c. 1810) on the Yeopim River near Edenton, they set out to make a living in their new community. In 1982, they bought the White-Bond House in the historic district. Built in 1901 by Fred White, a soldier of the Confederacy, the house is impressively large and superbly finished; an eloquent example of the late Queen Anne style. Shortly after renovation was completed and they opened the Lords Proprietors' Inn, Arch and Jane knew they wanted to expand. They acquired the adjoining Satterfield House (built in 1801), the oldest house on the block. Together, the two houses provided twelve lovely guest rooms, two parlors, and a library.

In 1988, another building was added to the two-acre site. The Pack House, built in 1915 as a tobacco storage barn, was cut in two and moved from Strawberry Hill plantation. Since the structure had few interior walls, Arch was able to design a building tailored to guest needs. The Pack House offers eight large guest rooms and features a huge parlor with two fireplaces, an overlooking balcony, and a wonderful porch.

To complete the Inn, Arch designed the Whedbee House, set on a patio, to provide a dining room and commercial kitchen. The Edwards serve a full breakfast daily and supper Tuesday through

Saturday to their guests. The evening meal prepared by Chef Kevin Yokley is exceptional. While the menu changes daily, an evening fare might include an appetizer of grilled barbecued quail, a salad of five greens, a choice of striped bass with pistachio vinaigrette or medallions of antelope with a porcini mushroom sauce, and end with Kevin's signature chocolate dessert or winter fruit poached in port with homemade filbert ice cream.

The Edwards have created a traditional village inn. The architecture and furnishings reflect periods from the Federal to the Victorian eras. Each guest room, with its own private bath, is large and meticulously decorated with antiques and fine reproductions. Cable TV, VCR, and touch-tone phones are in each room. Books and a selection of video tapes can be found in the library of the Satterfield House.

While in Edenton, be sure to see the historic district. The best way to do this is to take the guided walking tour from the Visitors Center. There is a self-guided tour, but the guided tour is inexpensive and provides a great deal of insight into the town's past and present. It is also the only way to enter the two museum houses, the Cupola House and the James Iredell House. Visits to nearby Hope Plantation and Somerset Place can provide further understanding of area and its history.

**The Lords Proprietors' Inn**
**300 N. Broad St.; Edenton, NC 27932**
**(919) 482-3641**
**Innkeepers: Arch & Jane Edwards**
Rooms: 20; Private Baths: 20; Rates: $$$-$$$$
Affiliations: IIA, PAII, Historic Hotels of America
Payment:   Amenities:

## Tranquil House Inn
## Manteo

I could have spent at least a week sitting on the porch watching the boats in the harbor and listening to the sounds of Shallowbag Bay. It wouldn't have taken that long to relax for we found the Tranquil House to be exactly what its name implies; calm, peaceful, relaxing.

Originally built in 1885, its hospitality was known world wide for almost 70 years. Early in the 1950s the Inn was lost to fire. It wasn't until 1988 that the new Tranquil House was built. Its architecture reflects the style of turn-of-the-century inns located along the Outer Banks. The designers incorporated elements from the original inn's architecture as well as from the Roanoke Hotel that was once located in downtown Manteo.

Custom cypress woodwork and stained glass decorate the interior of the Inn. The furnishings are of pine. Each of the 23 rooms are different in design and offer a multitude of choices from king- or queen-size to canopied or four-poster double beds. There are also two suites, complete with sitting area, available.

The 1587 Restaurant is on the first floor of the Tranquil House, its windows overlooking the dock and bay. While the name reflects the date of the first English settlement on Roanoke Island (1584-1587), the restaurant's decor is more modern. Sponge-painted walls, blond cypress trim and red oak floors greet you as you enter. Serving dinners only during the summer season, the choices include roasted duckling and lamb, beef tenderloin and New York strip. More than 20 million pounds of seafood is harvested in the area. Because of this, they offer seafood so fresh that they can't even list it on the menu.

Cable TV, private phones, and comfortable rooms made our stay pleasant. Yet the rockers on the porch were our favorite place to be while at

the Tranquil House. It was from the porch that the *Elizabeth II* sailing ship caught my eye. Just across the Bay, a State Historic Site gives guests a view into life at sea during the sixteenth century. The *Elizabeth II* represents a vessel much like the one that would have brought the first colonists to the area. During the summer, living history interpreters paint a grim picture of what life must have been like at sea.

Downtown Manteo is just outside the Inn door. Many shops and galleries provide an interesting view of Manteo's history as well as its present inhabitants. Fort Raleigh National Historic Site is a short drive from the Tranquil House. This 144-acre national park depicts the life and times of the first English settlement in the colonies.

Located next to the Fort is the *Lost Colony* outdoor drama. It is still America's premiere outdoor production after more than fifty years of performances. Its combination of dance, song and drama tells the story of the first English settlement and its mysterious disappearance.

Adjacent to the Fort and the *Lost Colony* drama is the Elizabethan Gardens. It was created in 1951 as a living memorial to the Lost Colony. The garden is a showplace with a combination of plants, trees, wildflowers and statues. While I fell in love with the porch and the bay, I quickly found Manteo offered much, much more.

---

**Tranquil House Inn**
**P.O. Box 2045; Manteo, NC 27954**
**(800) 458-7069; (919) 473-1404; Fax: (919) 473-1526**
**Innkeeper: Donny Just**
Rooms: 23; Private Baths: 25; Suites: 2; Rates: $$-$$$
Affiliations: AB&BA, NCHMA, OBHMA
Payment:  Amenities:  🖥 🛎 ♿

## First Colony Inn®
## Nags Head

Nags Head has been a resort since the 1830s. Hotels and cottages got their start in the early 1930s, in spite of the Great Depression. In 1931, a three-story inn was built in only four months on the ocean side of Nags Head. Leroy's Seaside Inn was wood framed with cypress shingles, and two floors of continuous wraparound verandas. For the next eighteen years, the inn operated with sixty rooms and only two bathrooms.

On the 350th anniversary of the Lost Colony (1937), the inn was sold to Capt. Cornelius and Miss Daisy Midgett and renamed First Colony Inn. The third owners, the Winslow family, did the only major renovation to the Inn in the early 1950s. They added bathrooms, enlarged the rooms, and reduced their number to 32.

Over the years, the inn changed hands again. By November of 1987, First Colony was closed. The new property owners hired demolition crews to tear down the inn. Locals, however, wanted to save the First Colony. Several attempts were made before the Lawrence family came to the inn's rescue.

They cut the Inn into three parts and moved it 3½ miles to a new five-acre site. National newspapers carried stories about the relocation. The move took place after midnight and area residents lined the street to cheer.

Today First Colony Inn has new life as a first class bed and breakfast. Richard and Camille, with the help of their four grown children and three daughters-in-law, have completely renovated the Inn. Each of its 26 rooms is an eclectic mix of traditional and antique English furnishings decorated with good taste. Rooms have been completely renovated and offer individual remote control heating and air-conditioning, four-

poster or canopied beds, over-stuffed chairs, private entrances, cable TV and private phones. All the rooms have microwaves and four have complete kitchenettes, including dishwashers. Two of the rooms offer a large divided bath with Jacuzzi. Bathrooms have been tiled, and each has a heated towel bar, a 50 gallon water heater, plush towels and thick, soft, terry robes.

Guests often gather in the upstairs library or on the verandas. The library has an extensive collection of Inn memorabilia, books, games and an antique pump organ. Others enjoy the 55-foot lap pool or take the boardwalk to a gazebo on a dune overlooking the beach.

From the complete continental buffet breakfast to afternoon tea complete with cookies, brownies or cake, First Colony Inn offers you all the amenities of a first class resort within a bed and breakfast.

Many good restaurants, shops and galleries are nearby. There is no limit of things to do while staying at First Colony Inn. To the south, Cape Hatteras National Seashore extends 72 miles across the tip of Bodie Island, and all of Hatteras and Ocracoke Islands. To the north is the Wright Brothers Memorial where the first flight took place. Further north, you can climb 214 steps to the top of Currituck Beach Lighthouse. From 158 feet in the air, you might get a glimpse of the wild horses. A short drive across the sound to the west takes you to Roanoke Island, home of Fort Raleigh, the Elizabethan Gardens and the *Lost Colony* outdoor drama.

---

**First Colony Inn**®
**6720 S. Virginia Dare Trail; Nags Head, NC 27959**
**(800) 368-9390; (919) 441-2343; Fax: (919) 441-9234**
**Innkeepers: The Lawrences**
Rooms: 20; Private Baths: 26; Suites: 6; Rates: $$-$$$$
Affiliations: AAA◆◆◆◆, PAII, NCHMA, AB&BA, AHMA, Mobil
Payment:  Amenities:

## Berkley Center Country Inn
## Ocracoke Island

The first English ships arrived in 1585. Sir Richard Greenville was on his way to establish a permanent colony on Roanoke Island. His flagship, the Tiger, ran hard aground on sand bar, and it is believed that the ponies that inhabit the Okracoke Island may be from stock lost from the Tiger.

By 1715, Ocracoke became a port of call for ships from around the world. The increase of trade brought a new problem to the coast: pirates! Robert Deal, Anne Bonney (wife of the infamous Major Bonney) and dozens of others terrorized the inhabitants of the islands. They robbed ships at sea, murdering crew and passengers. The days of the most notorious pirate, Blackbeard, ended in November of 1718, when Lt. Robert Maynard tracked the pirate's ship to Ocracoke Inlet, where *The Adventure* ran aground. In hand to hand fighting, an exchange of pistol balls wounded the pirate, and a cutlass fight ended with Blackbeard lying beheaded on deck.

In 1747, the Spanish took possession of the island and formed a blockade against British trade. During the American Revolution the island had a major role in supplying George Washington's army. The Civil War brought both Confederate and Union troops to the island. During WWII, islanders watched as German submarines sank merchant ships and tankers off the coast.

The pirates are long gone from Ocracoke Island, as is the naval base that was established in 1942. The only way to Ocracoke is by ferry, its gentle roll accompanied by sea gulls in flight. The island has no movie theaters, no crime, no barber shop or fast food restaurant. Many of the streets are only sandy paths. Now it's peace and quiet that draws visitors to the island with its many miles of pristine beaches on which nothing can be built since the beach is all National Seashore. Charter fishing boats are also available for ocean fishing in addition to surf casting on the beach.

Sam Jones, who grew up across the Pamlico Sound in Swan Quarter, built Berkley Center Country Inn back in the 1950s as a place to entertain customers of his foundry in Berkley, VA. He loved the island and built his retreat using the finest materials: cypress, redwood and red cedar from the West Coast. Jones used the facility until he died in 1977. In 1979, retired Col. Wes Egan and his wife, Ruth, purchased the inn and its 3.2 acres located near the ferry landing. They completely restored and refurbished the buildings.

Set back in the trees away from the road, Berkley is quiet and perfect for families. The nine rooms and one suite are spacious and furnished with reproduction antiques. Each morning, a continental breakfast of fresh breads, preserves and cereals is served in the breakfast room of the Manor House. On cool evenings, the guest lounge offers guests an opportunity to relax and meet one another by the fireplace.

Down the drive from the Inn, the Ocracoke Visitor Center, operated by the National Park Service, will introduce you to the history of the island. Escorted tours of the Coast Guard Station are available with advanced reservations. Across Silver Lake, the Ocracoke Lighthouse is the oldest (1823) and smallest (75 feet) of the lighthouses along the Outer Banks. The Pony Pens are located near the opposite end of the island. The ponies are a bit shy and your best vantage point for viewing them is the observation deck.

Ocracoke is an island paradise rich in history and beauty. It makes a perfect setting for Berkley Center Country Inn where life is gentler.

---

**Berkley Center Country Inn**
**P.O. Box 220; Hwy. 12; Ocracoke, NC 27960**
**(919) 928-5911**
**Innkeepers: Wes & Ruth Egan**
Rooms: 9; Private baths: 7; Shared baths: 2; Suites: 1; Rates: $$
Affiliations: SIA, NCBBI, Mobil, AHMA, Dare Co. Chamber, NCHMA
Payment: $$$ CHECKS  Amenities: A/C ▢ ⚞ ☺ ♿

## Four Gables Bed & Breakfast
## Plymouth

To the town of Plymouth, on the banks of the Roanoke River, the Civil War brought both the Union and Confederate armies. Its location as a designated port of entry complete with its own customs house and collector, had made it a major shipping center before the war. Hundreds of thousands of dollars in cypress shingles, lumber, turpentine, and other wood products were shipped to New York, Boston and the West Indies. Because of its importance, the city changed hands four times during the numerous fierce battles fought for control of the area. By the end of the war, only one in five houses and part of one church survived.

To this smoking ruin, Louis Henry "Larry" Hornthal came in 1866. Hornthal, born in Pahers, Bavaria, had first come to America before the war. He settled in Natchez, and enlisted in the 17th Mississippi Infantry when war broke out between the states. Captured in Tennessee in 1863, he was imprisoned for the rest of the war in Kentucky. When the war ended, instead of returning to Mississippi, he sought his fortune in North Carolina.

He was only 25 when he arrived in Plymouth. Within two years he had started a dry goods store, met and married Martha Bateman, and was ready to build a home for his new bride. Larry selected one of Plymouth's most fashionable streets as the site for his wedding gift. West Main Street, once called "Silk Stocking Row"—because only those who lived on that street could afford "silk stockings"—was a perfect setting for the new couple. The white Gothic Victorian served as home for the girl and three boys the couple raised. When Martha died at the age of 46, Larry moved to Norfolk, Virginia. His son, Phillip, took over both the Plymouth business and his father's house.

By the time that Norm and Brenda Conklin arrived in Plymouth to begin restoration of the Hornthal Mansion, they had already invested four years

of their lives in researching all facets of operating a bed and breakfast. They had contacted suppliers and insurance agents and visited bed and breakfasts in Virginia, Indiana and North Carolina. They even took an extension course through Duke University on how to be an innkeeper and spent two years as associate members of the North Carolina Bed & Breakfast Association before they even saw the mansion in Plymouth. But they believed in their dream and wanted to provide the very best for their guests. After buying the Hornthal house, another 15 months were required to restore and redecorate the it.

From the boxwoods in front to the collection of ancient magnolia, pecans and Japanese maples in the garden, Martha Hornthal would be pleased with the landscaping. With each room decorated in period antiques and lit by original chandeliers, the rooms are comfortable and offer the amenities needed to make your stay pleasant. When breakfast comes, you will find that Brenda really excels. Victorian style French toast with pecans and apple sauce, cornbread with egg cream sauce, gingerbread pancakes with lemon sauce or, in the fall, fresh apples with sausage and French toast stuffed with cream cheese.

Located in the center of the Historic Albemarle District, you will find that the history of North Carolina was written all around you. It's a land forged out of a wilderness by independent people who fought against tyranny. There are the Lost Colony of Manteo, the antebellum plantations of Somerset Place and Hope, and the Battle of Plymouth, the second largest Civil War battle in North Carolina. These are just a sampling of the attractions of the Albemarle District.

---

**Four Gables Bed & Breakfast**
**P.O. Box 538; 109 W. Main Street; Plymouth, NC 27962**
**(919) 793-6696**
**Innkeepers: Norman & Brenda Conklin**
Rooms: 4; Private baths: 4; Rates: $$
Affiliations: NCBBI, Washington Co. Chamber
Payment:      Amenities:

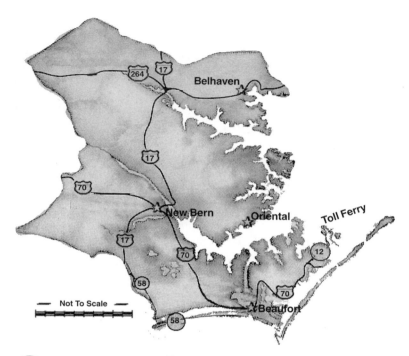

# Central
# Coast

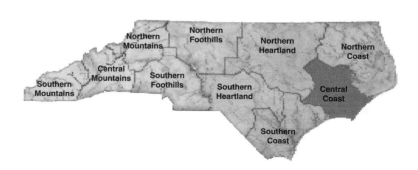

# Delamar Inn
# Beaufort

If you love history, intimate dining, quaint shops, and excellent bed and breakfasts, then Beaufort is a necessary stop for any visit to the eastern shore. Tourists have been coming to Beaufort for nearly 300 years. Why, even Blackbeard the pirate was a frequent guest and often stayed at the Hammock House (an inn or "ordinary") built in 1698. While the Hammock House is now a private residence, twentieth century visitors often stay at the Delamar Inn.

Jacob Gibble, a local merchant who owned a dry goods shop and the local lumber yard, built the house at the corner of Broad and Turner just after the Civil War in the fall of 1865. Most of his six children were born in the house. Over the years, the Gibble family intermarried with the Delamars. The property remained in the Delamar family until the late 1970s.

Tom and Mabel bought the house in 1989, and to their surprise the home was in remarkably good shape. They have done extensive renovation to the home but it required no structural restoration.

While decorated throughout with quality antiques, the Delamar is comfortable. There isn't the feeling that you sometimes have of being afraid to relax and prop your feet up. Each of the four guest bedrooms is decorated in its own style and period. Rooms offer features such as a king-size Jenny Lynn or canopy bed and private baths with claw-foot bathtubs.

One of the things we enjoyed was the first- and second-story porches where you could relax and just watch the world of Beaufort before you. Complimentary soft drinks and cookies, are available to be enjoyed in the upstairs sitting room and assorted wines can be sampled downstairs in front of the fireplace. Feel free to borrow a bicycle to tour the town or beach furniture to relax on the local shores.

Beaufort was surveyed in 1713, nearly 20 years before the birth of George Washington, and it is the third-oldest town in North Carolina. The town was named for Henry Somerset, the Duke of Beaufort, and was once a British customs port. The English influence is apparent in architecture and street names.

More than 100 historic structures are located in the community. The Beaufort Historical Association has moved several old structures to a plot just down the street from the Delamar Inn. Here, costumed guides will take you back in time to the days when Beaufort was a major deep-water port. A ride on an authentic English double-decker bus will take you through the town past many historic buildings while the guide tells the story of each.

With every step you take in Beaufort, the history of America seems to unfold: local militia saved the town from repeated raids by pirates in the 1740s. The town was pillaged by British dragoons after the defeat of Cornwallis during the Revolutionary War. Just across the sound at Fort Macon, Union and Confederate forces clashed during the Civil War. At the North Carolina Maritime Museum, you will learn how the sea played the most important part in Beaufort's history.

Each day you can take cruises of the sound on the Crystal Queen or the 65' tour boat Mystery. From ship rail you can see the wild horses of Shackleford Banks or the dolphins that come to the sound to feed.

Beaufort is rich in treasures, many of which can be found in the quaint shops along the waterfront. After a day of exploring, there are many fine restaurants in the area.

---

**Delamar Inn**
**217 Turner St.; Beaufort, NC 28516**
**(800) 349-5823; (919) 728-4300; Fax: (919) 728-1471**
**Innkeepers: Tom & Mabel Steepy**
Rooms: 4; Private baths: 4; Rates: $$; children over 10
Affiliations: AB&BA, PAII, AAA♦♦♦, MobilSSS, NB&BA
Payment:     Amenities:

## Langdon House Bed & Breakfast
## Beaufort

I knew within a few minutes after meeting Jimm Prest that I had found an exceptional innkeeper. Innkeeping is an art and Jimm has been perfecting his technique for over 12 years.

Staying at a bed and breakfast should always be an experience, and guests stay for different reasons. Sometimes we are just looking for a place to relax from the day-to-day stress. Other times we want to act out a fantasy such as a romantic weekend. For others it may be to take a glimpse into the past. One of the things that makes the Langdon House so unique is that Jimm views it as a stage. The guests are not only the actors, but the directors and script writers as well. It is Jimm's job make sure you know the many "props" you have to work with and to make sure the "production" goes smoothly.

Jimm feels the relationship between innkeeper and guest begins on the phone. That 15-20 minute call allows each to become familiar with the other. The guest learns what Jimm can and can not provide and Jimm learns what role he is to play in their special getaway.

The town of Beaufort was incorporated in 1722 by the British as a customs station because of the natural deep water port. Today, there are more than 100 historic structures in the community. The Langdon House is located in the heart of the district just one block from waterfront shops, restaurants and museums. Across the street, behind the old Ann Street Methodist Church, is a cemetery that dates into the 1730s. On the far side of the block is the Beaufort historical restoration complex where costumed guides take you back in time nearly 200 years.

The oldest part of the three-story Colonial Federal structure that Jimm restored was built in 1733. From the old books that line the bookcases to the spacious sitting room and two wide porches, you'll find the Langdon

House is comfortable, warm and inviting. Currier & Ives prints, original pine heartwood floors and an eclectic collection of antique furnishings make it a perfect stage for guests. It doesn't matter whether you're just looking for a peaceful getaway, a romantic weekend, or diving head first into the history of our eastern shore.

Jimm's eye for detail really shines at breakfast. Every plate is beautifully styled and filled with a variety of wonderful food. His specialties are waffles and French toast. In addition to a slab of ham almost a half-inch thick, you might find lemon, blueberry, or pineapple waffles or pecan waffles served with orange butter. Other mornings might include French toast stuffed with various meats, cheeses, fruits or herbs. There is such a variety of breakfast entrées that the menu will never be repeated no matter how long you stay. Breakfast is provided any time between 7 a.m. and 11 a.m. and sleeping late is considered a compliment to the innkeeper. Any dietary restrictions or preferences will be gladly accommodated with advanced notice to allow for preparations.

Acting as guide, local historian, and host, Jimm suggested the best places in town to see, as well as his favorite places to eat. During the day we wandered the streets, viewed the many historic structures, and took an authentic English double-decker bus for a tour of the town. By evening we were ready to try one of Jimm's suggestions for dinner. With Jimm's extensive knowledge of the varied restaurants, he goes to great lengths to match the guests' desire with the right restaurant.

---

**Langdon House Bed & Breakfast**
**135 Craven St.; Beaufort, NC 27516**
**(919) 728-5499**
**Innkeeper: Jimm Prest**
Rooms: 4; Private baths: 4; Rates: $$-$$$; children over 12
Affiliations: NCBBI, CCHMA
Payment:  $$$ CHECKS Amenities: A/C

# Pecan Tree Inn
# Beaufort

If I could move the mountains closer to Beaufort, I would live there. The downtown area with its charming shops and antique stores along the waterfront, its historic district, the warm and friendly people we met—all made me want to stay.

Joe and Susan Johnson were driving through the area and stopped for lunch. They fell in love with the area as I did, but they stayed and purchased what was once the Masonic Lodge. Within six months they completed extensive renovations to the property and opened the Pecan Tree Inn. In less than two years, their efforts have received national recognition, a three diamond award from AAA and a write-up in *Conde Nast Traveler* magazine.

Located just ½ block from the waterfront, the structure was built in 1866 as a Masonic Lodge. In the early 1900s, turrets, gingerbread trim, and additional rooms were added to the structure. The property at 116 Queen Street has been a school, Sunday school, doctor's office, tea house and apartments. It required major renovations to restore the charm of the Victorian era.

The Johnson family had been in the hardware business in New Jersey since 1890. Joe drew on this experience to complete the work quickly. He added central air-conditioning and private baths with showers for each guest room. A two-person jacuzzi was installed in the Bridal Suite. The town of Beaufort presented them an award for the restoration of the house. The Inn is now on the North Carolina Register of Historic Places.

The Pecan Tree has been carefully decorated and is without the cluttered look typically associated with the Victorian era. Refinished pine floors, Oriental and pattern berber rugs provide a perfect setting for

classic Queen Anne period antiques and reproductions. Each room carries a different theme. The Country Room has a queen-size pencil post bed, hand-tied canopy and carefully selected art work. The Bridal Suite has a private entrance from the back porch. Its king-size canopied bed was custom-made for Joe and Susan.

Susan's pride and joy at the Pecan Tree is the 5,500-square-foot flower and herb garden that she tends. In addition to its goldfish pond, there are more than 1,000 plants, each with identifying labels.

Sometimes a Victorian bed and breakfast looks out of place in its surroundings. This is not so with the Pecan Tree Inn. The town of Beaufort takes its heritage seriously. The Beaufort Historic Site on Turner Street has thirteen historic buildings including an apothecary shop, the old courthouse and jail. The Old Burying Ground on Ann Street, listed on the National Register of Historic Places, has tours available for a small fee.

I suggest a walk down Front Street. Stroll the waterfront boardwalk to the North Carolina Maritime Museum. This 18,000-square-foot wooden building is reminiscent of the U.S. Lifesaving buildings of the nineteenth century. It houses an impressive collection of nautical history, ship models and exhibits on costal birds, fish and animals.

---

**Pecan Tree Inn**
**116 Queen St.; Beaufort, NC 28516**
**(919) 728-6733**
**Innkeepers: Susan & Joe Johnson**
Rooms: 7; Private Baths: 7; Rates: $$-$$$; children over 12
Affiliations: NCBBI, NB&BA, PAII, Carteret Co. Chamber
Payment:  Amenities:

## River Forest Manor Inn & Marina
## Belhaven

Rich in history, the peninsula jutting out into Pamlico Sound includes communities like Swan Quarter, Stumpy Point, Frying Pan Landing, and Scuppernong. Here also is North Carolina's oldest incorporated town, Bath, chartered in 1705. Located on the Pamlico River, Bath was the first official port of entry into North Carolina. Just eighteen miles away, the community of Belhaven, on the Pungo River, didn't exist until the mid 1800s. It wasn't until the railroad arrived in 1891, that the town began to prosper.

During the summer of 1899, townspeople gathered in disbelief to watch John Aaron Wilkinson drive into town in a Stanley Steamer. This is believed to be the first automobile in the state. The same year, Wilkinson, President of the J.L Roper Lumber Company, and vice-president of Norfolk & Southern Railroad, began building an elaborate mansion on the bank of the river. A bachelor with an eye for detail, Wilkinson hired only the best craftsmen to build his splendid home. It took five years to complete. When finished, Ionic columns led the way to leaded glass doors. Elegant tapestries hung above mahogany wainscoting and crystal chandeliers were suspended from ornate plaster ceilings created by Italian craftsmen. Each of the eleven fireplaces featured beautifully carved oak mantels. Eight years after the showplace was completed, Wilkinson brought home a new bride from New York City.

The third owner of this magnificent home, Axson Smith, purchased the home in 1947 from J.W. Hines of Rocky Mount. Smith, who had extensive hotel management experience, partially gained at the famed Drake Hotel and The Palmer House in Chicago, had returned home to Belhaven to stay. He bought River Forest Manor right away, and married a local girl, Melba, in 1948.

The ambiance of River Forest has remained the same since its opening. Over the years a world-class restaurant, marina and shipyard have been added. The inn is famous for its Southern hospitality and charm, but also for its Southern cooking. Its rooms and 52-item smorgasbord have attracted the wealthy and

famous, with James Cagney, Robert Ripley, Harvey Firestone, Roy Clark, Neal Sedaka and Walter Cronkite numbered among its guest. Many guests arrive by boat, as the River Forest is famous among those who travel the Intracoastal Waterway.

There's always something to do at River Forest. Walk along the Pungo River, watch boats from all over the world pull into the marina, play tennis, take a dip in the pool, enjoy the hot tub, visit the new bar/lounge or just sit back on the spacious deck.

When you're ready to venture a bit farther afield, the Belhaven Memorial Museum is one of the 14 sites on the Historic Albemarle Tour. City Hall, where the museum is housed, is also on the National Register of Historic Places.

Bath, once the home to politicians and pirates (the notorious Blackbeard had a home here at one time), has several preserved historic structures open to the public. The oldest home, the Palmer-March House built in 1751, is where Edna Ferber stayed while researching *Showboat*. Across the Pamlico River in Aurora, a small museum exhibits fish fossils from the Pilocene period, some fiive million years ago.

To the east of Belhaven, the Lake Mattamuskeet Wildlife Refuge covers more than 50,000 acres of water, marsh, timber and croplands. During the winter, its shallow 40,000 acre lake is home to as many as 150,000 birds. Fishing for bass, bream and catfish is excellent in spring and fall.

---

**River Forest Manor Inn & Marina**
**600 E. Main St.; Belhaven, NC 27810**
**(800) 346-2151; (919) 943-2151; Fax: (919) 943-6628**
**Innkeeper: Mrs. Melba G. Smith**
Rooms: 12; Private baths: 12; Cottages: 1; Rates: $-$$
Affiliations: AB&BA, NCBBI, AAA, Mobil
Payment:  Amenities:

# Aerie
# New Bern

Located within a four block radius of the Aerie is the Attmore-Oliver House Museum, the Fireman's Museum, the Civil War Museum, New Bern Academy and the Tryon Palace. No other accommodation in New Bern is so conveniently located.

Built in 1882 by Samuel Street, the Street-Ward House, as it is known locally, remained a private residence for more than a century. In 1985 it was fully restored and redecorated as a Victorian style bed and breakfast. Decorated with Colonial and Victorian antiques and period reproductions, the bed and breakfast is reminiscent of early twentieth century homes along the coast. The sitting room, with its player piano and library, provides a comfortable gathering place for guests. Each of the seven guest rooms is large and very cozy. They provide amenities such as private bath, cable TV and private phone.

Your hosts, Howard and Dee Smith, provide complimentary wine and soft drinks as well as fresh baked cookies or cakes throughout the evening. In the afternoon, the dining room becomes "The Tea Room." It is becoming famous in the area as *the* place for afternoon tea or coffee served with scones, tarts and assorted tea cakes.

Breakfast at the Aerie is unique in that guests have a choice of three different entrées each day. Your choices might include Belgian waffles, an egg dish such as omelets, or stuffed French toast along with ham, sausage or bacon. Dee also serves fresh fruit, fruit juices, coffee, tea or milk with breakfast. Our breakfast was delightful and provided us the energy to explore the area.

More than 150 historic sites from the eighteenth and nineteenth centuries can be found in New Bern, the second-oldest city in the state. The best known place is the Tryon Palace Historic Sites and Gardens. Built in

1770, it was one of the most beautiful homes in the colonies. The Georgian style mansion served as both the capitol of the Colony of North Carolina as well as the private residence of Royal Governor William Tryon. The Palace has been fully restored to its former glory and is only one block from the Aerie.

The New Bern Academy focuses on early education in the colony. It also provides insights into the history of New Bern from its settlement in 1710 through the Civil War.

The Civil War itself is well documented at the Civil War Museum. It houses one of the largest private collections of Civil War weapons and memorabilia in the state. Many award-winning displays help bring a new perspective to the war between the states.

Take a ride on the *Belle of New Bern*, a 125-foot paddlewheel riverboat or visit the Fireman's Museum. An extensive collection of early firefighting equipment provides a unique glimpse into the past. The rare photographs, relics and other equipment along with the guide's narrative are very impressive.

New Bern is a beautiful community with a rich heritage. Yet history is not its only feature. The 157,000-acre Croatan National Forest is but a short drive. Here you'll find an abundance of wildlife and plant life.

---

**Aerie**
**509 Pollock St.; New Bern, NC 28560**
**(800) 849-5553; (919) 636-5553**
**Innkeepers: Howard & Dee Smith**
Rooms: 7; Private Baths: 7; Rates: $$
Affiliations: NCBBI, PAII
Payment:      Amenities:

# Harmony House Inn
# New Bern

There are many reasons people want to be innkeepers and I have probably heard most of them. However, none of the reasons impressed me as much as Ed and Sooki Kirkpatrick's.

Ed had been in the hotel industry for years. He believed that the last three years had seen a tremendous decline in the product and services many hotels and motels provided. Guest services, payroll and amenities had been cut. He felt that it had gotten to the point where many hotels and motels were just checking guests in and out. He almost knew each day he went to work there would be an angry guest just waiting to "pounce" on him. He loved working with the traveling public, but was not in a position where he could control the policies of the company or the product his hotel offered. With a bed and breakfast, he could provide the kind of service and amenities he felt was important to the traveler.

With this attitude Ed and Sooki began a quest to find the right location; the right bed and breakfast. They chose New Bern and Harmony House Inn. Harmony House had been a bed and breakfast for several years. The prior owners had built a very good reputation, yet Ed saw where he and Sooki could make changes and improvements.

Redecorating, adding a suite and a gift area filled with handmade items by his wife and other area artisans are only a few of the changes. They have a social hour for guests complete with white wine from 6-7 p.m. They put out port and sherry at 8 p.m. for the remainder of the evening. Guest rooms are large and well furnished with period antiques and reproductions. Many have four-poster canopy or pencil-poster beds. They are also air-conditioned, have ceiling fans, and include cable

TV. A guest refrigerator is on the first floor stocked with complimentary soft drinks and juice.

The location of Harmony House helped to convince the Kirkpatrick's that their choice was right. It is in the historic area and next door to the Craven County Visitor Center. They are in the heart of downtown New Bern, close to many of the more than 150 historic landmarks in the city, and the marina. Restaurants, gift and antique shops are all within walking distance.

Settled in 1710 by Swiss and German immigrants, New Bern is the second-oldest town in the state. You will find eighteenth and nineteenth century architecture to be plentiful. The centerpiece, however, is Tryon Palace. It is the restored home of the British Royal Governor William Tryon. The palace was built in 1770 to serve as capitol of the Colony of North Carolina and the Governor's private residence.

Built circa 1850, the Harmony House has its own interesting history. The house originally had only four rooms. The owner had six children so he made several additions to the house. Legend has it that the house was left to two of the sons. They had an argument and felt that they could no longer live in the same house. Because of this, they sawed the house in half and had one side moved nine feet to the right. They filled the gap with a new front door, a second set of stairs to the second floor and additional rooms.

**Harmony House Inn**
**215 Pollock St.; New Bern, NC 28560**
**(800) 636-3113; (919) 636-3810**
**Innkeepers: Ed & Sooki Kirkpatrick**
Rooms: 9; Private Baths: 9; Suites: 1; Rates: $$-$$$
Affiliations: IIA, NCBBI, PAII, AB&BA, AAA
Payment:        Amenities:

## The Tar Heel Inn
## Oriental

Our destination: The Oriental Cup Sailing Regatta, held each September in the sailing capital of North Carolina. Because of the busy weekend schedule, we were unable to stay at the Tar Heel Inn. However, I had the opportunity to meet the innkeeper Shawna Hyde and visit the Inn.

The structure was built in 1890, six years before the community of Oriental was formed. At that time, the house served as both home and millinery shop. While Oriental is a small community today, then it was quite a thriving area.

Lou Midyette, the first settler in Oriental, discovered it by accident. Sailing to New Bern from his home on the Outer Banks, a squall caused him to seek haven in the harbor. This deep water harbor is formed by six creeks that flow into the mouth of the Neuse River. Here, where the river is five miles wide, Lou found a place to bring his family. He returned home, packed, and became the first settler. As time passed, other people came to the area. Fishing became a major industry. When the lumber mill opened, the railroad came to the area. At one time both river steamer and rail served Oriental. After the burning of the mill in 1914, the only way to Oriental was by road.

Today the population of Oriental is only 800. There are actually more sailboats than people. Fishing is still a mainstay, but many come just to be near the water or to sail. Others come for a change of pace away from the hurried life of the city. This was the case for Shawna and Robert Hyde and their two daughters, Lindsay and Sarah.

The Tar Heel has been completely restored to capture the ambience of an English Country Inn from the turn of the century. From the fireplace in the parlor to the rough hewn beams in the dining room, they

have done exactly that. You'll find antiques and comfortable cushioned sofas and chairs in the parlor. English wallpaper and fabrics and antiques or period reproductions are in each of the eight guest rooms. Furnishings include king, queen, canopy or four-poster beds.

Breakfast includes entrees such as Southern pecan French toast, cheese blintzes with fruit sauce, quiche or casseroles and homemade breads or muffins. Breakfast is served at individual tables in the dining room or on the garden patio.

Shawna and Robert have owned the bed and breakfast only a short time, yet already you can see the changes they have made. By the time this book goes to press, their plans of a gazebo and Jacuzzi should be complete. A guest kitchen already provides a refrigerator and microwave. Shawna serves afternoon refreshments, such as brownies and iced tea. She makes soft drinks and popcorn available for late evening snacks.

Oriental is pleasant place to spend a romantic weekend or to get away for a few days. Shawna and Robert can help with suggestions for dinner, sailing charters or even a bicycle ride through the community.

**The Tar Heel Inn**
**P.O. Box 176; 205 Church St.; Oriental, NC 28571**
**(919) 249-1078**
**Innkeepers: Shawna & Robert Hyde**
Rooms: 8; Private Baths: 8; Rates: $$
Affiliations: NCBBI, PAII
Payment:     Amenities:

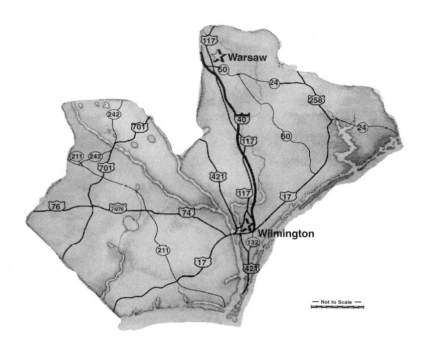

# Southern
# Coast

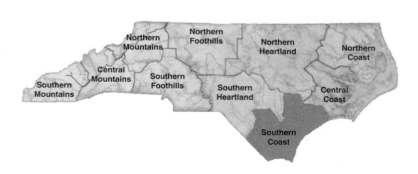

## The Squires Vintage Inn
## Warsaw

We found the Squires Vintage Inn to be so unique, we felt we should include it. You see, it isn't really a bed and breakfast nor is it a country inn. It's a small 12-room motel that has been converted to look and operate like a bed and breakfast. It doesn't end there. Next door is one of the most unique restaurants at which I have ever eaten.

It all started with the restaurant more than 34 years ago. A 200-year-old log cabin was converted into a restaurant. When it began in 1961, there was seating for only 76 guests. In 1967 an old house was added to it. By the early 1970s other additions were made and now there is seating for 456 people. In 1973, the owner, Joe West, built a small 12-room motel next door. The next year Joe hired an attractive young Scottish lass (Iris Lennon) to work as hostess and bookkeeper. Iris stayed with Joe until 1981. After the property was purchased by area businessmen, she was rehired to help manage the property. Finally, Iris purchased the entire property and continued to uphold the traditions that has made Squire's Vintage Inn and the Country Squire Restaurant successful.

Each of the rooms look out on the grounds with its winding brick sidewalks and trails leading to a large English garden and gazebo. Eleven of the rooms at the inn have two double beds, and one room has a king-size bed. The continental breakfast is brought to your room at your convenience (up to 10 a.m.). If you prefer, you could have breakfast on the sunken patio near the fountain. The birds and the squirrels are friendly, and wait patiently to see if you might have dropped a crumb or two.

Next door is the Country Squire Restaurant decorated with antiques. The many fireplaces and its torch and candle lighting gives it the feel of a colonial inn. There are small rooms with intimate seating like the "Pantry" while the "Jester's Court" will seat 200. Lunch and dinner are not included with the room rate, yet the prices are very reasonable. I am a filet mignon fan, and while researching this book have tried them all over the state. My steak at the Country Squire tied for first place.

Seven miles from the inn, in Kenansville, you will find the Cowan Museum. More than 1,500 rare tools, household furnishings and other items are in this restored Civil War-era home. Liberty Hall is a working plantation built in the early 1800s. The *Song of Liberty* outdoor drama is also in Kenansville and tells the story of two families (one black, one white) and the changes they had to face during the Revolutionary and Civil Wars.

**The Squires Vintage Inn**
**Rt. 2, Box 130-R; 748 NC 24&50; Warsaw, NC 28398**
**(910) 296-1831**
**Innkeeper: Iris Lennon**
Rooms: 12; Private Baths: 12; Rates: $$
Payment:       Amenities:

# Front Street Inn
# Wilmington

When Jay and Stefany Rhodes decided to open a bed and breakfast, they wanted to do it right. They wanted a place where guests could feel at home and have plenty of room to relax. Keeping this in mind, they created a bed and breakfast offering only suites.

Built in 1923, the building originally housed the Salvation Army and was used as such until 1980. In the following years the property served as an office building, apartments, a church and even a theater. The Rhodes' were fortunate to have large open spaces that allowed them to design nine large suites. Four of the suites offer full kitchens, others have wet bars. Only one of the suites does not have a refrigerator. Each suite provides guests with ceiling fans, individually-controlled heat and air conditioning, private entrances, cable television, VCR and private telephone. The rooms are soundproof and all the suites have large private baths.

Each suite is named and decorated accordingly. The Hemingway is reminiscent of Hemingway's home in Key West. The only missing items were his cats and an old manual typewriter. The Hemingway also includes a fireplace, Jacuzzi, and private balcony.

Other suites include the Nutcracker, the Monet, Pearl Buck, Kipling, Segovia, O'Keefe, the Molly Brown, and the Cousteau. All the rooms have king or queen beds. In addition, some have day beds as well. The Nutcracker is a favorite for families as it has a loft area for kids.

The continental breakfast is served on the main floor in the Sol y Sombra Bar and breakfast room. You'll find hard-crust rolls, croissants, yogurt, fresh muffins, fruits and fruit juices as well as cof-

fee and teas. The Sol y Sombra Bar works on the honor system offering wines, champagne and beer.

In the lower level, they are adding an exercise room. At the time of our stay, the billiard table, dart board and basic exercise equipment were already in place.

The Front Street Inn is only a few blocks from downtown Wilmington. The best way to see downtown Wilmington is by one of the horse-drawn carriage tours. You should then take the river taxi across Cape Fear to the USS *North Carolina* Battleship Memorial. While downtown, I recommend a stop at the Cotton Exchange. Thirty-three specialty shops and restaurants offer a unique feel of Wilmington when it was a major river port in the early nineteenth century. When you have finished your tour of downtown, take the Riverwalk back to Chandler's Wharf. Its cobblestone streets and a boardwalk that meanders along the river bank will take you back in time. In addition to the quaint shops in the area, you'll find Elijah's Oyster Bar. They serve very good food either inside or on the outdoor deck overlooking the Cape Fear River. Since the Front Street Inn is only a block away, it provides a pleasant walk after dinner.

**Front Street Inn**
**215 South Front Street; Wilmington, NC 28401**
**(910) 762-6442; Fax: (910) 762-8991**
**Innkeepers: Jay & Stephany Rhodes**
Suites: 9; Private Baths: 9; Rates: $$-$$$
Payment:  Amenities:

# James Place Bed & Breakfast
# Wilmington

Innkeepers Tony and Maureen Spataro's first experience at a bed and breakfast came on their honeymoon nearly ten years ago. Over the years since then, each time they visited another bed and breakfast, they talked about the things they would do when they had their own. The dream came true in March of 1995 when they had the opportunity to purchase James Place.

Once the boyhood home of General Westmoreland, the most decorated general from North Carolina, the house at 9 South Fourth Street has been a bed and breakfast since 1988. While we never had the opportunity to meet James Smith, the original innkeeper, I have been told by many that James reminded them of a favorite uncle. I can say that Tony is carrying on the same traditions.

Built in 1909, the four-square style house was the fourth house built on the block. Libby McIntosh, owner of the Colonial Inn Hotel, was the primary force in building homes on the block. During the years before it became a bed and breakfast, the house had a history of serving guests. During World War II, Wilmington was a major ship-building port and the house served as a boarding house.

While James Smith played a major role in the restoration of the home, the Spataros have taken the work even further. They have completely redone the main floor and added a third private bath upstairs complete with Jacuzzi. Their redecorating with country and shaker furnishings has added a great deal to James Place. Visitors find the home intimate and warm.

The Shaker Room, largest of the three, is an informal family room with a queen-size Shaker bed, pedestal table, and a twin bed for couples traveling with a child. The Nesting Suite, with canopy bed and its own sitting area, is a favorite of couples and newlyweds. The Renewal Room with its

Jacuzzi tub and private balcony overlooking the brick courtyard is the smallest of the three guest rooms.

As Maureen works full time for a local pharmaceutical company, breakfast chores fall to Tony, a task for which he is well prepared each morning. While they offer the early riser "continental breakfast," those who wait for Tony's breakfast will be well rewarded. One of his favorites is his "eggseptional" casserole, while another is overnight French toast. Of course there's also sausage, ham or bacon, plus fresh fruit, scrambled eggs and a variety of home baked breads.

The enclosed brick courtyard is home to the family pets, Watson, a Golden Retriever, Rusty, a Shetland Sheep dog, and Buddy, the cat. The brick courtyard is also where you will find the hot tub.

Wilmington is an almost magical city with much to offer visitors. A short stroll from James Place, the Wilmington Railroad Museum tells the history of the Wilmington and Weldon Railroad. When completed in 1840, its 161 miles of track comprised the longest rail line in the world. In the 1800s, the Port of Wilmington brought ships from around the world for trade. Today, many of the buildings along the river have been restored. The Cotton Exchange, with eight restored buildings connected by cobblestone walkways, offers more than 30 unique shops and restaurants. While you're near the river front, be sure to take the water taxi to the USS *North Carolina* Battleship Memorial. She has earned 15 battle stars and participated in every major naval offensive in the Pacific from Guadalcanal to Okinawa. She is dedicated to the men and women who defended this great country during WWII.

---

**James Place Bed & Breakfast**
**9 South Fourth Street; Wilmington, NC 28401**
**(800) 303-9444; (910) 251-0999; Fax: (910) 251-1150**
**Innkeepers: Tony & Maureen Spataro**
Rooms: 3; Private baths: 3; Rates: $$
Affiliations: PAII, NCBBI, Downtown Wilmington Assoc.
Payment:        Amenities:

# Rosehill Inn
# Wilmington

Wilmington is one of North Carolina's most inviting cities with one of the largest districts listed in the National Register of Historic Places (200 blocks). The city is a cultural center, its residents are friendly, and its diversity can be seen from Riverfront Park to the USS *North Carolina* Battleship Memorial.

It was the character of Wilmington that ended a three-year search by Laurel Jones and Dennis Fietsch for the perfect location for their bed and breakfast. In the heart of the historic district, the beautiful home built by Henry Russell Savage in 1848 provided them the working structure to create Rosehill Inn.

Savage, a prominent businessman and banker, purchased the entire block for only $600. He then parceled the block and sold most of it for a large profit. The home he built, a four-square in the Italian Renaissance style, while substantial for a bachelor of his position, was not very impressive on the outside. Savage died in 1868 and the property was, for a time, the childhood home of Henry Bacon, Jr., architect of the Lincoln Memorial.

The home changed hands again in 1909 when Percy Albright, the operating vice president of the Atlantic Coast Railroad, purchased it. It was Albright who first saw the potential of the home. In today's dollars, he spent the equivalent of $460,000 to create a gentleman's town home. The massive renovations changed the home from the Italian Victorian to a Greek Revival style with 23 columns on the porch. The entire millwork of the house changed as did the design of the foyer and grand staircase. Even a three-story hand-operated elevator was installed. When electricity came to Wilmington, Albright's home was one of the first lit by Edison lamps.

Over the years this beautiful home went the way of many others in the historic district. While there was no real decay, the beautiful wood throughout the house was painted and the pine heartwood flooring was carpeted. It required an extensive eight months of renovation to bring Rosehill Inn to life.

For Dennis, whose background is more than 20 years as a professional furniture restorer, the house provided him a canvas that needed to be prepared for Laurel to begin her magic. A fashion designer with her own line of swimwear, Laurel added the right blend of colors to the canvas to make Rosehill Inn a place to be remembered for a long time.

With quality antiques in each room and the addition of fabrics and paintings, Rosehill Inn has once again returned to the elegance of the past. In this author's eyes it offers comfortable romantic surroundings in which to rest after a day of exploring all that Wilmington has to offer.

Rosehill Inn is located only three blocks from the Cape Fear River, a short walk will take you to the shops and fine dining along the river front. The best way to really see and appreciate the historic district is by carriage. Each evening, during good weather, Springbook Farms offers rides throughout the district. Dennis can recommend any of a number of fine restaurants in Wilmington, but one of our favorites is Trails End. From the 35-pound Civil War cannon ball that closes the door through a series of ropes and pulleys to the mouth-watering steaks cooked to perfection over a slow-burning hardwood charcoal pit, the Trails End is an experience to be enjoyed.

Upon returning to Rosehill Inn, you will find your bed turned down, treats on your pillow, plush bath robes and oversized towels awaiting you. Each of the six guest rooms in the 7,500-square-foot house is large and private. A good night's rest and a generous breakfast of baked fruit dishes, broiled tomato steak with vermonto basil and feta cheese with a dessert of homemade cherry cheesecake will prepare you for another day of exploring this marvelous city.

---

**Rosehill Inn**
**114 S. Third St.; Wilmington, NC 28401**
**(800) 815-0250; (910) 815-0250; Fax: (910) 815-0350**
**Innkeepers: Laurel Jones & Donnis Fietsch**
Rooms: 6; Private baths: 6; Rates: $$-$$$; children over 12
Affiliations: NCBBI, PAII
Payment:  Amenities:

# The Taylor House Inn
# Wilmington

Innkeeper Glenda Moreadith's interest in bed and breakfasts dates back to when she was a young girl and her family moved to Sullivan's Island, South Carolina. They lived next door to an inn. Each day she would watch the guests coming and going. It took a few years, and a career as a Certified Registered Nurse Anesthetist, before the opportunity was available for her to have her own bed and breakfast. Now her stately home, located in the heart of the Historic District, welcomes guests from around the world.

Built in 1905 by John Allan Taylor, a wholesale grocery merchant, it remained in the Taylor family until 1969. The home has rich oak woodwork, high ceilings, enormous rooms, and beautiful wood floors. Rich oriental rugs, antique furnishings and period accessories decorate the rooms. Glenda has been collecting antiques and pieces of art throughout her life, and they have all found a place in this delightful home.

The guest rooms are quite large and have well-lighted sitting areas. While each of the rooms has its own private bath, three rooms feature claw-foot tubs original to the house. As in the rest of the house, the rooms are well-decorated with a collection of antique and period pieces. Beds vary from one room to the next and include brass and canopied beds. All are either king- or queen-sized. The Garden Room includes a gas-burning fireplace.

The house has an impressive appearance both inside and out. It was for this reason that it has been featured in two different made-for-television movies, *Against Her Will* and *Labor of Love*.

Each morning, breakfast is served family-style in the formal dining room. A sampling of Glenda's breakfast treats includes frozen fruit salad with strawberry purée, croissant a l'orange, Italian egg pie, breakfast bread pudding, and apple-cheddar quiche.

The historic area of Wilmington is one of the largest in the country comprised of more than 200 blocks. The area is pleasant for afternoon or evening walks, but my favorite mode of transportation through the district is by horse-drawn carriage. Glenda can help with arrangements and you can even be picked up at the door and taken for a ride to the waterfront. Here, a variety of outstanding restaurants, quaint shops and antique dealers await you.

Not to be missed is the Cotton Exchange. More than 30 shops and restaurants can be found in this fully restored 100 plus-year-old Cotton Exchange. After lunch, take a river taxi to the battleship USS *North Carolina*, pride of the Navy fleet during World War II.

The area has been shaped by history and geography. More than four centuries of history can be found in area museums such as the Cape Fear Museum, the Wilmington Railroad Museum and the Zebulon-Latimer House. The Cape Fear Museum includes life-sized dioramas, a scale model of the Wilmington waterfront in 1863 and a recreation of the battle of Fort Fisher.

The Orton and the Poplar Grove Plantations give insights into life in the South prior to the Civil War. Costumed guides recount the history while leading visitors to demonstrations of weaving, blacksmithing, and basket making.

The area is rich in its cultural heritage, and you will find an abundance of things to do and places to visit. Glenda and the well-trained staff at the Visitors Center can help with reservations and suggestions for a weekend getaway or an extended vacation.

---

**The Taylor House Inn**
**14 N Seventh Street; 14 N. Seventh Street; Wilmington, NC 28401**
**(800) 382-9982; (910) 763-7581**
**Innkeeper: Glenda Moreadith**
Rooms: 4; Private baths: 5; Suites: 1; Rates: $$$; children over 12
Affiliations: PAII, NCBBI, AAA, Mobil, Wilmington Chamber
Payment:  CHECKS MC VISA AMEX  Amenities:

# Worth House
# Wilmington

In the heart of one the largest historic districts listed in the National Register of Historic Places, the Worth House is a jewel that should not be missed. A bed and breakfast since 1985, this Queen Anne style Victorian has been carefully restored to its original beauty. Innkeepers John and Francie Miller have carefully decorated it with period antiques and artwork.

Charles Worth, who purchased the property in 1889, was a merchant involved in a number of different enterprises. While engaged in the wholesale grocery trade when he built his home, by 1905 he had interest in a number of Wilmington businesses. He was a commission merchant in cotton and naval stores, and president of the Cape Fear Machine Works. Although he was not a rich man, his income allowed him to move the house that was originally on the property and build a beautiful home for his wife, Emma.

By 1910, styles had changed, and the Worth house underwent major remodeling to give it a more neoclassical revival quality. The house was expanded and a corner tower was added. These changes added to the well-designed home and gave it more character.

The Worths had five daughters who lived in the home until Charles died in the early 1930s. During the shipbuilding boom in the 1940s, the home served as a boarding house. By the 1970s, it was abandoned for several years. Early in the 1980s, Herman and Betty Hossfeld saw the diamond in the rough, scraped off the layers of paint from the beautiful woodwork and restored the home to make it a bed and breakfast in 1985.

Today, the Millers are the fourth owners to operate the Worth House as a bed and breakfast and they have added greatly to the good reputation that preceded them. In fact, they have recently been awarded the three-diamond award by AAA.

While redecorating, the furnishings and artwork came not only from local antique stores but from stores in Atlanta, New Orleans and Charleston. Some of the an-

tiques, such as the queen bed in the Hibiscus Room, the hand-carved sea chest and the barrister's bookshelves in the library are as old as the house itself.

Francie varies her breakfast each morning. Offerings might include eggs Benedict, French toast, apple cobbler, or scrambled eggs and sausage. Angel appreciated the fresh squeezed orange juice and they were prepared for my request for fresh apple juice. Breakfast hours are flexible.

The guest refrigerator has a variety of complimentary soft drinks, and there's always coffee, tea and snacks available. For those who like to stay up late, two televisions both with VCRs, and a collection of movies can help to while away the hours.

Wilmington is a city to be explored. Since the Worth House is only a few blocks from the river front, a carriage ride along cobblestone streets to the Cotton Exchange might be the best place to start a day of wandering.

At the turn of the century, sailing ships from around the world delivered their treasures to the Port of Wilmington. Cotton was king and the cotton exchange was one of the largest in the world. Eight buildings have been restored and are connected by brick walkways to more than 33 unique specialty shops and restaurants. Paddy's Hollow has been a part of the Cotton Exchange since 1982. We always make it a stopping spot for lunch before continuing along the waterfront.

When you make your reservation at the Worth House, be sure to plan a couple of days in Wilmington. While the historic district is a perfect place to start your explorations, it will take time to see all the city has to offer.

---

**The Worth House**
**412 S. Third St.; Wilmington, NC 28401**
**(800) 340-8559; (910) 762-8562; Fax: (910) 763-2173**
**Innkeepers: John & Francie Miller**
Rooms: 5; Private baths: 7; Suites: 2; Rates: $$-$$$; children over 8
Affiliations: PAII, NCBBI, AAA, Mobil
Payment:   Amenities:

The following abbreviations are used:

$ .......................... 50 and under
$$ ........................ 51-100
$$$ ...................... 101-150
$$$$ .................... 151-250
$$$$$ ................. 251 and over

AAA ................... American Automobile Association
AB&BA ............. American Bed & Breakfast Association
AHA .................. American Hotel Association
AHMA ............... American Hotel & Motel Association
CCHMA ............ Crystal Coast Hotel & Motel Association
IIA ...................... Independent Innkeepers Association
NB&BA ............. National Bed & Breakfast Association
NCBBI ............... North Carolina Bed & Breakfasts & Inns
NCHMA ............ North Carolina Hotel & Motel Association
OBHMA ............ Outer Banks Hotel & Motel Association
PAII .................... Professional Association of Innkeepers International
SIA ..................... Southern Innkeepers Association
USB&B ............. United States Bed & Breakfast Association

# North Carolina Bed & Breakfasts and Inns

### Andrews

**The Walker Inn of Old Valleytown**
P.O. Box 1567, 39 Junaluska Rd
Andrews, NC 28901
(704) 321-5019
Innkeepers: Patricia & Peter Cook
Rooms: 4; Rates: $-$$
Affiliations: Andrews Chamber

### Asheboro

**The Doctor's Inn**
716 S. Park St.; Asheboro, NC 27203
(910) 625-4916
Innkeepers: Marion & Beth Griffin
Rooms: 2; Suites: 1; Rates: $-$$

### Asheville

**Abbington Green Bed & Breakfast Inn**
46 Cumberland Cir.; Asheville, NC 28801
(800) 251-2454; (704) 251-2454
Fax: (704) 251-2872
Innkeeper: Valerie Larrea
Rooms: 5; Suites: 1; Rates: $$-$$$
Affiliations: NCBBI, PAII

**Acorn Cottage Bed & Breakfast**
25 St. Dunstan's Circle; Asheville, NC 28803
(800) 699-0609; (704) 253-0609
Fax: (704) 253-0866
Innkeeper: Connie Stahl
Rooms: 4; Rates: $$
Affiliations: Asheville Chamber

**Albemarle Inn**
86 Edgemont Rd.; Asheville, NC 28801
(800) 621-7435; (704) 255-0027
Innkeepers: Dick & Kathy Hemes
Rooms: 10; Suites: 1; Rates: $$-$$$
Affiliations: NCBBI, PAII

**Beaufort House Victorian Bed & Breakfast**
61 N. Liberty St.; Asheville, NC 28801
(704) 254-8334; Fax: (704) 251-2082
Innkeepers: Robert & Jacqueline Glasgow
Rooms: 8; Suites: 1, Cottages: 3; Rates: $$-$$$$
*(25% off for AARP members Sun-Thu
excluding July, Aug and Oct)*

**Bird's Nest**
41 Oak Park Rd.; Asheville, NC 28801
(704) 252-2381
Innkeeper: Elizabeth Ann Wyndelts
Rooms: 7; Rates: $$

**The Bridal Path Inn**
30 Lookout Rd.; Asheville, NC 28804
(704) 252-0035
Innkeeper: Carol Halton
Rooms: 8; Suites: 2; Rates: $$-$$$
Affiliations: Asheville Chamber, AB&BA,
NB&BA, PAII
*On mountain over-looking downtown
Asheville. Breakfast on veranda.*

**Cairn Brae**
217 Patton Mountain Rd
Asheville, NC 28804
(704) 252-9219
Innkeepers: Milli & Ed Adams
Rooms: 3; Suites: 1; Rates: $$-$$$
Affiliations: NCBBI, AAA, PAII

**The Colby House**
230 Pearson Drive; Asheville, NC 28801
(800) 982-2118; (704) 253-5644
Fax: (704) 259-9479
Innkeepers: Everett & Ann Colby
Rooms: 4; Rates: $$-$$$
Affiliations: NCBBI, PAII, AB&BA, AAA

**Corner Oak Manor**
53 Saint Dunstans Rd.; Asheville, NC 28803
(704) 253-3525
Innkeepers: Karen & Andy Spradley
Rooms: 3; Cabins: 1; Rates: $$-$$$
Affiliations: NCBBI, NB&BA, Mobil

**Dogwood Cottage Inn**
40 Canterbury Rd. N; Asheville, NC 28801
(704) 258-9725
Innkeepers: Joan & Don Tracy
Rooms: 4; Rates: $$
Affiliations: NCBBI

**The Inn On Montford**
296 Montford Ave.; Asheville, NC 28801
(800) 254-9569; (704) 254-9569
Fax: (704) 254-9518
Innkeepers: Alexa & Lynn Royden
Rooms: 4; Rates: $$$
Affiliations: PAII, NCBBI

**Mountain Springs Cabins & Chalets**
P.O. Box 2; Asheville, NC 28715
(704) 665-1004; (704) 667-1581
Innkeepers: Sara & John Peltier
Rooms: 10; Suites: 2; Rates: $$-$$$
Affiliations: AAA◆◆◆

**Reed House**
119 Dodge St.; Asheville, NC 28803
(704) 274-1604
Innkeeper: Marge Turcot
Rooms: 3; Suites: 1; Rates: $-$$

**Richmond Hill Inn**
87 Richmond Hill Dr.; Asheville, NC 28806
(704) 252-7313; Fax: (704) 252-8726
Innkeeper: Susan Michel
Rooms: 33; Suites: 3; Rates: $$$-$$$$$
Affiliations: PAII, IIA, AB&BA

**The Scarlett Inn**
315 Pearson Dr.; Asheville, NC 28801
(704) 253-7888
Innkeepers: Greg & Bridgett Bounds
Rooms: 3; Cottages: 1; Rates: $$-$$$
Affiliations: Asheville Chamber

**The Wright Inn**
235 Pearson Drive; Asheville, NC 28801
(800) 552-5724; (704) 251-0789
Innkeepers: Carol & Art Wenczel
Rooms: 8; Carriage House: 1
Rates: $$-$$$$
Affiliations: NCBBI, PAII, AB&BA

## Atkinson

**Hawes House Bed & Breakfast**
301 S. 1st Ave.; Atkinson, NC 28421
(910) 283-5600
Innkeeper: Arlette Canning
Rooms: 4; Rates: $

## Balsam

**Balsam Lodge**
Valley Road; P.O. Box 279; Balsam, NC 28707
(800) 699-6528; (704) 456-6528
Innkeepers: Frank & Marti Shaver
Rooms: 4; Rates: $$
Affiliations: Jackson Co. Chamber, Haywood
Co. Chamber
*1908 renovated train depot. Four efficiency
units. Open year round. 1/4 mile off Parkway.
Elevation: 3500 ft.*

**Balsam Mountain Inn**
Seven Springs Drive; P.O. Box 40; Balsam, NC
28707
(704) 456-9498; Fax: (704) 456-9298
Innkeeper: Merrily Teasley
Rooms: 47; Suites: 3; Rates: $$-$$$
Affiliations: Mobil, AB&BA, PAII

## Banner Elk

**The Banner Elk Inn Bed & Breakfast**
Hwy. 194 N, Main St.; Rt. 3, Box 1134;
Banner Elk, NC 28604
(704) 898-6223
Innkeeper: Beverly Lait
Rooms: 4; Suites: 2; Rates: $$-$$$
Affiliations: AAA◆◆◆

## Hummingbird Lodge Bed & Breakfast
NC Hwy. 194; Rt. 4, Box 403
Banner Elk, NC 28604
(704) 963-7210
Innkeepers: Randy & Susan Hutchins
Rooms: 4; Rates: $$
Affiliations: Banner Elk & Boone Chambers

## Rainbow Inn Bed & Breakfast
317 Old Turnpike Road
Banner Elk, NC 28604
(704) 898-5611; Fax: (704) 898-5611
Innkeepers: Tammy & Steve Rondinaro
Rooms: 4; Rates: $$
Affiliations: NB&BA, NCBBI, Banner Elk
Chamber
*100-yr-old farmhouse filled with antiques and braided rugs. 4 miles from Beech Mtn. and Sugar Mtn. ski resorts. Grandfather Mtn. nearby.*

## The Tufts House Bed & Breakfast Inn
Rt. 2, Box 25A; Banner Elk, NC 28604
(704) 898-7944
Innkeepers: Nancy & Dean Barnett
Rooms: 4; Rates: $$
Affiliations: Banner Elk Chamber, High
Country Host
*North Carolina public television captured the essence of this secluded country inn with its cottage look and country flower and herb gardens.*

## Beaufort

## Captains' Quarters of Beaufort, Inc.
315 Ann St.; Beaufort, NC 28516
(919) 728-7711
Innkeepers: Ms. Ruby & Capt. Dick Collins
Rooms: 2; Suites: 1; Rates: $-$$
Affiliations: NCBBI, AB&BA

## Delamar Inn
217 Turner St.; Beaufort, NC 28516
(800) 349-5823; (919) 728-4300
Fax: (919) 728-1471
Innkeepers: Tom & Mabel Steepy
Rooms: 4; Rates: $$
Affiliations: AB&BA, PAII, AAA◆◆◆,
Mobil★★★, NB&BA

## Langdon House Bed & Breakfast
135 Craven St.; Beaufort, NC 27516
(919) 728-5499
Innkeeper: Jimm Prest
Rooms: 4; Rates: $$-$$$
Affiliations: NCBBI, CCHMA

## Pecan Tree Inn
116 Queen St.; Beaufort, NC 28516
(919) 728-6733
Innkeepers: Susan & Joe Johnson

Rooms: 7; Rates: $$-$$$
Affiliations: NCBBI, NB&BA, PAII, Carteret
Co. Chamber

## Belhaven

## River Forest Manor Inn & Marina
600 E. Main St.; Belhaven, NC 27810
(800) 346-2151; (919) 943-2151
Fax: (919) 943-6628
Innkeeper: Mrs. Melba G. Smith
Rooms: 12; Cottages: 1; Rates: $-$$
Affiliations: AB&BA, NCBBI, AAA, Mobil

## Black Mountain

## Black Mountain Inn
718 W. Old Hwy. 70
Black Mountain, NC 28711
(800) 735-6128; (704) 669-6528
Innkeeper: June Bergeron Colbert
Rooms: 7; Rates: $$
Affiliations: Black Mountain Chamber

## Friendship Lodge
P.O. Box 877; Black Mountain, NC 28711
(704) 669-9294
Innkeepers: Bob & Sarah LaBrant
Rooms: 10; Rates: $$

## Petworth Inn
103 Orchard; Black Mountain, NC 28711
(704) 669-4517
Innkeeper: Doris T. Hanisco
Rooms: 1; Rates: $

## Blowing Rock

## Gideon Ridge Inn
6148 Gideon Ridge Rd.; P.O. Box 1929;
Blowing Rock, NC 28605
(704) 295-3644; Fax: (704) 295-4586
Innkeepers: Jane & Cobb Milner/Cindy &
Cobb Milner, III
Rooms: 10; Rates: $$-$$$
Affiliations: IIA

## Hound Ears Lodge & Club
P.O. Box 188; Blowing Rock, NC 28605
(704) 963-4321
Innkeeper: Lillian Smith
Rooms: 27; Suites: 1; Rates: $$$$

## The Inn at Ragged Gardens
203 Sunset Drive; P.O. Box 1927; Blowing
Rock, NC 28605; (704) 295-9703
Innkeepers: Lee & Jama Hyett
Rooms: 8; Suites: 2; Cottages: 1; Rates: $$$
Affiliations: PAII, Blowing Rock Chamber,
High Country Host

**The Lindridge House Bed & Breakfast**
5447 US Hwy 221 S
Blowing Rock, NC 28605
(704) 295-7343
Innkeepers: Suzann French & Lou Gutheil
Rooms: 2; Suites: 1; Rates: $$-$$$
Affiliations: NCBBI, Blowing Rock Chamber,
High Country Host

**Maple Lodge**
Sunset Dr.; P.O. Box 1236
Blowing Rock, NC 28605
(704) 295-3331
Innkeepers: Marilyn & David Bateman
Rooms: 10; Suites: 1; Rates: $$-$$$
Affiliations: PAII, Blowing Rock Chamber,
Boone Area Chamber, High Country Host

**Rocking Horse Inn**
445 Rocking Horse Lane; P.O. Box 629;
Blowing Rock, NC 28605
(704) 295-3311
Innkeepers: Bill & Glenda Howard
Rooms: 7; Cottages: 1; Rates: $$-$$$
Affiliations: Blowing Rock Chamber
*Surround yourself with peace and quiet,*
*birdsong & rocking chairs on porches!*

**Stone Pillar Bed & Breakfast**
144 Pine St.; P.O. Box 1881
Blowing Rock, NC 28605
(704) 295-4141
Innkeepers: George Van Nuys & Ron Tharp
Rooms: 6; Rates: $-$$

**Boone**

**Eagle's Retreat**
333 Eagle Dr.; Boone, NC 28607
(704) 264-3007
Innkeepers: Suzanne & Jim Fletcher
Suites: 2; Rates: $$
Affiliations: Blowing Rock Chamber, High
Country Host

**The Gragg House**
Rt. 6, Box 1205; 210 Ridge Point Drive;
Boone, NC 28607
(704) 264-7289; Fax: (704) 264-7289
Innkeepers: Robert & Judy Gragg
Rooms: 3; Rates: $$

**Grandma Jean's Bed & Breakfast**
254 Meadowview Drive; Boone, NC 28607
(704) 262-3670
Innkeeper: Dr. Jean Probinsky
Rooms: 4; Rates: $-$$
Affiliations: High Country Host, Blowing
Rock Chamber

**The Lion's Den**
P.O. Box 1327; Boone, NC 28607
(800) 963-5785; (704) 963-5785
Innkeepers: Tom & Kay Shervington
Rooms: 4; Suites: 1; Rates: $$-$$$
Affiliations: Boone Chamber, Blowing Rock
Chamber

**Lovill House Inn**
404 Old Bristol Rd.; Boone, NC 28607
(800) 849-9466; (704) 264-4204
Innkeepers: Tim & Lori Shahen
Rooms: 5; Rates: $$-$$$
Affiliations: PAII, NCBBI, AAA♦♦♦, Mobil,
Boone Chamber, High Country Host

**Brevard**

**The Inn at Brevard**
410 E. Main St.; Brevard, NC 28712
(704) 884-2105
Innkeepers: Eileen & Bertrand Bourget
Rooms: 15; Suites: 1; Rates: $$-$$$

**Red House Inn Bed & Breakfast**
412 W. Probart St.; Brevard, NC 28712
(704) 884-9349
Innkeeper: Marilyn Ong
Rooms: 4; Rates: $$

**The Womble Inn**
301 W. Main St.; Brevard, NC 28712
(704) 884-4770
Innkeepers: Beth & Steve Womble
Rooms: 6; Rates: $$

**Bryson City**

**Hemlock Inn**
P.O. Drawer EE; Bryson City, NC 28713
(704) 488-2885
Innkeepers: Morris & Elaine White
Rooms: 19; Cottages: 3; Rates: $$$-$$$$
Affiliations: IIA

**Nantahala Village**
9400 Hwy. 19 W.; Bryson City, NC 28713
(800) 438-1507; (704) 488-2826
Innkeepers: John Burton & Jan Letendre
Rooms: 14; Cabins: 45; Rates: $-$$$$

**Randolph House Country Inn**
223 Fryemont Road; P.O. Box 816
Bryson City, NC 28713
(800) 480-3472; (704) 488-3472
Innkeepers: Bill & Ruth Randolph Adams
Rooms: 7; Suites: 1; Rates: $$-$$$$ wk

**West Oak Bed & Breakfast**
948 Richmond St.; Bryson City, NC 28713
(704) 488-2438
Innkeeper: Mercedith Bacon
Rooms: 10; Rates: $$

## Burnsville

**A Little Bit Of Heaven**
937 Bear Wallow Rd.; Burnsville, NC 28714
(704) 675-5379
Innkeepers: Shelley & John Johnson
Rooms: 4; Rates: $$

**Hamrick Inn**
7787 Hwy. 80-S; Burnsville, NC 28714
(704) 675-5251
Innkeepers: Neal & June Jerome
Rooms: 4; Rates: $-$$
Affiliations: Yancey Co. Chamber

**Nu Wray Inn**
Town Square; P.O. Box 156
Burnsville, NC 28714
(800) 368-9729; (704) 682-2329
Innkeepers: Chris & Pam Strickland
Rooms: 26; Suites: 5; Rates: $$-$$$
Affiliations: PAII, Mobil, AAA, AB&BA

**The Terrell House**
109 Robertson St.; Burnsville, NC 28714
(704) 682-4505
Innkeepers: Pat & John Terrell
Rooms: 4; Suites: 2; Rates: $$

## Buxton

**Cape Hatteras Bed & Breakfast**
P.O. Box 490; Buxton, NC 27920
(800) 252-3316; (919) 995-4511
Fax: (919) 995-6004
Innkeeper: Cathy Moir
Rooms: 6; Rates: $-$$
Affiliations: NCBBI, Outer Banks Chamber,
Hatteras Business Assoc.

## Candler

**Owl's Nest Inn at Engadine**
2630 Smokey Park Highway
Candler, NC 28715
(800) 665-8868; (704) 665-8325
Innkeepers: Mary & Jim Melaugh
Rooms: 4; Rates: $$-$$$
Affiliations: NCBBI, PAII, Asheville Chamber

**Pisgah View Ranch**
Rt. 1; Candler, NC 28715
(704) 667-9100
Innkeepers: Phyllis Parris & Max Cogburn

24 cabins (41 rooms; 7 suites); Rates: $-$$
Affiliations: Asheville Chamber

## Carolina Beach

**The Beacon House Inn Bed & Breakfast**
715 Carolina Beach Ave. N
Carolina Beach, NC 28428
(910) 458-6244
Innkeepers: Mary & Larry Huhn/Peggy &
Jerry Emerson
Rooms: 9; Cabins: 2; Rates: $$
Affiliations: PAII, NCBBI, Carolina Beach
Chamber

**Harbour Lodge**
222 Canal Dr.; P.O. Box 1015
Carolina Beach, NC 28428
(800) 458-3645; (910) 458-3644
Innkeepers: Mike & Johanna Purgason
Rooms: 3; Rates: $$

## Carthage

**The Blacksmith Inn**
703 McReynolds St.; P.O. Box 1480
Carthage, NC 28327
(800) 284-4515; (910) 947-1692
Fax: (910) 295-5798
Innkeepers: Gary & Shawna Smith
Rooms: 4; Rates: $
Affiliations: AB&BA

## Cashiers

**Laurelwood Mountain Inn**
Hwy. 107 N.; P.O. Box 188
Cashiers, NC 28717
(800) 346-6846; (704) 743-9939
Innkeepers: Bob & Lise Dews
Rooms: 17; Suites: 2; Rates: $$
Affiliations: PAII, AAA, Cashiers Chamber,
Highlands Chamber
*Conveniently located in the heart of Cashiers.
Walk to shops and restaurants.*

**Millstone Inn Bed & Breakfast**
P.O. Box 949; Cashiers, NC 28717
(704) 743-2737
Innkeepers: Paul & Patricia Collins
Rooms: 7; Suites: 4; Rates: $$-$$$
Affiliations: NCBBI, PAII

## Cedar Mountain

**The Sassy Goose**
Reasonover Dr.; P.O. Box 228; Cedar
Mountain, NC 28718
(704) 966-9493
Innkeepers: Bob & Bette Vande Weghe

Rooms: 3; Cabin suites: 2; Rates: $$
*Open May-November*

### Chapel Hill

**The Inn at Bingham School**
NC 54 at Mebane Oaks Road; P.O. Box 267
Chapel Hill, NC 27514
(800) 566-5583; (919) 563-5583
Fax: (919) 563-9826
Innkeepers: Francois & Christina Deprez
Rooms: 5; Suites: 1; Rates: $$-$$$
Affiliations: NCBBI, PAII

### Charlotte

**601 Poplar Street Bed & Breakfast**
601 N. Poplar St.; Charlotte, NC 28202
(800) 545-2851; (704) 358-1464
Innkeeper: Ashley Parlier
Rooms: 3; Rates: $$
Affiliations: NCBBI

**The Homeplace Bed & Breakfast**
5901 Sardis Rd.; Charlotte, NC 28270
(704) 365-1936; Fax: (704) 366-2729
Innkeepers: Frank & Peggy Dearien
Rooms: 2; Suites: 1; Rates: $$-$$$
Affiliations: NCBBI, AAA

**The Inn Uptown**
129 N. Poplar St.; Charlotte, NC 28202
(800) 959-1990; (704) 342-2800
Fax: (704) 342-2222
Innkeeper: Elizabeth J. Rich
Rooms: 6; Rates: $$-$$$
Affiliations: NCBBI, PAII

**Still Waters Bed & Breakfast**
6221 Amos Smith Rd.; Charlotte, NC 28214
(704) 399-6299
Innkeepers: Janet & Rob Dyer
Rooms: 3; Rates: $$
Affiliations: NCBBI, PAII

### Cherokee

**Carriage Inn**
P.O. Box 1506; Cherokee, NC 28719
(704) 488-2398
Innkeepers: Saeed & Nayyer Khan
Rooms: 25; Suites: 1; Rates: $-$$

### Chimney Rock

**The Dogwood Inn Bed & Breakfast**
US 74 Hwy.; P.O. Box 159
Chimney Rock, NC 28720
(800) 992-5557; (704) 625-4403
Fax: (704) 625-8825

Innkeepers: Marsha & Mark Reynolds
Rooms: 10; Rates: $$
Affiliations: NCBBI, PAII

**Esmeralda Inn**
Hwy. 74A; P.O. Box 57
Chimney Rock, NC 28720
(704) 625-9105
Innkeepers: Ackie & JoAnne Okpych
Rooms: 13; Suites: 3; Rates: $$
Affiliations: Hickory Nut Chamber, Asheville
Chamber. Rutherfordton Chamber

### Clemmons

**Tanglewood Manor House B & B Inn**
P.O. Box 1040; Clemmons, NC 27012
(910) 766-0594; Fax: (910) 766-8723
Tanglewood Park; Innkeeper: Angela Schultz
Rooms: 10; Rates: $$-$$$

### Clinton

**The Shield House & Courthouse Inns**
216 Sampson St.; Clinton, NC 28328
(800) 462-9817; (910) 592-2634
Innkeepers: Juanita McLamb & Anita Green
15; Suites: 2; Rates: $$
Affiliations: NCBBI, NCHMA, Clinton Area
Chamber

### Clyde

**Windsong: A Mountain Inn**
120 Ferguson Ridge; Clyde, NC 28721
(704) 627-6111
Innkeepers: Gale & Donna Livengood
Rooms: 4; Cabins: 1; Rates: $$-$$$
Affiliations: NCBBI, AB&BA

### Columbia

**Heart's Delight**
802 Green Street; P.O. Box 447; Columbia,
NC 27925
(704) 796-2321
Innkeepers: Nancy & Philip House
Rooms: 3; Rates: $-$$

### Cullowhee

**Cullowhee Bed & Breakfast**
150 Ledbetter Rd.; Cullowhee, NC 28723
(704) 293-5447
Innkeepers: Charles & Janet Moore
Rooms: 4; Rates: $$
Affiliations: NCBBI, PAII

## Dillsboro

**Applegate Inn Bed & Breakfast**
163 Hemlock St.; P.O. Box 567
Dillsboro, NC 28725
(704) 586-2397
Innkeepers: Judy & Emil Milkey
Rooms: 4; Efficiencies: 3; Rates: $$
Affiliations: AAA, NB&BA, PAII, Jackson Co.
Chamber

**The Jarrett House**
P.O. Box 219; Dillsboro, NC 28725
(800) 972-5623; (704) 586-0265
Innkeepers: Jim & Jean Hartbarger
Rooms: 18; Suites: 3; Rates: $$
Affiliations: PAII, SIA

**Olde Towne Inn**
300 Hayood Rd.; P.O. Box 485
Dillsboro, NC 28725
(704) 586-3461
Innkeepers: Gretchen & Dave Dilks
Rooms: 3; Rates: $$
Affiliations: Jackson Co. Chamber, Dillsboro
Merchant's Assoc.

## Duck

**The Sanderling Inn Resort**
1461 Duck Road; Duck, NC 27949
(800) 701-4111; (919) 261-4111
Fax: (919) 261-1638
Innkeeper: Tina Berger
Rooms: 77; Suites: 10; Rates: $$$-$$$$$

## Durham

**Arrowhead Inn**
106 Mason Rd.; Durham, NC 27712
(800) 528-2207; (919) 477-8430
Fax: (919) 477-8430
Innkeepers: Barbara & Jerry Ryan
Rooms: 8; Suites: 2; Rates: $$-$$$
Affiliations: NCBBI, PAII

**The Blooming Garden Inn**
513 Holloway St.; Durham, NC 27701
(919) 687-0801
Innkeepers: Frank & Dolly Pokrass
Rooms: 2; Suites: 2; Rates: $$-$$$
Affiliations: NCBBI

**Old North Durham Inn**
922 N. Magnum St.; Durham, NC 27701
(919) 683-1885; Fax: (919) 682-2645
Innkeepers: Debbie & Jim Vickery
Rooms: 4; Suites: 1; Rates: $$-$$$
Affiliations: PAII, NCBBI, Durham Chamber
*This early 1900 Colonial Revival Home is*
*located just one mile from Duke University &*
*the Durham Bulls Baseball Park. Complimen-*
*tary tickets available for all Bulls home games.*

## Eagle Springs

**The Inn at Eagle Springs**
P.O. Box 56; Eagle Springs, NC 27242
(800) 472-0842; (910) 673-2722
Fax: (910) 673-7740
Innkeeper: Wes Smith
Rooms: 5; Rates: $-$$

## Edenton

**Captain's Quarters Inn**
202 West Queen Street; Edenton, NC 27932
(919) 482-8945
Innkeepers: Bill & Phyllis Pepper
Rooms: 6; Suites: 2; Rates: $$
Affiliations: NCBBI

**Granville Queen Inn**
108 S. Granville St.; Edenton, NC 27932
(919) 482-5296
Innkeepers: Marge & Ken Dunne
Rooms: 8; Rates: $$

**The Lords Proprietors' Inn**
300 N. Broad St.; Edenton, NC 27932
(919) 482-3641
Innkeepers: Arch & Jane Edwards
Rooms: 20; Rates: $$$-$$$$
Affiliations: IIA, PAII, Historic Hotels of
America

## Elizabeth City

**Culpepper Inn**
609 W. Main Street; Elizabeth City, NC 27909
(919) 335-1993; Fax: (919) 335-1555
Innkeepers: Judy Smith & Henry D. Brinkman
Rooms: 11; Rates: $$-$$$
Affiliations: PAII, NCBBI, AAA, Dasquotank
Tourism Board, Elizabeth City Chamber
*A hidden treasure that will transport you from*
*everyday life. Arrive in time for the nightly*
*evening social, feed the goldfish, take a dip in*
*the pool or just relax.*

**Elizabeth City Bed & Breakfast**
108 E. Fearing St.; Elizabeth City, NC 27909
(919) 338-2177
Innkeepers: Darla & Joe Semonich
Rooms: 4; Rates: $$
Affiliations: NCBBI

### Faison

**Magnolia Hall Bed & Breakfast**
701 W. Main St.; P.O. Box 728
Faison, NC 28341
(910) 267-9241
Innkeeper: Verna Taylor
Rooms: 4; Suites: 1; Rates: $$
Affiliations: Duplin Co. Chamber

### Flat Rock

**Highland Lake Inn**
Highland Lake Drive; P.O. Box 1026
Flat Rock, NC 28731
(800) 762-1376; (704) 693-3868
Fax: (704) 696-8951
Innkeepers: The Lindsey Family
Rooms: 58; Suites: 6; Cottages: 6; Cabins: 10;
Rates: $$-$$$

### Franklin

**Blaine House Bed & Breakfast**
661 Harrison Avenue; Franklin, NC 28734
(704) 349-4230; Fax: (704) 349-4230
Innkeepers: Suzy Chandler & Karin Gorboff
Rooms: 2; Suites: 1; Rates: $$
Affiliations: NCBBI, Franklin Chamber
*Experience a touch of elegance and a wealth of hospitality. Within walking distance of - shops, restaurants, museums.*

**Buttonwood Inn**
50 Admiral Drive; Franklin, NC 28734
(704) 369-8985
Innkeeper: Liz Oehser
Rooms: 4; Rates: $$
Affiliations: NCBBI

**Country Time Bed & Breakfast**
506 Potts Branch Drive; Franklin, NC 28734
(704) 369-3648
Innkeepers: Greg & Darlene Kimsey
Rooms: 4; Rates: $-$$

**The Franklin Terrace**
67 Harrison Ave.; Franklin, NC 28734
(800) 633-2431; (704) 524-7907
Innkeeper: Helen Hanson
Rooms: 9; Cottages: 1; Rates: $$

**Heritage Inn**
101 Heritage Hollow; Franklin, NC 28734
(704) 524-4150
Innkeeper: Sally Wade
Rooms: 4; Cabins: 1; Rates: $$
Affiliations: Franklin Chamber, Smoky Mountain Host
*Private entrances, baths/and porches. Waterfall extending length of veranda.*

**The Summit Inn**
125 E. Rogers St.; Franklin, NC 28734
(704) 524-2006
Innkeeper: Charles Harshman
Rooms: 14; Rates: $-$$

**Wayah Creek Cottages**
610 Wayah Rd.; Franklin, NC 28734
(704) 524-2034
Innkeepers: Larry & Jackie Clark
Rooms: 2; Suites: 5; Rates: $$

### Gastonia

**York-Chester Bed & Breakfast**
310 S. Chester St.; Gastonia, NC 28052
(800) 327-5067; (704) 853-2700
Innkeeper: Lynn J. Stepp
Rooms: 3; Suites: 1; Rates: $$
Affiliations: NCBBI, AAA

### Germanton

**MeadowHaven Bed & Breakfast**
Hwy. 8; P.O. Box 222; Germanton, NC 27019
(910) 593-3996
Innkeepers: Samuel & Darlene Fain
Rooms: 3; Suites: 4; Rates: $$-$$$$
Affiliations: PAII

### Glendale Springs

**Mountain View Lodge & Cabins**
164 Mountain View Lodge Drive; P.O. Box 90;
Glendale Springs, NC 28629
(800) 209-8142; (910) 982-2233
Innkeepers: Elton & Joann Derden
Cabins: 10; Suites: 4; Rates: $-$$
Affiliations: Ashe, Boone, Blowing Rock, &
Wilkes Co. Chambers, High Country Host
*On Blue Ridge Parkway milepost 256. Open year-round. Pets are welcomed.*

### Grassy Creek

**River House**
1896 Old Field Creek Road
Grassy Creek, NC 28631
(910) 982-2109; Fax: (910) 982-2109
River House, Inc.; Innkeeper: Gayle Winston
Rooms: 9; Rates: $$-$$$
Affiliations: Chamber members in three counties

### Greensboro

**The Biltmore Greensboro Hotel**
111 W. Washington St
Greensboro, NC 27401
(800) 332-0303; (910) 272-3474

Fax: (910) 275-2523
Innkeepers: Michael Mellor & Terry Jordan
Rooms: 21; Suites: 4; Rates: $$-$$$
Affiliations: AAA, Mobil

**Greenwood Bed & Breakfast**
205 N. Park Drive; Greensboro, NC 27401
(800) 535-9363; (910) 274-6350
Fax: (910) 274-9943
Innkeepers: Mike & Vanda Terrell
Rooms: 4; Rates: $$
Affiliations: NCBBI, PAII, AAA

**The Troy-Bumpass Inn Bed & Breakfast**
114 S. Mendenhall Street
Greensboro, NC 27403
(800) 370-9070; (910) 370-1660
Fax: (910) 274-3937
Innkeepers: Charles & Gwen Brown;
Rooms: 4; Rates: $$-$$$
Affiliations: PAII, NCBBI, Greensboro
Chamber
*True antebellum ambiance & romance in one
of Greensboro's oldest historic districts.
"Come share the history"*

## Hayesville

**Broadax Inn**
Rt. 1, Box 289-A; Hayesville, NC 28904
(704) 389-6987
Innkeepers: Roger & Ruth Young
Rooms: 5; Rates: $$

## Henderson

**La Grange Plantation Inn**
Nutbush Road; Rt. 3, Box 610
Henderson, NC 27536
(919) 438-2421
Innkeepers: Jean & Dick Cornell
Rooms: 5; Rates: $$
Affiliations: NCBBI

## Hendersonville

**The Claddagh Inn**
755 N. Main St.; Hendersonville, NC 28792
(800) 225-4700; (704) 697-7778
Fax: (704) 697-8664
Innkeepers: August & Geraldine Emanuele
Rooms: 12; Suites: 2; Rates: $$
Affiliations: AAA, Hendersonville Chamber

**Havenshire Inn**
3483 Cummings Road; Rt. 13, Box 366;
Hendersonville, NC 28739
(704) 692-4097
Innkeeper: Cindy Findley
Rooms: 7; Cabins: 2; Rates: $$-$$$

Affiliations: Brevard Chamber
*An English country manor, circa 1882. The
Blue Ridge Parkway and Pisgah National
Forest are minutes away!*

**Mountain Home Bed & Breakfast**
10 Courtland Blvd.; P.O. Box 234;
Hendersonville, NC 28758
(800) 397-0066; (704) 697-9090
Innkeepers: Bob & Donna Marriott
Rooms: 5; Suites: 1; Rates: $$-$$$$
Affiliations: NCBBI, NB&BA, AAA◆◆◆

**The Waverly Inn**
783 N. Main St.; Hendersonville, NC 28792
(800) 537-8195; (704) 693-9193
Fax: (704) 692-1010
Innkeepers: John & Diane Sheiry
Rooms: 14; Suites: 1; Rates: $$-$$$$
Affiliations: NCBBI, IIA, PAII, Asheville
Chamber, Hendersonville Chamber

## Hiddenite

**Hidden Crystal Inn**
Sulpher Springs Rd.; P.O. Box 58
Hiddenite, NC 28636
(704) 632-0063; Fax: (704) 632-3562
Innkeeper: Lynn S. Hill
Rooms: 12; Suites: 1; Rates: $$-$$$
Affiliations: NCBBI, AB&BA

## Highlands

**4 1/2 Street Inn**
22A 4 1/2 St.; Highlands, NC 28741
(704) 526-4464
Innkeepers: Tom & Linda Clark
Rooms: 10; Rates: $$-$$$

**Colonial Pines Inn**
Rt. 1, Box 22B; P.O. Box 2309
Highlands, NC 28741
(704) 526-2060
Innkeepers: Chris & Donna Alley
Rooms: 6; Suites: 2; Rates: $$

**The Guest House**
Rt. 2, Box 649-N; Highlands, NC 28741
(704) 526-4536
Innkeeper: Juanita Hernandez
Rooms: 4; Rates: $$

**The Lodge**
155J Whiteside Cove Rd
Highlands, NC 28741
(704) 526-9644
Innkeepers: Tom & Linda Clark
Rooms: 5; Rates: $$$

**Long House Bed & Breakfast**
29 Cottage Row; P.O. Box 207-B
Highlands, NC 28741
(800) 833-0020; (704) 526-4394
Innkeepers: Lynn & Valerie Long
Rooms: 4; Rates: $$
Affiliations: PAII, Highlands Chamber
*A rustic and comfortable mountain getaway*
*4,000 feet up in the Blue Ridge.*

**Mirror Lake Lodging**
23 Cullasaja Drive; Highlands, NC 28741
(704) 526-5947
Innkeeper: Raymond H. Bisbing
Rooms: 1; Suites: 1; Rates: $$-$$$

**Mitchell's Motel**
P.O. Box 1717; Highlands, NC 28741
(800) 522-9874; (704) 526-2267
Innkeepers: Al & Renee Bolt
Rooms: 12; Suites: 7; Rates: $-$$$

**Phelps House Bed & Breakfast Inn**
Rt. 1, Box 55; Highlands, NC 28741
(704) 526-2590
Innkeeper: Carol Williams
Rooms: 21; Rates: $$

**Ye Olde Stone Bed & Breakfast**
1337 S. Fourth Street; Highlands, NC 28741
(704) 526-5911
Innkeeper: James Ramsdell, Jr.
Rooms: 4; Cabins: 2; Rates: $$-$$$
Affiliations: Highlands Chamber

## Hillsborough

**The Colonial Inn**
153 W. King St.; Hillsborough, NC 27278
(919) 732-2461
Innkeepers: Carlton & Sara McKee
Rooms: 8; Rates: $$

**The Hillsborough House Inn**
209 E. Tryon St.; P.O. Box 880; Hillsborough,
NC 27278
(800) 616-1660; (919) 644-1600; Fax: (919)
644-1600
Innkeepers: Katherine & Bev Webb
Rooms: 5; Suites: 1; Rates: $$-$$$$
Affiliations: NCBBI, AAA, PAII

## Hot Springs

**The Brick House**
P.O. Box 462; Hot Springs, NC 28743
(704) 622-3425
Innkeepers: Frank & Donna Fraquelli
Rooms: 11; Bedrooms: 5; Rates: $$

## Kill Devil Hills

**Cherokee Inn**
500 N. Virginia Dare Trail
Kill Devil Hills, NC 27948
(800) 554-2764; (919) 441-6127
Fax: (919) 441-1072
Innkeepers: Bob & Kaye Combs
Rooms: 6; Rates: $$
Affiliations: AB&BA, PAII

## Kitty Hawk

**3 Seasons Bed & Breakfast**
P.O. Box 1429; Kitty Hawk, NC 27949
(800) 847-3373
Innkeepers: Tom & Susie Gardner
Rooms: 4; Rates: $$$$
Affiliations: PAII

## Kure Beach

**Ocean Princess Bed & Breakfast Inn**
824 Fort Fisher Blvd. S
Kure Beach, NC 28449
(800) 762-4863; (910) 458-6712
Fax: (910) 458-6712
Innkeeper: Jeff Youngblood
Rooms: 9; Rates: $$-$$$
Affiliations: Carolina-Kure Beaches Chamber

## Lake Junaluska

**Providence Lodge**
207 Atkins Loop; Lake Junaluska, NC 28745
(704) 456-6486
Innkeepers: Ben & Wilma Cato
Rooms: 16; Rates: $$

## Lake Lure

**Lodge on Lake Lure**
Rt. 1, Box 529-A; P.O. Box 519, Charlotte
Drive; Lake Lure, NC 28746
(800) 733-2785; (704) 625-2789
Fax: (704) 625-2421
Innkeepers: Jack & Robin Stanier
Rooms: 10; Suites: 2; Rates: $$-$$$
Affiliations: NCBBI, PAII

## Lake Toxaway

**Earthshine Mountain Lodge**
Rt. 1, Box 216-C; Lake Toxaway, NC 28747
(704) 862-4207
Innkeepers: Kim Maurer & Marion Boatwright
Rooms: 8; Cabins: 1; Rates: $$$$

## Greystone Inn
Greystone Lane; Lake Toxaway, NC 28747
(800) 824-5766; (704) 966-4700
Fax: (704) 862-5689
Innkeepers: Tim & Boo Boo Lovelace
Rooms: 32; Suites: 1; Rates: $$$$-$$$$$
Affiliations: IIA, SIA

## Twin Streams Bed & Breakfast
P.O. Box 314; Lake Toxaway, NC 28747
(704) 883-3007
Innkeepers: Mel & Emma Hochstetler
Rooms: 3; Rates: $$

## Lake Waccamaw

## Bed & Breakfast by the Lake
404 Lake Shore Dr.; P.O. Box 218
Lake Waccamaw, NC 28450
(910) 646-4744
Innkeeper: Max Garrell
Rooms: 3; Rates: $$
Affiliations: NCBBI

## Laurel Springs

## Burgiss Farm Bed & Breakfast
Elk Knob Road; Laurel Springs, NC 28644
(800) 233-1505; (919) 359-2995
Innkeepers: Nancy & Tom Burgiss
Rooms: 1; Suites: 1; Rates: $$

## Doughton Hall Bed & Breakfast Inn
Rt. 1, Box 1; Laurel Springs, NC 28644
(910) 359-2341
Innkeepers: Pam & Eddie Hall
Rooms: 5; Rates: $$
Affiliations: NCBBI

## Louisburg

## Hearthside Inn Bed & Breakfast
305 North Main St.; Louisburg, NC 27549
(919) 496-6776
Innkeepers: John & Susan McKay
Rooms: 4; Rates: $$
Affiliations: NCBBI, PAII

## Madison

## The Boxley Bed & Breakfast Inn
117 E. Hunter St.; Madison, NC 27025
(919) 427-0453
Innkeepers: Monte McIntosh; JoAnn McIntosh
Rooms: 4; Rates: $$

## Maggie Valley

## Smokey Shadows Lodge
Fie Top Rd.; P.O. Box 444

Maggie Valley, NC 28751
(704) 926-0001
Innkeepers: Bud & Ginger Shinn
Rooms: 12; Cabins: 2; Rates: $-$$
Affiliations: Haywood Co. Chamber

## Wynne's Creekside Lodge Bed & Breakfast
Rt. 2, Box 365; Maggie Valley, NC 28786
(800) 849-4387; (704) 926-8300
Innkeepers: Les & Gayle Wynne
Rooms: 3; Suites: 1; Rates: $$-$$$
Affiliations: Maggie Valley Chamber, Smoky
Mountain Host

## Manteo

## Scarborough Inn
P.O. Box 1310; Manteo, NC 27954
(919) 473-3979
Innkeepers: Phil & Sally Scarborough
Rooms: 12; Rates: $-$$

## Tranquil House Inn
P.O. Box 2045; Manteo, NC 27954
(800) 458-7069; (919) 473-1404
Fax: (919) 473-1526
Innkeeper: Donny Just
Rooms: 23; Suites: 2; Rates: $$-$$$
Affiliations: AB&BA, NCHMA, OBHMA

## Marion

## The Inn at Blue Ridge
Rt. 3, Box 295; Marion, NC 28752
(800) 845-8430; (704) 756-7017
Fax: (704) 756-4267
Innkeeper: Cristina Graham
Rooms: 13; Rates: $$

## Mars Hill

## Baird House Bed & Breakfast
41 S. Main Street; P.O. Box 749
Mars Hill, NC 28754
(704) 689-5722
Innkeepers: Yvette K. Wessel
Rooms: 5; Suites: 1; Rates: $
Affiliations: Madison Co. Chamber

## Marshall

## Marshall House Bed & Breakfast Inn
5 Hill St.; Marshall, NC 28753
(704) 649-9205; Fax: (704) 649-2999
Innkeepers: Ruth & Jim Boylan
Rooms: 9; Rates: $-$$
Affiliations: Asheville Chamber, Madison Co.
Chamber

**The Mashburn House**
1 Mashburn Hill Rd.; P.O. Box 937
Marshall, NC 28753
(704) 649-3509
Innkeepers: Carl O. Gutmann & Betsy
Williams
Rooms: 5; Rates: $-$$

## Mebane

**The Old Place Bed & Breakfast Inn**
1600 Saddle Club Rd.; Mebane, NC 27302
(919) 563-1733
Innkeepers: Joe & Avis Rice
Rooms: 4; Rates: $$

## Milton

**Woodside Inn**
P.O. Box 197; Milton, NC 27305
(919) 234-8646
Innkeepers: Paul & Angela Larkin
Rooms: 3; Cabins: 1; Rates: $$-$$$

## Mocksville

**Boxwood Lodge**
132 Becktown Road; Mocksville, NC 27028
(704) 284-2031
Innkeeper: Martha Hoffner
Rooms: 8; Suites: 1; Rates: $$
Affiliations: NCBBI, PAII, Mocksville
Chamber

## Mooresville

**Spring Run Bed & Breakfast**
172 Spring Run Drive; Mooresville, NC 28115
(704) 664-6686
Innkeeper: Mary Farley
Rooms: 2; Rates: $$
Affiliations: AAA♦♦♦, North Mecklenburg
Chamber, South Iredell Chamber

## Morehead City

**Morehead Manor**
107 N. 10th St.; Morehead City, NC 28557
(919) 726-9233
Innkeepers: Bob & Brenda Thorne
Rooms: 8; Rates: $$
Affiliations: NCBBI

## Mount Airy

**Mayberry Bed & Breakfast**
329 W. Pine St.; Mount Airy, NC 27030
(910) 786-2045
Innkeepers: Jack & Hazel Fallis
Rooms: 2; Rates: $

**The Merritt House**
618 N. Main St.; Mount Airy, NC 27030
(800) 290-6290; (910) 786-2174
Innkeepers: Pat & Rich Mangels
Rooms: 4; Rates: $$
Affiliations: NCBBI

**Pine Ridge Inn**
2893 W. Pine St.; Mount Airy, NC 27030
(910) 789-5034; Fax: (910) 786-9039
Innkeepers: Ellen & Manford Haxton
Rooms: 6; Rates: $$-$$$
Affiliations: NCBBI, AB&BA, AAA, Mobil

## Murphy

**The Hilltop House**
104 Campbell St.; Murphy, NC 28906
(704) 837-8661
Innkeepers: Don & Jacqueline Heinze
Rooms: 3; Rates: $-$$
Affiliations: Murphy Chamber
*1902 step back into time the "ole" porch swing rocking chairs "Grandma's" house*

**Hoover House**
306 Natural Springs Drive; Murphy, NC 28906
(704) 837-8734
Innkeeper: Sugie Kovach
Rooms: 4; Rates: $$-$$$
Affiliations: AAA

**Huntington Hall Bed & Breakfast**
500 Valley River Ave.; Murphy, NC 28906
(800) 824-6189; (704) 837-9567
Fax: (704) 837-2527
Innkeepers: Bob & Kate DeLong
Rooms: 5; Rates: $$
Affiliations: NCBBI, PAII, AAA

**Stone Manor Inn**
505 Peachtree St.; Murphy, NC 28906
(704) 837-8676
Innkeeper: Sue Sechler
Rooms: 4; Rates: $$

## Nags Head

**First Colony Inn**
6720 S. Virginia Dare Trail
Nags Head, NC 27959
(800) 368-9390; (919) 441-2343
Fax: (919) 441-9234
Innkeepers: The Lawrence family
Rooms: 20; Suites: 6; Rates: $$-$$$$
Affiliations: AAA♦♦♦♦, PAII, NCHMA,
AB&BA, AHMA, Mobil

## Nebo

**Merry Heart Cabin**
Rt. 2, Box 768; 1414 Merry Heart Lane
Nebo, NC 28761
(704) 584-6174
Innkeeper: Connie Smart
Rooms: 3; Rates: $$

## New Bern

**The Aerie**
509 Pollock St.; New Bern, NC 28560
(800) 849-5553; (919) 636-5553
Innkeepers: Howard & Dee Smith
Rooms: 7; Rates: $$
Affiliations: NCBBI, PAII

**Harmony House Inn**
215 Pollock St.; New Bern, NC 28560
(800) 636-3113; (919) 636-3810
Innkeepers: Ed & Sooki Kirkpatrick
Rooms: 9; Suites: 1; Rates: $$-$$$
Affiliations: IIA, NCBBI, PAII, AB&BA, AAA

**King's Arms Inn**
212 Pollock St.; New Bern, NC 28560
(800) 872-9306; (919) 638-4409
Innkeepers: Richard & Pat Gulley
Rooms: 9; Rates: $$
Affiliations: PAII, AAA, Mobil

**The Lighthouse**
315 George St.; New Bern, NC 28562
(919) 633-9488; Fax: (919) 633-9488
Innkeepers: Art & Ruthann Moran-Salinger
Rooms: 2; Rates: $$
Affiliations: NCBBI

**New Berne House Inn**
709 Broad St.; New Bern, NC 28560
(800) 842-7688; (919) 636-2250
Innkeepers: Marcia Drum & Howard Bronson
Rooms: 7; Rates: $$

## Ocean Isle Beach

**The Winds-Clarion Carriage House Inn**
310 E. First St.; Ocean Isle Beach, NC 28469
(800) 334-3581; (910) 579-6275
Fax: (910) 579-2884
Innkeepers: Helen & Miller Pope
Rooms: 67; Suites: 40; Rates: $-$$$$$
Affiliations: SIA, AAA, Mobil, South
Brunswick Islands Chamber
*Oceanfront rooms & suites overlooking
subtropical gardens & island beach. Heated
pool, bicycle & sailboat rentals.*

## Ocracoke

**Berkley Center Country Inn**
Hwy. 12; P.O. Box 220; Ocracoke, NC 27960
(919) 928-5911
Innkeepers: Wes & Ruth Egan
Rooms: 9; Suites: 1; Rates: $$
Affiliations: SIA, NCBBI, Mobil, AHMA,
Dare Co. Chamber, NCHMA

**Eugenia's Bed & Breakfast**
P.O. Box 611; Ocracoke, NC 27960
(919) 928-1411
Innkeeper: Jean M. Fletcher
Rooms: 4; Rates: $$

**OSCAR'S HOUSE**
Rt. 12, Box 206; Ocracoke Island, NC 27960
(919) 928-1311
Innkeeper: Ann Ehringhaus
Rooms: 4; Rates: $-$$
Affiliations: Okracoke Civic & Business Assoc.

## Old Fort

**The Inn at Old Fort**
116 West Main Street; P.O. Box 1116
Old Fort, NC 28762
(704) 668-9384
Innkeepers: Chuck & Debbie Aldridge
Rooms: 4; Suites: 1; Rates: $-$$

## Oriental

**The Cartwright House Bed & Breakfast**
301 Church St.; P.O. Box 310
Oriental, NC 28571
(919) 249-1337
Innkeeper: Christina
Rooms: 5; Suites: 1; Rates: $$-$$$

**The Tar Heel Inn**
205 Church St.; P.O. Box 176
Oriental, NC 28571
(919) 249-1078
Innkeepers: Shawna & Robert Hyde
Rooms: 8; Rates: $$
Affiliations: NCBBI, PAII

## Penland

**Chinquapin Inn**
P.O. Box 145; Penland, NC 28765
(704) 765-0064
Innkeepers: Bill & Sue Ford
Rooms: 4; Suites: 1; Rates: $-$$

**Pine Bluff**

**Pine Cone Manor**
450 E. Philadelphia Ave.; P.O. Box 1208
Pine Bluff, NC 28373
(910) 281-5307
Innkeeper: Virginia H. Keith
Rooms: 4; Rates: $-$$
Affiliations: NCBBI

**Pinehurst**

**Pine Crest Inn**
P.O. Box 879, Dogwood Rd
Pinehurst, NC 28374
(910) 295-6121; Fax: (910) 295-4880
Innkeeper: Peter Barrett
Rooms: 36; Suites: 4; Rates: $-$$
Affiliations: American Hotel Assoc.

**Pinnacle**

**Scenic Overlook Bed & Breakfast**
144 Scenic Overlook Lane
Pinnacle, NC 27043
(910) 368-9591
Innkeepers: Gayle & Alan Steinbicker
Rooms: 1; Suites: 3; Rates: $$-$$

**Trails Inn**
129 Santa Fe Trail; Pinnacle, NC 27043
(910) 325-3268
Innkeepers: Sam & Suzanne Fowler
Rooms: 4; Rates: $$
*Horse accommodations on premises. Near bridle & hiking trails of Pilot Mtn.*

**Pisgah Forest**

**The Pines Country Inn**
719 Hart Rd.; Pisgah Forest, NC 28768
(704) 877-3131
Innkeepers: Tom & Mary McEntire
Rooms: 22; Rates: $$

**Plymouth**

**Four Gables Bed & Breakfast**
109 W. Main Street; P.O. Box 538
Plymouth, NC 27962
(919) 793-6696
Innkeepers: Norman & Brenda Conklin
Rooms: 4; Rates: $$
Affiliations: NCBBI, Washington Co. Chamber

**Raleigh**

**The William Thomas House**
530 North Blount Street; Raleigh, NC 27604
(919) 755-9400; Fax: (919) 755-3966

Innkeepers: Jim & Sarah Lofton
Rooms: 4; Rates: $$
Affiliations: NCBBI, PAII

**Ridgecrest**

**Mote's Mountain View**
P.O. Box 146; Ridgecrest, NC 28770
(704) 669-4714
Innkeepers: Henry & Polly Mote
Rooms: 4; Rates: $
Affiliations: Black Mountain Chamber

**Robbinsville**

**Snowbird Mountain Lodge**
275 Santeetlah Rd.; Robbinsville, NC 28771
(704) 479-3433
Innkeepers: The Lenz family
Rooms: 22; Rates: $$$
Affiliations: IIA

**Rocky Mount**

**Sunset Inn**
1210 Sunset Ave.; Rocky Mount, NC 27804
(800) 786-7386; (919) 446-9524
Innkeepers: Herbert & Dale Fuerst
Rooms: 2; Suites: 2; Rates: $$
Affiliations: NCBBI, AAA

**Rutherfordton**

**Carrier Houses**
423 N. Main Street; Rutherfordton, NC 38139
(704) 287-4222
Innkeepers: Barbara & Boyce Hodge
Rooms: 8; Suites: 2; Rates: $-$$
Affiliations: AB&BA. Rutherford Co. Chamber

**Pinebrae Manor**
Hwy. 108, RR 5, Box 479-A; Rutherfordton, NC 28139
(704) 286-1543; Fax: (704) 287-3755
Innkeepers: Allen & Charlotte Perry;
Rooms: 4; Rates: $-$$
Affiliations: NCBBI

**Salisbury**

**Rowan Oak House**
208 S. Fulton Street; Salisbury, NC 28144
(800) 786-0437; (704) 633-2086
Innkeepers: Leslie & Barbara Coombs
Rooms: 4; Rates: $$-$$$
Affiliations: NCBBI, AAA◆◆◆

## Saluda

**Ivy Terrace Bed & Breakfast Inn**
Hwy. 176; Main Street; Saluda, NC 28773
(800) 749-9542; (704) 749-9542
Innkeepers: Diane & Herbert McGuire
Rooms: 8; Rates: $$-$$$
Affiliations: AB&BA, NB&BA, NCBBI, PAII

**The Oaks**
Rt. 1, Box 10; Saluda, NC 28773
(800) 893-6097; (704) 749-9613
Fax: (704) 749-9613
Innkeepers: Crowley & Terry Murphy
Rooms: 4; Guest houses: 1; Rates: $$-$$$
Affiliations: NCBBI, AAA

**The Orchard Inn**
P.O. Box 725; Saluda, NC 28773
(800) 581-3800; (704) 749-5471
Fax: (704) 749-9805
Innkeepers: Veronica & Newell Doty
Rooms: 9; Suites: 3; Rates: $$$-$$$$
Affiliations: PAII, IIA

## Sapphire

**Woodlands Inn of Sapphire**
1305 US 64 W.; Sapphire, NC 28774
(704) 966-4709; Fax: (704) 966-4544
Innkeepers: Sherry & Bill Coy
Rooms: 12; Suites: 2; Rates: $-$$
Affiliations: NCHMA

## Shelby

**The Inn at Webbley**
403 S. Washington St.; P.O. Box 1000
Shelby, NC 28151
(800) 852-2346; (704) 481-1403
Fax: (704) 487-0619
Innkeepers: O. Max Gardner III & Victoria
Harwell-Gardner
Rooms: 5; Rates: $$$
Affiliations: NCBBI, PAII. AAA◆◆◆◆

## Siler City

**Bed & Breakfast at Laurel Ridge**
3188 Siler City—Snow Camp Road
Siler City, NC 27344
(800) 742-6049; (919) 742-6049
Innkeepers: David Simmons & Lisa Reynolds
Rooms: 2; Suites: 1; Cottages: 1; Rates: $$-$$$
Affiliations: PAII, NCBBI

## Southern Pines

**Jefferson Inn**
150 W. New Hampshire Ave
Southern Pines, NC 28387
(910) 692-8300; Fax: (910) 692-8315
Innkeepers: Glenn & Claire Golcher
Rooms: 7; Suites: 1; Rates: $$

**Knollwood House**
1495 W. Connecticut Ave
Southern Pines, NC 28387
(910) 692-9390
Innkeepers: Dick & Mimi Beatty
Rooms: 2; Suites: 2; Rates: $$-$$$
Affiliations: NCBBI

## Southport

**The Indian Oak Inn**
120 W. Moore Street; 120 W. Moore Street
Southport, NC 28461
(910) 457-0209
Innkeepers: John & Norma Kluttz
Rooms: 4; Suites: 3; Rates: $$-$$$
Affiliations: AB&BA, PAII, NCBBI,
Southport-Oak Island Chamber

## Sparta

**Alleghany Inn & Restaurant**
531 North Main Street; P.O. Box 995
Sparta, NC 28675
(910) 372-2501
Innkeeper: Mary Lou Edwards
Rooms: 49; Rates: $
Affiliations: Alleghany Co. Chamber

**Mountain Hearth Lodge**
Rt. 1, Box 228-E; Sparta, NC 28675
(910) 372-8743
Innkeepers: Ernest, Eleanor & Sherry Rancourt
Rooms: 3; Suites: 4; Rates: $$

**Turby Villa**
Star Route 1, Box 48; Sparta, NC 28675
(910) 372-8490
Innkeeper: Maybelline R. Turbiville
Rooms: 3; Rates: $-$$

## Spruce Pine

**The Fairway Inn Bed and Breakfast**
110 Henry Lane; Spruce Pine, NC 28777
(704) 765-8559; Fax: (704) 765-8559
Innkeepers: Margaret & John Stevens
Rooms: 2; Suites: 2; Rates: $$
Affiliations: NCBBI

## Statesville

**Aunt Mae's Bed & Breakfast**
532 E. Broad St.; Statesville, NC 28677
(800) 448-6862; (704) 873-9525

Innkeepers: Richard & Sue Rowland
Rooms: 2; Rates: $$
Affiliations: NCBBI

**Cedar Hill Farm Bed & Breakfast**
778 Elmwood Rd.; Rt. 1, Box 492
Statesville, NC 28677
(800) 484-8457; (704) 873-4332
Innkeepers: Jim & Brenda Vernon
Rooms: 1; Suites: 1; Rates: $$
Affiliations: NCBBI

**Madelyn's Bed & Breakfast**
514 Carrol St.; Statesville, NC 28677
(704) 872-3973
Innkeepers: Madelyn & John Hill
Rooms: 3; Rates: $$
Affiliations: NCBBI, AAA◆◆◆

## Stokes

**Sheppard Mill Farm Bed & Breakfast**
Rt. 1, Box 240; Stokes, NC 27884
(919) 757-0992
Innkeepers: Sonia & Pat Fiscus
Rooms: 4; Rates: $$
Affiliations: Greenville Chamber

## Sugar Grove

**Galloways' Rivendell Lodge**
P.O. Box 211; Sugar Grove, NC 28679
(704) 297-1685
Innkeepers: Gary & Sandy Galloway
Rooms: 4; Rates: $$
Affiliations: NCBBI

**Olde Cobblestone Chimney Inn**
P.O. Box 102; Sugar Grove, NC 28679
(704) 297-5111
Innkeepers: Billie & Mersch Merschdorf
Rooms: 3; Rates: $$-$$$

**Sugar Grove Inn & Robin's Nest Cabin**
P.O. Box 215; Sugar Grove, NC 28679
(704) 297-3336
Innkeepers: Robin & Elizabeth Atkiss
Rooms: 2; Suites: 1; Rates: $$-$$$
Affiliations: Boone Chamber, High Country
Host

## Supply

**Doe Creek Inn Bed & Breakfast**
843 Ocean Hwy. W; Rt. 3, Box 36
Supply, NC 28462
(910) 754-7736
Innkeeper: Mark Owens
Rooms: 8; Rates: $-$$

## Swan Quarter

**Cutrell Inn Bed & Breakfast**
P.O. Box 125; Swan Quarter, NC 27885
(800) 263-1708; (919) 926-9711
Innkeeper: Delores C. Emory
Rooms: 3; Rates: $
Affiliations: Hyde Co. Chamber

## Swansboro

**Scott's Keep Bed & Breakfast**
P.O. Box 1425; Swansboro, NC 28584
(800) 348-1257; (910) 326-1257
Innkeepers: Frank & Norma Scott
Rooms: 3; Rates: $

## Tabor City

**Four Rooster Inn**
403 Pireway Road; Tabor City, NC 28463
(910) 653-3878
Innkeepers: Gloria & Bob Rogers
Rooms: 3; Rates: $-$$
Affiliations: NCBBI

## Tarboro

**Lady Ann of Tarboro Bed & Breakfast**
1205 Main St.; Tarboro, NC 27886
(919) 641-1438
Innkeeper: Linda A. Tharrington
Rooms: 3; Rates: $-$$
Affiliations: Tarboro-Edgecombe Chamber

**Little Warren Bed & Breakfast, estab. 1984**
304 E. Park Ave.; Tarboro, NC 27886
(800) 309-1314; (919) 823-1314
Innkeepers: Patsy & Tom Miller
Rooms: 3; Rates: $$
Affiliations: NCBBI

**The Main Street Inn**
912 Main St.; Tarboro, NC 27886
(919) 823-2560
Innkeepers: Karen & Paul Andrus
Rooms: 3; Suites: 1; Rates: $$
Affiliations: NCBBI

## Taylorsville

**Barkley House Bed & Breakfast**
2522 NC Hwy 16 S.; Taylorsville, NC 28681
(800) 474-4652; (704) 632-9060
Innkeeper: Phyllis Barkley
Rooms: 3; Rates: $$

## Tryon

**Fox Trot Inn**
800 Lynn Rd.; Tryon, NC 28782
(704) 859-9706
Innkeepers: Mimi Colby & Betty Daugherty
Rooms: 2; Suites: 2; Rates: $$-$$$

**Mimosa Inn**
One Mimosa Lane; Tryon, NC 28782
(704) 859-7688
Innkeepers: Jay & Sandi Franks
Rooms: 9; Rates: $$

**Pine Crest Inn**
200 Pine Crest Lane; Tryon, NC 28782
(800) 633-3001; (704) 859-9135
Innkeepers: Jeremy & Jennifer Wainwright
Rooms: 23; Suites: 9; Rates: $$$-$$$$$
Affiliations: IIA, AAA, Mobil

**Stone Hedge Inn**
300 Howard Gap Rd.; P.O. Box 366
Tryon, NC 28782
(704) 859-9114
Innkeepers: Ray & Anneliese Weingartner
Rooms: 6; Rates: $$

**Tryon Old South Bed & Breakfast**
107 Markham Rd.; Tryon, NC 28782
(704) 859-6965; Fax: (704) 859-2756
Innkeepers: Mike & Terry Cacioppo
Rooms: 4; Rates: $-$$
Affiliations: NCBBI, USB&B

## Valle Crucis

**Bluestone Lodge**
SR 1112, Bluestone Wild Road; P.O. Box 736
Valle Crucis, NC 28691
(704) 963-5177
Innkeepers: Merry Lee Benore & Bill Benore
Rooms: 2; Suites: 2; Rates: $$-$$$$
Affiliations: Boone Chamber, High Country
Host
*Pool. Kitchenettes.*

**Cat Pause Inn**
P.O. Box 697; Valle Crucis, NC 28691
(704) 963-7297
Innkeeper: Mary Alice Smith
Rooms: 2; Rates: $$
Affiliations: Boone Area Chamber, Banner Elk
Chamber
*Distinctly decorated for people who love cats
and enjoy antiques.*

**The Inn at the Taylor House**
P.O. Box 713; Valle Crucis, NC 28691
(704) 963-5581; Fax: (704) 963-5818

Innkeepers: Chip & Roland Schwab
Rooms: 5; Suites: 2; Rates: $$$
Affiliations: IIA, PAII

**Mast Farm Inn**
P.O. Box 704; Valle Crucis, NC 28691
(704) 963-5857; Fax: (704) 963-6404
Innkeepers: Sybil & Francis Pressly
Rooms: 9; Cabins: 3; Rates: $$-$$$$
Affiliations: IIA, PAII

## Warsaw

**The Squires Vintage Inn**
748 NC 24&50; Rt. 2, Box 130-R
Warsaw, NC 28398
(910) 296-1831
Innkeeper: Iris Lennon
Rooms: 12; Rates: $$

## Washington

**Acadian House Bed & Breakfast**
129 Van Norden St.; Washington, NC 27889
(919) 975-3967
Innkeepers: Johanna & Leonard Huber
Rooms: 3; Suites: 1; Rates: $-$$

**Pamlico House Bed & Breakfast**
400 E. Main St.; Washington, NC 27889
(800) 948-8507; (919) 946-7184
Fax: (919) 946-9944
Innkeepers: Jeanne & Lawrence Hervey
Rooms: 4; Rates: $$
Affiliations: NCBBI, PAII

## Waynesville

**Belle Meade Inn**
5170 S. Main Street; P.O. Box 1319
Waynesville, NC 28786
(704) 456-3234
Innkeepers: Gloria & Al Dinofa
Rooms: 4; Rates: $$
Affiliations: NCBBI, Haywood Co. Chamber
*Built in 1908, a charming craftsman style home
w/carved stone fireplace, chestnut woodwork
throughout. Great breakfasts. Mystery weekends.*

**Boyd Mountain Log Cabins**
Rt. 2 Box 167; Waynesville, NC 28786
(704) 926-1575
Innkeepers: Dan & Betsy Boyd
Rooms: 3; Rates: $$-$$$

**Grandview Lodge**
809 Valley View Circle Rd
Waynesville, NC 28786
(800) 255-7826; (704) 456-5212
Fax: (704) 452-5432

Innkeepers: Stan & Linda Arnold
Rooms: 9; Suites: 2; Rates: $$-$$$
Affiliations: Mobil, Haywood Co. Chamber,
Smoky Mtn. Host

**Hallcrest Inn**
299 Halltop Circle; Waynesville, NC 28786
(800) 334-6457; (704) 456-6457
Innkeepers: Martin & Tesa Burson
Rooms: 11; Rates: $$
Affiliations: PAII, Haywood Co. Chamber

**Haywood House Bed & Breakfast**
409 South Haywood Street
Waynesville, NC 28786
(704) 456-9831
Innkeepers: Lynn & Chris Sylvester
Rooms: 4; Rates: $$
Affiliations: Haywood Co. Chamber

**The Palmer House**
108 Pigeon St.; Waynesville, NC 28786
(704) 456-7521
Innkeepers: Jeff Minick & Kris Gillet
Rooms: 7; Rates: $$

**The Swag Country Inn**
Hemphill Rd.; Rt 2, Box 280-A
Waynesville, NC 28786
(800) 789-7672; (704) 926-0430
Fax: (704) 926-2036
Innkeeper: Deener Matthews
Rooms: 14; Cabins: 3; Rates: $$$$-$$$$$
Affiliations: PAII, IIA, NCHMA, AHMA
*(Open May-October)*

**The Way Inn**
299 S. Main St.; Waynesville, NC 28786
(704) 456-3788
Innkeeper: Barbara Rhoads
Rooms: 6; Rates: $$

**Weaverville**

**Dry Ridge Inn**
26 Brown St.; Weaverville, NC 28787
(800) 839-3899; (704) 658-3899
Innkeepers: Paul & Mary Lou Gibson
Rooms: 7; Rates: $$
Affiliations: NCBBI, PAII

**Gypsy's End Cottages**
159 Arrowood Rd.; Weaverville, NC 28787
(704) 645-9828
Innkeeper: Burton Smith
Rooms: 4; Rates: $$
Affiliations: Asheville Chamber

**Inn on Main St.**
88 S. Main St.; P.O. Box 1153

Weaverville, NC 28787
(704) 645-3442
Innkeepers: Joel & Melba Goldsby
Rooms: 6; Rates: $-$$
Affiliations: Asheville Chamber

**Weaverville Featherbed & Breakfast**
3 Le Perrion Drive; Weaverville, NC 28787
(704) 645-7594; Fax: (704) 658-3905
Innkeepers: Sharon Ballas & Shelley Burtt
Rooms: 3; Suites: 3; Rates: $$-$$$
Affiliations: AAA

**Weldon**

**Weldon Place Inn**
500 Washington Ave.; Weldon, NC 27890
(800) 831-4470; (919) 536-4582
Innkeepers: Andy & Angel Whitby
Rooms: 4; Rates: $$
Affiliations: NCBBI, AAA

**Whittier**

**The Chalet Inn**
Rt. 2, Box 99; Whittier, NC 28789
(704) 586-0251
Innkeepers: George & Hanneke Ware
Rooms: 4; Suites: 2; Rates: $$-$$$
Affiliations: Jackson Co. Chamber, Swain Co.
Chamber
*Experience European ambience, gracious lodg-*
*ing and genial hosts in a mountain cove. Close*
*to Great Smoky Mountains National Park, Blue*
*Ridge Parkway, and Nantahala River. Private*
*balconies & modern baths; brook, hiking trails,*
*lawn games picnic area.*

**Wilmington**

**219 South 5th Bed & Breakfast**
219 South 5th Ave.; Wilmington, NC 28401
(800) 219-7634; (910) 763-5539
Innkeepers: Bob Beecher & Connie Donkin
Rooms: 3; Suites: 1; Rates: $$

**Anderson Guest House**
520 Orange street; Wilmington, NC 28401
(910) 343-8128
Innkeepers: Landon & Connie Anderson
Rooms: 2; Rates: $$

**Catherine's Inn**
410 South Front St.; Wilmington, NC 28401
(800) 476-0723; (910) 251-0863
Innkeepers: Catherine & Walter Ackiss
Rooms: 3; Rates: $$
Affiliations: NCBBI, AB&BA, NB&BA

**Front Street Inn**
215 South Front Street
Wilmington, NC 28401
(910) 762-6442; Fax: (910) 762-8991
Innkeepers: Jay & Stephany Rhodes
Suites: 9; Rates: $$-$$$

**James Place Bed & Breakfast**
9 South Fourth Street; Wilmington, NC 28401
(800) 303-9444; (910) 251-0999
Fax: (910) 251-1150
Innkeepers: Tony & Maureen Spataro
Rooms: 3; Rates: $$
Affiliations: PAII, NCBBI, Downtown
Wilmington Assoc.

**Market Street Bed & Breakfast**
1704 Market St.; Wilmington, NC 28403
(800) 242-5442; (910) 763-5442
Innkeeper: Jo Anne Jarrett
Rooms: 4; Rates: $$
Affiliations: NCBBI, NB&BA

**Rosehill Inn**
114 S. Third St.; Wilmington, NC 28401
(800) 815-0250; (910) 815-0250
Fax: (910) 815-0350
Innkeepers: Laurel Jones & Donnis Fietsch
Rooms: 6; Rates: $$-$$$
Affiliations: NCBBI, PAII

**The Taylor House Inn**
14 N Seventh Street; Wilmington, NC 28401
(800) 382-9982; (910) 763-7581
Innkeeper: Glenda Moreadith
Rooms: 4; Suites: 1; Rates: $$$
Affiliations: PAII, NCBBI, AAA, Mobil,
Wilmington Chamber

**The Worth House**
412 S. Third St.; Wilmington, NC 28401
(800) 340-8559; (910) 762-8562
Fax: (910) 763-2173
Innkeepers: John & Francie Miller
Rooms: 5; Suites: 2; Rates: $$-$$$
Affiliations: PAII, NCBBI, AAA, Mobil

## Wilson

**Miss Betty's Bed & Breakfast Inn**
600 W. Nash St.; Wilson, NC 27893
(800) 258-2058; (919) 243-4447
Innkeepers: Betty & Fred Spitz
Rooms: 7; Suites: 3; Rates: $$
Affiliations: AB&BA, NCBBI, AAA, Mobil

## Winston-Salem

**Augustus T. Zevely Inn**
803 South Main Street

Winston-Salem, NC 27101
(800) 928-9299; (910) 748-9299
Zevely House Assoc.; Innkeeper: John Seitz
Rooms: 12; Suites: 1; Rates: $$-$$$$
Affiliations: AB&BA, AAA

**Brookstown Inn**
200 Brookstown Ave
Winston-Salem, NC 27101
(800) 845-4262; (910) 725-1120
Fax: (910) 773-0147
Innkeeper: Deborah Bumgardner
Rooms: 40; Suites: 31; Rates: $$$-$$$$
Affiliations: NCHMA

**Colonel Ludlow Inn**
Summit & W. Fifth St
Winston-Salem, NC 27101
(800) 301-1887; (910) 777-1887
Fax: (910) 777-1890
Innkeeper: Constance Creasman
Rooms: 8; Rates: $$-$$$$
Affiliations: PAII, AHMA

**Henry F. Shaffner House**
150 S. Marshall St
Winston-Salem, NC 27101
(800) 952-2256; (910) 777-0052
Fax: (910) 777-1188
Innkeeper: Betty Falls
Rooms: 6; Suites: 2; Rates: $$-$$$$
Affiliations: NCBBI

**Lady Anne's Victorian Bed & Breakfast**
612 Summit St.; Winston-Salem, NC 27101
(910) 724-1074
Innkeeper: Shelley Kirley
Rooms: 2; Suites: 3; Rates: $$-$$$
Affiliations: NB&BA, Winston-Salem B&B
Assoc.

**Mickle House Bed & Breakfast**
927 W. Fifth St.; Winston-Salem, NC 27101
(910) 722-9045
Innkeeper: Barbara Garrison
Rooms: 2; Rates: $$
Affiliations: NCBBI, PAII, AAA◆◆◆

**Thomas-Welch House**
618 Summit Street; Winston-Salem, NC 27101
(910) 723-3586; Fax: (910) 631-5750
Innkeepers: Trish Pegram & Buck Skillen
Rooms: 4; Rates: $$
Affiliations: NCBBI

**Wachovia Bed & Breakfast, Inc.**
513 Wachovia St.; Winston-Salem, NC 27101
(910) 777-0332
Innkeeper: Susan Bunting
Rooms: 5; Rates: $$

# Index

NOTES

## We'd love to hear from you...

Comments about the Getaways Series books are always welcome. If you have suggestions for improvements we can make to the books, corrections which should be made, or comments based on your stays at B&Bs/Country Inns featured in Getaways Series books, please use the space below to let us know about them. We will do our best to respond to you personally.

Sincerely,
Don Vandeventer

Comments:

_____

_____

_____

_____

_____

_____

_____

_____

_____

Please mail to:

Don Vandeventer
c/o Down Home Publications
P.O. Box 1899-B
Candler, NC 28715

The Getaways Series is available at bookstores everywhere and is distributed to the book trade by John F. Blair, Publisher.

☎ To order by phone call toll-free 1-800-306-7668.

📄 Fax orders: (540) 997-0289

📧 To order by mail: Hummingbird Books, P.O. Box 147, Goshen, VA 24439-0147

| Title: | # of copies | Price each: |
|---|---|---|
| North Carolina Getaways | | $14.95 |
| Tennessee Getaways | | $12.95 |
| | | |
| Total Amount for Books | | |
| Shipping & Handling: add $2.55 per copy | | |
| Virginia Residents, add 4.5% Sales Tax | | |
| Total Amount of Order: | | |

Payment by: ☐ check/money order (payable to Hummingbird Books)

☐ credit card

☐ AMEX ☐ DISCOVER ☐ MC ☐ VISA

Credit Card No.: _____

Expiration Date: _____

Signature: _____

Ship to: _____

Address: _____

City: _____ State:____ Zip: _____